TRAGEDY AS A CRITIQUE OF VIRTUE

Scholars Press
Studies in the Humanities Series

TRAGEDY AS A CRITIQUE
OF VIRTUE
The Novel and Ethical Reflection

John D. Barbour

Scholars Press
Chico, California

TRAGEDY AS A CRITIQUE OF VIRTUE
The Novel and Ethical Reflection

John D. Barbour

© 1984
Scholars Press

Library of Congress Cataloging in Publication Data

Barbour, John D.
   Tragedy as a critique of virtue.

   (Scholars Press studies in the humanities series ; no. 2)
   1. American fiction—History and criticism. 2. Tragic,
The. 3. Virtue in literature. 4. Ethics in literature.
5. Conrad, Joseph, 1857–1924. Nostromo.
I. Title. II. Series.
PS374.T66B3   1984   813'.009'16   83–20028
ISBN 0–89130–661–7
ISBN 0–89130–662–5 (pbk.)

CONTENTS

JOHN D. BARBOUR is Assistant Professor of
Religion at St. Olaf College. He earned his B.A.
from Oberlin College and his M.A. and Ph.D.
from the University of Chicago Divinity School.

ACKNOWLEDGMENTS

Many persons have helped me in this inquiry, not all of whom can be thanked here. Among my teachers, I owe a special debt of gratitude to Anthony Yu, who has long encouraged my interest in tragedy and supported my work in many ways. James Gustafson, Stanley Hauerwas, and James Miller, Jr. provided valuable insights and counsel. The Deans of the Divinity School of the University of Chicago, Joseph Kitagawa and Franklin Gamwell, as well as the Divinity School's Institute for the Advanced Study of Religion, made possible the fellowships which allowed me to work on this project. Giles Gunn offered very valuable advice on the manuscript. Lynn Poland read an earlier draft of this project and made helpful comments.

Chapter VII has appeared previously in *The Journal of Religion* 63 (1983), pp. 1–25; a version of chapter II is published in *Arizona Quarterly* in 1984.

The suggestions of my mother, Deane Kern Barbour, have improved a number of pages I have written here. Both she and my father, Ian G. Barbour, have supported and influenced my work in so many ways, for so many years, that I could never express the extent of my intellectual and personal indebtedness. Finally, Meg Ojala, my wife, has made this project, as well as my life, immeasurably the richer.

Introduction

Tragedy depicts the downfall of a good man or woman. "A good man" is a person with a particular kind of moral excellence, someone who embodies his culture's idea of virtue. Despite his moral goodness, the protagonist of a tragedy suffers or dies in an unusually disturbing way. A central theme of tragic literature is that human virtue does not suffice for happiness because of the possibility of tragic error. In fact, it is often as a consequence of his most morally admirable actions that a character makes a tragic error and suffers his fate; a less virtuous individual would have escaped disaster. The very virtue of the central figure in tragedy, then, contributes to his or her downfall.

The central thesis of this study is that tragedy involves a critique of virtue. Tragedy assesses the implications of a particular form of virtue by affirming its value and significance while recognizing its inherent limitations and dangerous potential in certain circumstances. Tragedy tests a form of virtue to discover two kinds of potential danger: its tendency to bring suffering for the central protagonist himself, and the role of virtue in contributing to a moral evil the hero inflicts on others.

This study focuses on four narrative tragedies: Henry James's *The Princess Casamassima*, Herman Melville's *Billy Budd*, Joseph Conrad's *Nostromo*, and Robert Penn Warren's *All the King's Men*. Most of the criticism and theory of tragedy has been based on works of drama. Though it has been claimed that the modern novel is the authentic heir to the tradition of classical tragic drama, or that the novel often has important tragic dimensions, no study of the modern tragic novel has focused on the specific ethical issues at the heart of tragedy: the ambiguity of virtue in different social contexts and the nature of a tragic error. The intention of this study is not to propose a definition of the genre of tragedy or the tragic novel, but to explore the central ethical situation of these works: the phenomenon of a basically good person bringing about suffering and his own destruction. We seek to understand both the ways in which tragedy explores the moral qualities of individual characters, and the ways that tragedy investigates problems and conflicts between different moral values within a culture.

The central virtue treated in each novel is not always one of the classical virtues discussed in philosophical and theological ethics. With the exception of prudence in Melville's *Billy Budd*, the virtues under analysis may appear somewhat unusual or unorthodox to systematic ethical thought. However, it seems more sensitive to each literary text to seek to determine what its operative conception of moral excellence is, rather than to impose on it a concept of virtue derived from some nonliterary source. Thus analysis of *The Princess Casamassima* elucidates what James means by characterizing Hyacinth Robinson as the sort of person "on whom nothing was lost." Interpretation of Conrad's *Nostromo* focuses on the qualities of idealism and skepticism, which are pivotal in the destinies of all the characters in that novel. In *All the King's Men*, Willie Stark's political program is based on his ideal of "making good out of bad"; my interpretation of this novel centers on the cultural sources of this understanding of political ethics.

These four novels have been selected for analysis because they are broadly representative of the tragic novel but have received relatively little attention from critics. While all the works treated in the present study have been discussed before in terms of their tragic dimensions, each has been neglected in comparison with certain other works. *The Princess Casamassima* has not received nearly the amount of attention given to *The Portrait of a Lady* and *The Wings of the Dove*, the works usually interpreted as James's closest approximations of tragedy. *Billy Budd* has hardly lacked critical acclaim since the 1920s, but its tragic dimensions remain highly controversial. *Lord Jim* and *Heart of Darkness* occupy such central positions in the Conrad canon that the tragic form and themes of *Nostromo* have not been adequately studied. And though *All the King's Men* is by now a classic of the American literary tradition, Warren's novels have been overshadowed by Faulkner's tragedies, especially *Absalom, Absalom*. Each of the novels to be discussed in this study deserves a close study in the light of tragic theory. There are important differences among the novels, and a comparative approach should reveal the diversity of literary techniques and thematic concerns within the tradition of narrative tragedy. It is hoped that something can be suggested as to the richness and profundity of these novels apart from their connection with the central ethical themes of this study. It is also hoped that my thesis—that these narrative tragedies all involve a critique of a form of virtue—will disclose new aspects of their significance.

My approach to the ethical aspects of the four novels will focus on key issues which will be identified in the first chapter's discussion of the history of tragic theory. Chapters II through V will seek to show how the conception of tragedy as a critique of virtue can be useful in illuminating the narratives selected for analysis. Initially, the virtue of the protagonist and its literary representation will be analyzed. We need to understand both the motivations of individual characters and the ways in which their societies shape them. Next, the discussion of each novel will look at the connection between a character's virtues and his tragic error. For the heart of the moral ambiguity of tragedy is that a virtuous person brings about his own destruction. How is the hero's tragic error related to his moral guilt and to his responsibilities in society? Is the hero's destruction presented as justified in the eyes of those in his society? To what extent does his death reveal contradictions and unresolved conflicts of value in his society? Each chapter will discuss how the novel offers a critique of the virtue in question, assessing both its significance and its possible failure. And each chapter will show how a character's tragic error reveals not only the complexities of the individual's moral agency, but the potential conflicts between different virtues or values within his culture. We inquire as to whether the novel criticizes or affirms the cultural values and ideals which underlie and justify a society's idea of virtue. Finally, we will ask about the broader implications of each novel. Is the problem of the failure of a virtuous person presented as a universal one, because of the limitations and fallibility of virtue in any community? If so, is recognition of the universal scope of the problem presented as a liberating factor in moral experience, or does it induce despair? Does the recognition of the fallibility of a form of virtue involve a kind of religious affirmation or denial? Chapter VI will summarize the analysis of these issues in the four novels and discuss the moral structure of tragic literature in terms of my conception of tragedy as a critique of virtue.

The purpose of this investigation of modern tragedy is to raise the question of how literary tragedy may nourish ethical reflection. Tragedy can be profoundly disturbing because it seems to reveal the structure of the world at odds with the deepest moral aspirations of humankind. Ethical thinkers have often bypassed or avoided the philosophical and religious problems raised by tragedy, precisely because the phenomenon of a virtuous person's downfall has been perceived as destructive of moral initiative and confidence. The issues raised in the literature of tragedy call for a consideration of the ways that ethical thinkers have accounted for, or failed to account for, the tragic dimensions of moral experience. This study culminates, therefore, in a discussion of how tragedy has been perceived as a problem for ethical reflection and might serve as an incentive to further ethical reflection.

Thus the structure of this study will take the following form. The first chapter is an evaluation of the treatment of tragedy's ethical dimensions in literary criticism and theory. Three areas are discussed: the tragic literature of the Greeks, the history of tragic theory through the nineteenth century, and modern developments in the theory and criticism of tragedy. Four chapters are then devoted to close analysis of the ethical themes in the focal texts: *The Princess Casamassima*, *Billy Budd*, *Nostromo*, and *All the King's Men*. And finally, two concluding chapters discuss the significance of tragedy for ethical reflection. The first of these, chapter VI, interprets the moral structure of narrative tragedy in terms of the notion of a critique of virtue. The last chapter explains why tragedy has been seen as a problem for ethical reflection, and has led to an impasse or to failure to confront the issues raised by tragedy; it concludes by elaborating the significance of tragedy as an incentive for further ethical reflection.

1

The Ethical Dimensions of Tragedy
in Literary Criticism and Theory

Since Aristotle's *Poetics*, literary critics and theorists have recognized that a striking moral situation lies at the heart of tragedy. Tragedy recounts deeds in the lives of individuals who are admirable or heroic, or who in some way surpass normal human standards of character. Tragedy deals with excellence of human character, with virtue in its broadest sense, even when that virtue becomes corrupted. Tragedy depicts heroic characters succumbing to a terrible disaster or misfortune that seems partly to have been inflicted on the protagonists and partly to have been brought about through their own activity. This is the moral phenomenon at the heart of tragedy: that the highest standard of human virtue sometimes leads to the greatest extreme of suffering and misfortune. To a significant degree, the tragic spectacle has fascinated literary critics through the ages because of its moral significance. Tragedy has revealed something of crucial importance about the human moral condition in an unforgettable way which is at once emotionally terrifying, aesthetically beautiful, and intellectually provocative.

Even though literary critics have often been struck by tragedy's moral significance, they have conceived of this dimension of tragedy in very different ways, as we shall see in this chapter. It seems essential to evaluate at the outset of this study these different conceptualizations of the ethical dimensions of tragedy in literary criticism and theory. This subject has intrinsic interest and importance, and yet has not been analyzed from a historical perspective. It will be helpful before interpreting four modern tragic narratives to reflect on how other critics have approached the ethical dimensions of tragedy. We can then appropriate the insights and interests that have proved to have enduring value in literary criticism, rather than approaches that are vague, parochial, or moralistic in a dogmatic, didactic sense. Analysis of the strengths and weaknesses of previous discussions of the ethical significance of tragedy will help us to conceptualize the most fruitful approach to the four narrative tragedies. Thus our notion of narrative tragedy as a critique of virtue is elaborated initially through comparison with other theories of tragedy's moral significance. Chapter VI will summarize and explain our final understanding of tragedy as a critique of virtue, as this notion is worked out in the analyses of the four novels.

The history of ethical approaches to tragedy has been divided here into three parts. First, the present chapter assesses interpretations of Greek tragedy, focusing on how critics have understood the central ethical themes in the *Iliad* and in Greek tragic drama. Three key issues are discussed: the significance of *hamartia* (tragic error), tragedy's representation of Greek ideas of virtue, and the implications of tragedy's depiction of the gods. Each of these issues raises important questions about the similarities and differences between Greek and modern tragedy.

A second section discusses the history of tragic theory from the Italian Renaissance through the late nineteenth century, insofar as literary theorists have sought to conceptualize the ethical significance of tragedy. This analysis culminates in a discussion of Hegel's work, which has great originality and power and has proven to be of practical value in the criticism of A. C. Bradley.

In the last section of this chapter, modern tragic theories are assessed under two rubrics. First, attention will be given to the ways that modern critics have differed about whether tragedy focuses on a representation of evil within the individual tragic hero or within his society. Secondly, an evaluation is made of recent attempts to characterize "the tragic vision" or the central moral significance of the modern tragic novel. Treatment of these issues influences this study's basic approach to tragedy in modern narratives.

These issues seem to be the principle topics which have shaped discussions of the ethical dimensions of tragedy in literary criticism and theory. Careful assessment of the moral issues involved guides our discussion below; we cannot do justice to the full-blown tragic theories of, for instance, Aristotle, Nietzsche, Hegel, or Murray Krieger.

I. *Greek Tragedy*

Interpretations of hamartia

Scholarship on Greek tragedy's moral implications continues to center on Aristotle's discussion in the *Poetics* of *hamartia*, which has been translated variously as "tragic error," "tragic guilt," "flaw of character," "fatal mistake," etc. The treatment of *hamartia* occurs in the context of Aristotle's examination of how the plot of a drama can best produce tragedy's unique emotional effects. The answer to this question follows from the premise that "for the finest form of tragedy, the Plot must be not simple but complex; and further, that it must imitate actions arousing fear and pity, since that is the distinctive function of this kind of imitation" (1452b: 30–2).[1] Three kinds of plot should be avoided: a pre-eminently good man's passage from happiness to misery, a bad person passing from misery to happiness, and a bad man falling from happiness into misery. Each of these plots fails in a different way to arouse both of the tragic emotions, for "pity is occasioned by undeserved misfortune, and fear by that of one like ourselves" (1453a: 5–6). Tragedy should deal instead with "an intermediate kind of personage" whose misfortune comes about through *hamartia*, translated here as "error of judgement":

> There remains, then, the intermediate kind of personage, a man not pre-eminently virtuous and just, whose misfortune, however, is brought upon him not by vice and depravity but by some error of judgement, of the number of those in the enjoyment of great reputation and prosperity; e.g., Oedipus, Thyestes, and the men of note of similar families. The perfect Plot, accordingly, must have a single, and not (as some tell us) a double issue; the change in the hero's fortune must be not from misery to happiness, but on the contrary from happiness to misery; and the cause of it must lie not in any depravity, but in some great error on his part; the man himself being either such as we have described, or better, not worse, than that. . . . The theoretically best tragedy, then, has a Plot of this description. (1453a: 7–16, 23)

Until relatively recently, Aristotle was interpreted as having said that the tragic hero should come to ruin because he sins. The *Poetics* was taken as the basis for a moralistic theory in which tragedy was supposed to show a correlation between the hero's guilt and his consequent suffering, between crime and punishment. Beginning early in the twentieth century, however, a scholarly consensus has been established that the meaning of *hamartia* in the *Poetics* is closer to "error of judgement" than to "moral guilt."[2] J. M. Bremer's systematic and thorough discussion of all the evidence pertaining to the meaning of *hamartia* summarizes this consensus.[3] Bremer argues against the moralistic view of *hamartia* first on the basis of Aristotle's overall attitude to tragedy, which is broadly concerned with the construction of plot rather than with demonstrating drama's moral effect on its audience. Aristotle's underlying

[1] Aristotle, *Poetics*, trans. Ingram Bywater, in *Introduction to Aristotle*, ed. Richard McKeon (New York: Modern Library, 1947).

[2] Despite differences of opinion about the precise definition of *hamartia*, the moralistic interpretation of Aristotle's passage in chapter 13 was criticized by Ingram Bywater, in *Aristotle on the Art of Poetry*, trans. Ingram Bywater with a preface by Gilbert Murray (1909; Oxford: Clarendon Press, 1976); P. van Braam, "Aristotle's Use of [*Hamartia*]," *CQ* 6 (1912), 266–72; I. M. Glanville, "Tragic Error," *CQ* 43 (1949), 47–56; and Gerald Else, *Aristotle's "Poetics": The Argument* (Cambridge: Harvard University Press, 1957). In the title of van Braam's work, as elsewhere in this study, all Greek words have been transliterated.

[3] J. M. Bremer, *Hamartia: Tragic Error in the "Poetics" of Aristotle and in Greek Tragedy* (Amsterdam: Adolf Hakkert, 1969).

premise is that pity and fear will only be aroused in the audience if the hero's downfall takes a certain form, which involves the hero's *hamartia* rather than crime or wickedness. Furthermore, the list of mythological examples Aristotle gives to illustrate good plots emphasizes figures famous for crimes committed in ignorance, not persons with notable defects of character. Aristotle's use of *hamartia* in the *Poetics* may also be compared with his analysis of voluntary and involuntary action in the *Nicomachean Ethics* and elsewhere. An act of *hamartia* is one in which an agent causes some harmful action but is not fully responsible morally because of his ignorance about some crucial circumstance (instrument, object, effect of the action, etc.). A person's misfortune is not blameworthy if it results from ignorance of factual information (the minor premise of a moral syllogism) rather than from ignorance about a general moral principle (the major premise). Finally, an exhaustive semantic study of the use of *hamartia* and its cognates by Aristotle and other Greek authors proves that these words "are virtually never used to describe an action which is felt to be wrong."[4] Bremer concludes that "it is justified to define *hamartia* in *Poetics* 1453a: 10–15 as 'tragic error,' i.e., a wrong action committed in ignorance of its nature, effect, etc., which is the starting point of a causally connected train of events ending in disaster."[5]

Aristotle's view of *hamartia*'s role in tragedy accounts for an important ethical dimension in the spectator's response, pointing out the fact that only a certain kind of dramatic situation calls for the type of ethical judgment which is a condition of the "proper pleasure" of tragedy. The nature of this relationship between dramatic structure, ethical judgment, and aesthetic pleasure needs to be explained. The requirement that tragedy produce pity and fear is central to Aristotle's analysis. Pity and fear are emotions which depend partly upon intellectual and moral considerations. We feel fear for the misfortune of a certain kind of person—someone like ourselves or a little better—because we can imagine ourselves in his place. We pity someone who suffers when we judge that his suffering is undeserved, or at least disproportionate to the mistake by which he brought suffering upon himself. Thus pity and fear will be felt, according to Aristotle, only for the unjustified suffering of a person we admire and respect. As Else makes clear, the peculiar tragic pleasure involves a relationship between intellectual and moral judgments and the emotions of pity and fear:

> The purification of the *pathos*, that is the exculpation of the hero's motive from polluted intent, is precedent to our feeling pity for him. The pity has to be authorized by reason before it can be released. . . . Thus the 'special pleasure' of tragedy—that is, of the best tragedy—is neither simply intellectual

4 Ibid., p. 62.
5 Ibid., p. 63.

nor simply emotional, but has its roots in both realms. It is a pleasure springing from emotion, but an emotion authorized and released by an intellectually conditioned structure of action. The emotion flows unimpeded *because* when we feel it we feel it as justified and inevitable.[6]

Thus the basically aesthetic criticism of tragedy in the *Poetics* involves an essential element of ethical judgment about the injustice of the hero's suffering. Aristotle's reference to *hamartia* calls attention to the spectator's judgment that, because a hero's choices were not fully culpable, his suffering is not morally deserved, and therefore may be pitied.

Though scholars now agree that Aristotle's use of *hamartia* in the *Poetics* does not mean moral guilt, there is substantial disagreement about the exact meaning of the term and its range of applicability. Some scholars see it as a fairly precise concept. Gerald Else narrows the concept's meaning to a specific kind of ignorance: that of the true identity of a blood relative.[7] In the *Poetics*, *hamartia* refers to the literary device which exploits the emotional potential inherent in the threat of violence between two "dear ones" who do not recognize each other. Arthur Adkins interprets Aristotle's *hamartia* as an ethical term applying only to the narrow category of acts involving a mistake of fact. Aristotle does not use it in connection with all of the full range of moral situations which the term can cover in the ordinary usage of Greek thought— situations that we would distinguish as due to moral error, to failure, and to simple ignorance or mistake of fact.[8]

However, most scholars do not see *hamartia* in the *Poetics* functioning as a carefully defined technical term, whether referring to a specific dramatic technique or to a precise ethical category.[9] Rather, Aristotle is interpreted as calling attention to the fact that the hero's route to misfortune must not be attributable to his being punished for an intentional transgression, but is rather the consequence of some factor which provides him with an excuse. While Bremer claims that only an action based on ignorance or an error of judgment will satisfy Aristotle's conditions for a tragic error, Stinton makes clear that the concept of *hamartia* also encompasses voluntary actions which are not fully culpable because of compulsion or the influence of strong passion. Furthermore, *hamartia* "is a general term: it can mean specific acts, specific decisions leading to

---

[6] Else, *Aristotle's "Poetics,"* pp. 447, 449. A similar interpretation of the relationship between moral judgments and aesthetic pleasure was briefly outlined by Charles Reeves in "The Aristotelian Concept of the Tragic Hero," *AJP* 73 (1952), 184–88.

[7] Else, *Aristotle's "Poetics,"* pp. 381–83.

[8] Arthur W. H. Adkins, "Aristotle and the Best Kind of Tragedy," *CQ* 16 (new series) (1966), 82.

[9] Bremer, *Hamartia*; R. D. Dawe, "Some Reflections on Atē and Hamartia," *Harvard Studies in Classical Philology* 72 (1967), 89–123; and T. C. W. Stinton, "*Hamartia* in Aristotle and Greek Tragedy," *CQ* 25 (1975), 221–54.

acts, or dispositions, which may vary from some kind of ignorance to some defect of character."[10] What is common to all the situations involving *hamartia* is not the element of ignorance, but the fact that the moral agent's culpability is reduced in some way. By using the notion of *hamartia*, Aristotle called attention to a crucial ethical judgment spectators make in witnessing a tragic work. A wide range of actions will satisfy the conditions for this judgment.

The significance of Aristotle's approach to tragedy is not his precise definition of *hamartia*, but rather his noticing that a work must secure by some means the spectator's judgment that the hero's downfall, though caused by his own actions, is not entirely deserved. Oedipus's situation of ignorance is not the definition of *hamartia* but only an example of one kind of tragic error. The extenuating circumstances which partially exculpate the hero's actions are not limited to cases in which disaster comes about through ignorance or an error of intellectual judgment. An audience also pities and fears for a character such as Phaedra, who is not morally faultless, but whose suffering far exceeds her culpability for her passion. We respond in a similar way to Antigone, who is fully conscious of her dilemma, but caught in an impossible choice between two moral obligations. A person need not be absolutely blameless for his or her fall to be pitiable; what is essential for tragedy is a disproportion between their fault, if any, and their suffering. There are various ways in which different plays can elicit this kind of judgment from spectators; there is a wide range of degrees of extenuation and moral approval, and consequently of pity and fear which we extend to different protagonists. What is necessary in tragedy is not the presence of one particular technique by which it is elicited, but the fact of this judgment, secured in various ways but indispensable if the protagonist's downfall is to produce the tragic emotions. The analysis of tragic errors in modern novels will explore the various means by which authors show a character's fate as self-induced but not fully culpable because of extenuating circumstances. "Tragic error" will therefore be used to cover not only decisions reached in ignorance of factual information, but also other morally significant actions which precipitate a chain of events leading to disaster.

Tragedy and the Greek Virtues

To focus the entire moral significance of a tragedy on the hero's isolated *hamartia* tends to make the downfall merely an instance of sheer bad luck. A tragic error has deeper roots in conflicts of value within the author's culture, and in the Greek view of the gods' role in human affairs. Aristotle remarked that tragedy deals with men "like ourselves or a little better," but he did not develop this point. Greek tragedy depicts

[10] Stinton, "*Hamartia*," p. 254.

characters who are both nobly born and basically good in terms of Greek standards of morality—at least until their tragic error. In many ways, the heroes and heroines of Athenian drama embody that culture's ideals of virtue, or moral excellence. Yet these characters suffer and die wretchedly; their virtue does not guarantee their success or happiness in life. In fact, it is often a hero's most morally praiseworthy actions that bring about his destruction. Prometheus's horrible suffering is brought about by his determination to help mankind and his courage in defying the punishment of Zeus. Oedipus's fate is realized through the energy and intelligence with which he persists in his search for the murderer of Laius. Both Antigone and Creon justify their actions in terms of the most fundamental moral and religious obligations due to family and state. These and other Greek tragedies show virtuous characters acting in situations in which they are unable to avoid their own destruction in carrying out their moral duties. Their tragic errors seem to grow out of their very striving for moral virtue.

James Redfield has shown how the tragic literature of the Greeks explores that culture's moral norms and tests their possible implications. Redfield sees the story of Hector in the *Iliad* as that of "an admirable man who falls into error without ceasing to be admirable and who dies a death which is tragic because we find it inevitable and in some sense his own fault, but undeserved."[11] He argues that to understand the *Iliad* requires a study of the Homeric poet's cultural values, specifically the heroic ethic of warfare. The poet is "a student of culture" who "puts the rules of culture to use under intelligible constraints and asks how they would then function. He imaginatively tests the limits of his culture's capacity to function."[12] In the *Iliad* Homer inquires into the limitations and self-contradictions of the heroic ethic. Redfield sets the crucial notion of tragic error in the broad context of the poet's study of his culture's ideas of moral virtue:

> The poet's inquiry into culture is both a criticism of culture—for it shows culture to be a source of error—and an affirmation of culture—for it shows error to be properly punished. . . . Error, in any case, is from this point of view the pivotal tragic event, and the interpretation of error is the focus of the poet's inquiry. In his error the actor enacts the limitations and self-contradictions of his culture; through his imitation of error, the consequences of error, and the healing of error, the poet leads us, not to a rejection of culture, but to a reaffirmation of it on a new level of troubled awareness.[13]

This interpretation of tragic error in the light of a culture's ideas about

---

[11] James Redfield, *Nature and Culture in the "Iliad": The Tragedy of Hector* (Chicago: University of Chicago Press, 1975), p. ix.
[12] Ibid., p. 80.
[13] Ibid., p. 91.

virtue explains why *hamartia* does not simply consist in bad luck or a trivial accident. A tragic error seems so perplexing and so significant because it is the kind of mistake which would only be made by a character who embodies the virtues most valued by his culture. The failure of virtue to be "good" in certain circumstances reveals basic conflicts and recurring moral dilemmas that a culture is unable to eliminate or solve. And a tragic figure's story becomes especially significant when it reveals not only the hidden implications of a particular culture's norms, but the general form of human life-in-culture. My interpretation of modern narrative tragedies uses Redfield's study of the *Iliad* as a theoretical model, taking a basically thematic approach to tragedy by focusing on how the depiction of a tragic error reveals conflicts of value in the poet's culture.

However, an approach to modern tragedy needs to take into account differences between Greek and modern ethical assumptions. If Greek assumptions about virtue are an essential presupposition of the first tragedies, then their difference from modern ethical ideas may mean that tragedy is no longer possible. Arthur Adkins explains the basic differences between the "results culture" of ancient Greece and the moral presuppositions of modern Western democracies in terms of the relative unimportance of the concept of responsibility in Greek ethics: "For any man brought up in a western democratic society the related concepts of duty and responsibility are the central concepts of ethics; and we are inclined to take it as an unquestionable truth, though there is abundant evidence to the contrary, that the same must be true of all societies. In this respect, at least, we are all Kantians now."[14] Adkins holds that the Greeks put a supreme value on the "competitive" virtues or excellences (the ideal of merit or *aretē*). In judgments about this kind of virtue, the success or failure of an action was of paramount importance. Only a secondary value was placed on the "cooperative" or "quiet" virtues, the moral qualities related to justice and fairness. As a result, judgments about an agent's intentions were not as important an aspect of moral evaluation in Greek thought as such judgments are to modern ethical thought based on the concepts of duty and responsibility. But though Greek society placed supreme value on the successful outcome of action, it recognized that it was possible for a virtuous man not to meet with success in life. Such a recognition forms the structure of Greek tragedy, and it underlies Aristotle's statements that the possession of virtue is only a potentiality for success and happiness, and that happiness does not consist in a person's possession of virtue, but in the exercise of virtue in

---

[14] Arthur W. H. Adkins, *Merit and Responsibility* (Chicago: University of Chicago Press, 1960) p. 2.

propitious circumstances.[15] The phenomenon of a virtuous man acting in circumstances which lead to failure and misfortune has been a deeply disturbing problem to many thinkers, but it was especially so for the Greeks. Thus it might seem that a presupposition of tragedy is a "results culture" that places supreme value on the successful outcome of action. Adkins's distinction between the Greek ideal of *aretē* and the modern concept of responsibility raises the question of the extent to which one can legitimately interpret modern tragedy as a critique of virtue.

Granting the differences between the moral concepts of Greek and modern thought, a fundamental pattern in the moral structure of tragedy can be discerned. Tragedy is based on a radical discrepancy between the good intentions that motivate an action and the actual consequences of action. This basic pattern is based on the fact that any culture must consider the moral significance of both human intentionality and the objective consequences of actions. As does modern ethical thought, Greek thought distinguished error from deliberate wrongdoing. Though the Greeks judged the importance of intentions in a different way than modern ethics, they clearly distinguished cases of voluntary wrongdoing or crime from cases of damage due to accident, mistake, or error. This is precisely the distinction Aristotle makes in his discussion of the hero's *hamartia* in the *Poetics*, and on it depends the whole structure of tragic pleasure. Both Greek and modern ethical thought must also judge and reward or punish the consequences of actions; any functioning society is to some extent a "results culture." Good intentions and well-meaning efforts influence judgment about but do not completely excuse actions which in fact prove harmful. Both Greek and modern moral thought evaluate the objective results of actions and make judgments about the culpability of the moral agents involved. Both cultures recognize that harmful actions can be performed by a person who is not fully culpable. And, in both Greek and modern culture, the genre of tragedy explores certain difficult cases which confuse moral assessment: situations in which characters act harmfully but are not fully culpable largely because of their well-meaning and even praiseworthy efforts to act rightly.

---

[15] Aristotle, *Nicomachean Ethics*, trans. W. D. Ross, in *Introduction to Aristotle* (New York: Modern Library, 1947): "With those who identify happiness with virtue or some one virtue our account is in harmony; for to virtue belongs virtuous activity. But it makes, perhaps, no small difference whether we place the chief good in possession or in use, in state of mind or in activity. . . . As in the Olympic Games it is not the most beautiful and the strongest that are crowned but those who compete (for it is some of these that are victorious), so those who act win, and rightly win, the noble and good things in life" (1098b: 30–99a: 7). Happiness depends partly on "external goods" and propitious circumstances, for "it is impossible, or not easy, to do noble acts without the proper equipment. . . . Happiness seems to need this sort of prosperity in addition; for which reason some identify happiness with good fortune, though others identify it with virtue" (1099a: 31–99b: 7).

On the other hand, certain differences between the Greek ideal of *aretē* and modern understandings of virtue have important implications for our interpretation of modern tragedy as a critique of virtue. The moral stature of the central figure in a modern tragedy usually does not depend upon his aristocratic social status or his military prowess, but rather on qualities such as integrity, fairness to others, or responsibility in meeting some difficult set of obligations. The highest value of such a protagonist may be not his status in the eyes of his community, but his own moral self-respect. Consequently, his fall may entail primarily an internalized sense of corruption and guilt, rather than shame before others. The suffering the hero undergoes may result not from his community's swift act of judgment, but from his own protracted state of internal conflict and moral anguish. The "recognition" of Aristotle's *Poetics*, involving the hero's sudden realization that his position in his community has been destroyed, may be replaced by a halting struggle to understand the protagonist's moral responsibility for evil—and the locus of such recognition may be displaced in a narrative tragedy from the hero himself to a more reflective character or the narrator.

Because of the differences between Greek and modern ethics, then, certain modifications are necessary in taking Redfield's approach to the *Iliad* as a model for interpreting modern narrative tragedy. However, we should not lose sight of the continuity of the tradition of tragic literature as a series of explorations of the conditions in which a particular form of virtue leads to self-destructive and morally evil actions. In modern tragic novels, too, the roots of tragic error lie in the cultural values and the ideals of virtue that help form a character's moral intentions and purposes.

Tragedy and the Gods

The second level on which tragic error has deeper roots than Aristotle indicates is its close connection with the idea of *atē* or divine blinding. Like *hamartia*, the term *atē* is used in a variety of senses in Greek literature. The orginal meaning of *atē* in the Homeric epics is "a kind of moral blindness or damaged deliberative capacity" or "a temporary clouding or bewildering of the normal consciousness."[16] *Atē* expresses the conjunction of a number of elements: a person's mental or moral delusion, the implication that demonic powers are somehow involved, and the outcome of this mysterious process in a disastrous event. In different contexts the term can refer primarily to the mental confusion in which a character brings about his own ruin or to the actual blow which damages his mental processes. There are numerous affinities between the

---

[16] Redfield, *Nature and Culture*, p. 97; E. R. Dodds, *The Greeks and the Irrational* (Boston: Beacon Press, 1951), p. 5.

ideas of *hamartia* and *atē*. *Atē* is a more archaic word and is not used at all by Euripedes or Aristotle. But although they belong to different periods of Greek thought, *atē* and *hamartia* refer to the same phenomenon of a good person's self-caused but unwilled destruction:

> Both *atē* and *hamartia* point to one and the same human reality: tragic error, but in different ways. The Homeric conception of *atē* relates the error to an arbitrary and malicious interference of the gods with human action, causing infatuation in man and resulting in disaster. Aristotle's *hamartia*, seen in the whole of his theory, is a link in a coherent chain of events, for according to Aristotle every event "must arise out of the very structure of the plot." . . . In this theory there is no place for divine interference.[17]

Dawe sees the concept of *atē* as the "missing link" between those theories of tragedy which emphasize a character's own responsibility for his downfall and those which see men as the victims of the gods: "Often in [tragedy] the means by which the gods send men to their doom is to cause them to commit an error that will lead to their downfall. The gods consign men to destruction not with the thunderbolt, but by interfering with the correct functioning of the mind and its judgment."[18] It is by exploiting human weaknesses that the gods work their will. But Aristotle sees this whole process in terms of human decision and action. Aristotle's use of *hamartia* refers to the psychological aspects of the phenomenon that Homer, Aeschylus, and Sophocles called *atē*—an old and superstitious notion which Aristotle did not accept. As an interpretation of tragedy, Aristotle's idea of *hamartia* is only partially accurate with respect to the causes of the hero's downfall, for he completely neglects the role of the gods in the dramatic action. "Greek poetry was a representation of men *and gods*. One half of this world has disappeared from Aristotle's field of view."[19] The close connection between *hamartia* and *atē* in the thinking of the tragic poets calls for a consideration of tragic error in the context of Greek drama's implied understanding of the gods.

In Greek tragic drama the downfall of a hero is sometimes ascribed at once to the malevolence of a god, fate, the ill will of another character, and the hero's own mistaken decisions. E. R. Dodds has explained how, for example, Agamemnon's explanations of his actions in the *Iliad* are "overdetermined," that is, attributed to a number of different causes.[20] To the modern reader these explanations appear contradictory, but each discloses a significant aspect of the dramatic events. It is important to emphasize that the suggestion that gods are involved in the action does not

[17] Bremer, *Hamartia*, pp. 111–12.
[18] Dawe, "Reflections on *Atē*," p. 100.
[19] Else, *Aristotle's "Poetics*," pp. 474–75.
[20] Dodds, *The Greeks and the Irrational*, p. 7.

make questions about moral agency illusory, or imply a systematic Greek belief in determinism. A character's attribution of some event to the influence of Zeus or *moira* (fate or one's lot) does not provide an excuse for moral error: "The belief in non-human causation of human action has practically no effects on the ascription of responsibility."[21] At the same time, the depiction of the influence of the gods on human action has serious theological implications. The direct relationship between tragic error and the activity of a deity raises the disturbing religious problem of theodicy. Human responsibility is not negated by evidence of divine involvement in events; but neither does the fact that human agents help cause their own ruin diminish the significance of the portrayal of gods putting a person in a situation in which he or she has little choice but to make the decision which leads to self-destruction.

The ways that the ethical issues raised in tragedy bear on theological matters have been conceptualized in two ways. Hugh Lloyd-Jones holds that Greek drama affirms the justice (*dike*) of Zeus, and that the sufferings of men are always deserved, though it is often difficult for humans to understand the "violent grace" with which Zeus punishes transgressions:

> Since it is far removed from Christian or other modern notions of justice, Sophoclean justice is even harder for us to understand than it was for Sophocles' contemporaries. *Dike* means not only "justice," but "the order of the universe," and from the human point of view that order often seems to impose a natural rather than a moral law. Yet Sophocles believed that the gods were just, and just in a sense in which the word was in his day applied to men. What made it hard, he thought, for men to understand the justice of the gods was the immense extent of time which may separate cause from punishment, and the complex interweaving within human history of different causal chains of injustice followed by chastisement.[22]

Lloyd-Jones justifies the fates of many of Aeschylus's protagonists in terms of beliefs about family solidarity and inherited guilt, which asserted that a person's crime may be punished by the suffering of his descendents. However, the principal weakness of the thesis of "the justice of Zeus" is that it does not offer a satisfying explanation of why the

---

[21] Adkins, *Merit*, p. 25. Though this passage summarizes Adkins's view of responsibility in Homeric society, he finds the same pattern in later Greek thought, including tragic drama. In his discussion of "external interference" with human agency (chapter six), Adkins argues that belief in an inherited curse does not diminish the responsibility of the heroes of Aeschylus's plays: "Aeschylus asserts that even in the extreme case of the accursed family, though some may be predisposed towards evil by supernatural agency, none are so predestined. Though the choice may be harder for some than for others, there is always a choice; and hence no one may escape responsibility for his actions on these grounds" (pp. 123–24).

[22] Hugh Lloyd-Jones, *The Justice of Zeus* (Berkeley: University of California Press, 1971), p. 128.

divine must appear demonic to humans: it does not fully account for the way that tragedy raises the problem of evil. One could dispute Lloyd-Jones's interpretations of numerous plays, particularly *Prometheus Bound*.[23] This interpretation of Greek tragedy fails to account for the portrayal of divine power as at least morally ambiguous, and in some cases blatantly unjust and arbitrary.

The other major interpretation of Greek tragedy's implied theology, Paul Ricoeur's *The Symbolism of Evil*, stresses the moral ambiguity or actual evil of the gods' actions. For Ricoeur, the hidden and "unavowable" theology of tragedy is that the gods blind mortals and lead them to destruction: this is "the scandalous theology of predestination to evil."[24] Ricoeur thinks tragedy discloses evil's origin as being in the demonic side of divine power as much as in man's will. Though some thinkers attempted to moralize the jealousy of the gods as a punishment for human pride, such attempts involved a loss of the central tragic vision of the "wicked god." Yet, according to Ricoeur, tragedy does not simply picture man as a passive victim of the gods; man's share in the genesis of evil is fully recognized. The tragic vision implies a dialectic of human and divine responsibility; it establishes a shifting relationship between the aggression of the gods—"a hostile transcendence"—and the resistance of a human agent—"a freedom that *delays* the fulfillment of fate."[25] Taken alone, neither the wrath of the gods nor human pride would be tragic; the "crux of the tragic" is found where these two elements are conjoined. Tragedy thus implies a double view of human moral responsibility: the protagonists of Greek drama are at once morally guilty for the consequences of their "destructive freedom" and victims of malevolent divine power. Tragedy involves a sort of anti-theodicy, by revealing the impossibility of trying to "justify the ways of god to man":

> The theme of the wrath of God, the ultimate motive of the tragic consciousness, is invincible to the arguments of the philosopher as well as the theologian. For there is no rational vindication of the innocence of God; every explanation of the Stoic or Leibnizian type is wrecked, like the naive arguments of Job's friends, on the suffering of the innocent. They leave intact the opacity of evil and the opacity of the world "in which such a thing is possible."[26]

It is very difficult to generalize about the works of even one author, so we must be extremely cautious about drawing conclusions about the "theology" implied by Greek tragedy as a whole. Yet it seems indisputable that

---

[23] For an interpretation of the "twin masks of Zeus," see Anthony C. Yu, "New Gods and Old Order: Tragic Theology in the *Prometheus Bound*," *JAAR* 39 (1971), 19–42.

[24] Paul Ricoeur, *The Symbolism of Evil*, trans. Emerson Buchanan (Boston: Beacon Press, 1967), p. 212.

[25] Ibid., p. 220.

[26] Ibid., p. 326.

the portrayal of gods as implicated in a mortal's destruction raises in nearly every tragedy at least the *question* of whether the strongest powers in the cosmos are ultimately opposed to human happiness, regardless of how or whether this question is finally resolved. Dodds's theory of the over-determination of irrational action by both divine and human causes, the studies by Bremer and Dawe linking *hamartia* and *atē*, and Ricoeur's interpretation of the dialectic between human freedom and a hostile transcendence: all these studies show that Greek tragedy was preoccupied—even obsessed—with the demonic aspects of the divine. But the ways tragic situations are represented in different works suggest various conceptions of man's relation to the gods. In a work like *Oedipus Rex*, the fate of the protagonist shows a world in which human existence is terribly precarious because of the inability of even the keenest human intelligence to escape the destruction worked by divine power. Such a depiction of the awful suffering which may be one's fate at the hands of a hostile deity implies what may be called a tragic *vision* or worldview. Other works present an invividual's or family's tragic *situation*, but do not imply that the relation of the gods to humans is inevitably one of tyranny and malice. In the *Oresteia*, the release of Orestes and the conversion of the Erinyes to Eumenides offers hope for an end to tragic suffering. The spectacle of a good person's destruction usually raises the disturbing question of whether the gods and the structures of the universe are inimical to the possibility of human happiness, but particular dramatic works imply different answers to that question, or simply leave the question unresolved.[27] Therefore, the common basis of the genre of tragedy is better conceptualized in terms of the thematic issues raised (or the questions asked) rather than in terms of the various solutions or resolutions (if any) given to those issues.

It needs to be emphasized that works which do not imply a totally tragic vision of man's relation to the cosmos are still worth calling "tragedy." What makes a work of literature a tragedy is its depiction of the serious and significant suffering of a good person. This spectacle is thought-provoking because it raises the question of whether the universe is ultimately hostile to humankind, especially in its essential moral aspirations. A particular work may or may not imply an explanation of the disturbing situation in terms of a conception of the divine.

This discussion of tragic theology is not irrelevant to a study of modern narrative tragedy, even though no gods are depicted in the novels to be discussed. For modern novels, too, show the error which leads to a

---

[27] This distinction between a tragic situation and a tragic vision (and between a question raised by tragedy and an answer which may be implied) is similar to one made by Albin Lesky in *Greek Tragedy*, trans. H. A. Frankfort (London: Ernest Benn Limited, 1965), p. 13. The distinction is a rough one, and there is room for a good deal of debate about particular plays.

character's ruin as "forced" by certain impersonal powers. These forces may be hereditary influences, psychological impulses, or social and historical pressures, but their effect on a character's moral agency is in many ways analogous to the role played by the gods in Greek tragedy. For example, Thomas Hardy portrays Jude Fawley and Tess as caught between their needs for love and the power of social conventions about sexuality. There are tragic aspects of the situations of George Eliot's Lydgate and Dorothea Brooke, for these characters' desires for a meaningful vocation are thwarted as much by inflexible social institutions and customs as by their own follies. In modern works, overpowering impersonal forces seem to crush just those individuals who strive to realize their moral ideals or aspirations. Such works may imply that the world's order—or disorder—is ultimately hostile to human happiness: a vision similar in many ways to that represented in certain Greek tragedies. Though a character's own choices contribute to his or her downfall, the appalling waste of human goodness may be presented as an indication of an essential flaw in the structure of the world rather than simply as a flaw in the character or judgment of the person destroyed. When an individual is destroyed because his actions express the only way his essential dignity or integrity can be affirmed, such an event is profoundly upsetting because it reveals the structure of the world at odds with the deepest needs of human nature. But the repercussions of the spectacle of an admirable person's downfall can be presented in various ways. As in Greek drama, depiction of a tragic moral situation may not be presented as evidence for a full-blown tragic vision of existence. This can only be determined by a study of each individual work, not by deduction from a theory of tragedy. In short, our discussion of Greek tragedy's portrayal of the gods raises the question of whether certain modern novels imply a vision of man's position in the universe and his chances of being both morally virtuous and happy. We will ask, in the case of *The Princess Casamassima*, *Billy Budd*, *Nostromo*, and *All the King's Men*, whether the depiction of a tragic moral situation implies a wider vision of human life.

In summary, this assessment of Greek tragedy raised three issues that reveal important ethical aspects of later tragic literature. The discussion of *hamartia* in Greek drama and Aristotle's *Poetics* indicated the decisive role played by tragic error in bringing about the protagonist's downfall. Aristotle's crucial insight was that an audience only feels the "proper pleasure" of tragedy if the hero's fall comes about as a result of his ignorance, misjudgment, or other extenuating circumstances rather than from deliberate wrongdoing. Second, Redfield's interpretation of the *Iliad* showed that a tragic error can be understood in the context of a culture's ideal of virtue; the tragedy of a good man reveals the poet's assessment of conflicts among his culture's moral values. The issue of whether Greek tragedy involves a kind of theology raises the question of whether a modern novel's depiction of a tragic moral situation implies a wider vision of human existence in the world.

II. *Tragic Theory through the Nineteenth Century*

Neoclassical and Romantic Views

The few comments on tragedy before the Italian Renaissance deal primarily with rhetorical and stylistic issues, rather than with ethical ones. A rebirth of interest in tragedy during the sixteenth century followed the publication of editions of Homer, Euripedes, and Sophocles, and the rediscovery of Aristotle's *Poetics*. The Greek plays served as models for fresh attempts to write tragedy, and numerous commentaries on the *Poetics* were written. Two passages in Aristotle's work became the foundation of the theory that tragedy should have a moral effect on spectators. The *hamartia* passage was interpreted as requiring that the hero be destroyed because of his sin. And Aristotle's reference to *catharsis* was taken to mean that tragedy should improve the moral condition of spectators by purging undesirable passions. The tremendous value placed on Aristotle's theory continued in the French neoclassical tradition, which represents the height of the moralistic theory of tragedy. Other influences on the neoclassical theory were Seneca's plays, showing his Stoic view of passion as the cause of human suffering, and Christian morality plays during the Middle Ages, portraying the wickedness of fallen man and the catastrophe that befalls those who place their trust in Fortune. Because of the Church's suspicion of the theater, there were numerous "defenses" of poetry, and the claim that drama has a beneficial moral effect on spectators usually offered tragedy as the chief example. Political leaders were often singled out as the special object of tragedy's moral purpose. As Sidney put it, tragedy "maketh kings fear to be tyrants, and tyrants manifest their tyrannical humours; [and] teacheth the uncertainty of this world, and upon how weak foundations gilden roofs are bilded."[28]

The seventeenth century French theory of drama was founded on a negative evaluation of human passion, coupled with an interpretation of catharsis as a process of moral improvement. Racine's Preface to *Phèdre* (1677) illustrates this moralistic interpretation of tragedy:

> I have not made one [play] where virtue is put in a more favorable light than in this one; the least faults are severely punished; the very thought of a crime is regarded with as much horror as the crime itself; the weaknesses of love are shown as true weaknesses; the passions are displayed only to show all the disorder of which they are the cause; and vice is everywhere

---

[28] Philip Sidney, "An Apology for Poetry," in *Criticism: The Major Texts*, ed. Walter Jackson Bate (New York: Harcourt Brace Jovanovich; enlarged edition, 1970), p. 94.

depicted in colors which make the deformity recognized and hated. That is properly the end which every man who works for the public should propose to himself; and it is that which the first tragic poets kept in sight above everything.[29]

A latent conflict existed between the moralistic idea of tragic error and the French doctrine of the decencies (les bienséances), which demanded that the poet free his characters of all unseemly qualities or manners. Racine had to argue by Aristotle's authority for the right to show his heroes as anything less than morally perfect: "Aristotle, far from asking of us perfect heroes, wants, on the contrary, that tragic characters . . . should be neither entirely good, nor entirely wicked. . . . It is therefore necessary for them to have a moderate goodness, that is to say a virtue capable of weakness, and that they should fall into misfortune by some fault which makes them pitied without making them detested."[30] Corneille emphasized drama's role in purging the mind of destructive passions: tragedy purges the causes of the major vices, while comedy deals with the minor ones. In 1692 Andre Dacier linked the ideas of *hamartia* and catharsis, holding that the hero's error results from the same kind of passion from which the spectators are released.

Similar views of tragedy's moral effect were expressed in England during the seventeenth century. In 1679 Dryden wrote of "the end or scope of tragedy, which is, to rectify or purge our passions, fear, and pity," and thus cure us of the two main vices, "pride and want of commiseration."[31] Milton's Preface to *Samson Agonistes* (1671) expresses the common view of catharsis as a purge for unhealthy and dangerous passions, a purge which operates medicinally like the remedy of "physic" for bad humors:

> Tragedy, as it was anciently composed, hath been ever held the gravest, moralest, and most profitable of all other poems: therefore said by Aristotle to be of power, by raising pity and fear, or terror, to purge the mind of those and suchlike passions, that is, to temper and reduce them to just measure with a kind of delight, stirred up by reading or seeing those passions well imitated. Nor is Nature wanting in her own effects to make good his assertion; for so in physic, things of melancholic hue and quality are used against melancholy, sour against sour, salt to remove salt humors.[32]

---

[29] Preface to *Phèdre*, in *Racine: Five Plays*, trans. with an introduction by Kenneth Muir (New York: Farrer, Straus, and Giroux, 1960), p. 177.

[30] Preface to *Andromaque*, in *Five Plays*, pp. 2–3.

[31] John Dryden, "Preface to *Troilus and Cressida*," in Barrett H. Clark, ed., *European Theories of the Drama: An Anthology of Dramatic Theory and Criticism* (New York: D. Appleton & Co., revised edition, 1929), p. 194.

[32] Milton's Preface to *Samson Agonistes*, in *The Portable Milton*, ed. with an introduction by Douglas Bush (New York: The Viking Press, 1949), p. 610.

The moralistic theory that tragedy should show the punishment of vice and the reward of virtue was codified as the "doctrine" of "poetic justice" by Thomas Rymer in 1678.

Samuel Johnson represents the height of the neoclassical tradition in many ways, yet his common sense and insight as a practical critic saved him from the rigidity of the age's many doctrines and rules, and his opinions influenced the romantic reaction against didacticism. On the one hand, Johnson sometimes held that the poet's obligation to present good examples of moral conduct required a "just distribution of good and evil" to his characters. Thus the first of the faults Johnson finds in Shakespeare is the playwrite's casual attitude to poetic justice:

> Shakespeare's first effect is that to which may be imputed most of the evil in books or men. He sacrifices virtue to convenience, and is so much more careful to please than to instruct, that he seems to write without any moral purpose. . . . He makes no just distribution of good or evil, nor is always careful to shew in the virtuous a disapprobation of the wicked; he carries his persons indifferently through right or wrong, and at the close dismisses them without further care, and leaves their examples to operate by chance. This fault the barbarity of his age cannot extenuate; for it is always a writer's duty to make the world better, and justice is a virtue independent of time or place.[33]

Johnson therefore defended Nahum Tate's revision of *King Lear*, in which Lear triumphs in the end, the villains are dethroned, and Cordelia and Edgar are happily married. A reader's "natural ideas of justice" should lead him to prefer the version of the play which distributes reward and punishment according to moral standards: "A play in which the wicked prosper, and the virtuous miscarry, may doubtless be good, because it is a just representation of the common events of human life: but since all reasonable beings naturally love justice, I cannot easily be persuaded, that the observation of justice makes a play worse; or, that if other excellencies are equal, the audience will not always rise better pleased from the final triumph of persecuted virtue."[34]

But though Johnson criticized Shakespeare for frequently neglecting opportunities to instruct his audience, he recognized that Shakespeare's genius transcends the conventions and requirements of the moralistic critic, and he justified the Bard's plays as giving an accurate representation of "the real state of sublunary nature." In defending Shakespeare from censure for mixing comic and tragic scenes, Johnson claimed that "there is always an appeal open from criticism to nature":

[33] Johnson's "Preface to Shakespeare," in *Samuel Johnson: Selected Poetry and Prose*, ed. with an introduction and notes by Frank Brady and W. K. Wimsatt (Berkeley: University of California Press, 1977), p. 307.

[34] Johnson's "Preface to *King Lear*," in *The Selected Writings of Samuel Johnson*, ed. with an introduction by Katharine Rogers (New York: New American Library, 1981), p. 295.

Shakespeare's plays are not in the rigorous and critical sense either tragedies or comedies, but compositions of a distinct kind; exhibiting the real
state of sublunary nature, which partakes of good and evil, joy and sorrow,
mingled with endless variety of proportion and innumerable modes of
combination; and expressing the course of the world, in which the loss of
one is the gain of another; in which, at the same time, the reveler is hasting
to his wine, and the mourner burying his friend; in which the malignity of
one is sometimes defeated by the frolic of another; and many mischiefs and
many benefits are done and hindered without design.[35]

The appeal to nature could justify tragedy's depiction of the actual state
of humankind's moral affairs, including the downfall of the virtuous and
the prosperity of the wicked. Johnson defended Addison's play *Cato* on
these grounds even though it violated the norm of poetic justice. Johnson, then, is a transitional figure in the theory of tragedy. He often
expressed the typical neoclassical critic's demand for a just distribution
of reward and punishment. Yet his appeal to nature in defending certain
works anticipated the romantic critics' concern with tragedy's depiction
of evil and suffering in the context of history or nature.

Renaissance and neoclassical theory was preoccupied in large part
with questions of style, method, and dramatic effect. Deeper problems of
moral conflict and the meaning of suffering in human history could not
be raised, given the common understandings of morality as a matter of
rational self-control and passion as a vice leading to sin and punishment.
Romantic literary criticism and Hegel's writings show the emergence
in tragic theory of a new concern with metaphysical questions about
human finitude and the meaning of suffering, producing a radically
different view of tragedy's moral significance. During the nineteenth
century, thinking about tragedy's moral dimensions developed in two
new directions. First, literary theories increasingly emphasized human
character. Partly because of the enormous popularity of *Hamlet*, critics
defended as an artistic end in itself the depiction of the complications
and moral dilemmas of individual personalities. Second, romantic theories of tragedy reveal a new preoccupation with the phenomenon of "*the
tragic*" in life: criticism of dramatic tragedy both gives rise to and is
itself shaped by philosophical speculations about necessity and freedom,
about universality and individuality. As we shall see in the theories of
Hegel and A. C. Bradley, these two tendencies come together in the
conception of the tragic protagonist (and also the poet) as a heroic figure
who bears the burdens of finitude.

Romantic literary theory marks a change in critical orientation from
the neoclassical interest in literature's mirroring of reality and its rhetorical effects on an audience to a new emphasis on the poet's expression of

[35] Johnson's "Preface to Shakespeare," in *Selected Prose*, ed. Wimsatt and Brady,
pp. 303–4.

his own personal thoughts and feelings.[36] Most romantic critics conceived of literature's primary moral dimension not in terms of a poet's
didactic intentions in relation to readers, but in terms of humanistic
values implicit in the creative process. Particularly valued was the poet's
power of uniting in his work the poles of reality that become separated
in human experience: subject and object, word and thing, feeling and
thought, and so forth. Romantic writers sought to liberate poetry from
the typical neoclassical demand for moral instruction. Yet the romantic
movement's proclamations of the poet's freedom from didactic requirements were usually based on a broader, if less specific, conception of
literature's moral dimensions. Morality was thought to be important not
as the basis for a poet's conscious attempt to inculcate virtue, but rather
as an essential aspect of human nature which would find expression
inevitably and spontaneously in an author's depiction of reality, in his
"subject."

The new view of morality is revealed in romantic statements about
tragedy. Tragedy was seen as the depiction and glorification of a heroic
soul able to endure or defy a cruel fate. Tragedy's moral dimension was
seen as an essential aspect of the work's subject matter—the heroic
character—or as an aspect of the poet's genius. Both the tragic hero and
the dramatist himself were thought to show the greatness of the human
soul, its power to contain the antinomies of the world within itself. Since
the moral dimension of tragedy should find expression naturally, the
poet need not labor to inculcate virtue. Goethe's views are representative: "If there be a moral in the subject, it will appear, and the poet has
nothing to consider but the effect and artistic treatment of the subject. If
a poet has as high a soul as Sophocles, his influence will always be moral,
let him do what he will." Greek tragedy did not make "moral beauty" its
special objective, but "pure humanity in its whole extent. . . . The morality of *Antigone* was not invented by Sophocles, but was contained in the
subject."[37]

An important reason for the romantic reconception of literature's
moral dimensions was its affirmative attitude towards the expression of
human feeling. This new appreciation of feeling in tragedy had roots in
an earlier "sentimental" interpretation of *catharsis*:

> The Aristotelian catharsis of undesirably soft emotions (pity and fear) slides
> conveniently into a new and sentimentalized version of catharsis—such as
> that which Dryden in the Preface to his *Troilus and Cressida* adapts from
> Rapin: not catharsis (or "abatement") of fear and pity, but abatement of

[36] Meyer Abrams, *The Mirror and the Lamp: Romantic Theory and the Critical Tradition* (Oxford: Oxford University Press, 1953).
[37] From *Conversations of Goethe with Eckerman and Soret*, trans. John Oxenford, in
Clark, *Theories of Drama*, pp. 333, 335.

such aggressive and evil emotions as pride and anger through the *feeding and watering* of the soft-hearted emotions of fear and pity. Thus the most nearly amenable classical doctrine became, by a sufficient deflection, an authority on the side of the coming ethics of benevolent feeling.[38]

Whereas the neoclassical theory saw passion as the root of vice, and therefore the object of discipline and reform through the catharsis of tragedy, romantic writers approved of the poet's expression of the deepest passions of the heart as a moral end in itself. Tragedy came to be seen as a representation of the conflict of passions within one heroic figure, whose division of feeling finally destroyed him.

Romantic critics recognized important differences between contemporary tragedy and ancient works and attempted to explain them with theories of "classic" and "romantic" art. Largely through the various activities of A. W. Schlegel, Shakespeare's plays became paradigmatic as the finest example of a kind of tragedy qualitatively different from, but just as valuable as, Greek drama. Schlegel was the translator who made Shakespeare's plays accessible in Germany, and the critic who not only defended Shakespeare as a tragedian in the tradition of the Greeks (as had Lessing), but viewed Shakespearean tragedy as an equally valid but different kind of drama, based upon the grand division of classic and romantic art. Schlegel was an early defender of attempts to write modern bourgeois tragedies; he had a decisive impact on the aesthetic theories of Coleridge; and he was one of the first critics to undertake extensive analysis of the special moral qualities of individual Shakespearean characters.[39] The effect of all of these activities was to establish the common assumption in Germany as in England that Shakespeare's focus on complexities of character created the possibility of a new romantic tragedy different from Greek drama.

Schlegel also exemplifies the second main characteristic of romantic tragic theory: its focus on the philosophical issues raised by the phenomenon of "the tragic" in life. Schlegel's view of the "tragic tone of mind" contemplating the unbridgeable gap between the finite and the infinite resembles Kant's conception of the sublime in art, though Schlegel suggests a somewhat different emotional response to the phenomenon:

> As soon as we begin to call ourselves to account for our actions, reason compels us to fix this aim higher and higher, till we come at last to the highest end of our existence: and here that longing for the infinite which is inherent in our being is baffled by the limits of our finite existence. All that we do, all that we effect, is vain and perishable. . . . When we think upon all this every heart which is not dead to feeling must be overpowered by an inexpressible melancholy for which there is no other counterpoise than the

---

[38] William K. Wimsatt and Cleanth Brooks, *Literary Criticism: A Short History* (New York: Knopf, 1957), pp. 206–7.
[39] For an evaluation of Schlegel's criticism of Shakespeare, see Arthur M. Eastman, *A Short History of Shakespearean Criticism* (New York: Norton, 1968), chapter three.

consciousness of a vocation transcending the limits of this earthly life. This is the tragic tone of mind; and when the thought of the possible issues out of the mind as a living reality, when this tone pervades and animates a visible representation of the most striking instances of violent revolutions in a man's fortunes, either prostrating his mental energies, or calling forth the most heroic endurance—then the result is *Tragic Poetry*.[40]

Schlegel's definition of tragedy in terms of a conception of the tragic in life influenced English literary theory, for example Coleridge's essay on "Greek Drama" (1818): tragedy raises "the emotions, the fears, and the hopes, which convince the inmost heart that their final cause is not to be discovered in the limits of mere mortal life, and forces us into a presentiment, however dim, of a state in which those struggles of inward free will with outward necessity, which form the true subject of the tragedian, shall be reconciled and solved."[41] It was chiefly in Germany, though, that tragic theory was dominated by metaphysical speculations about human destiny. While a thorough study of the philosophical issues raised by German tragic theory is beyond the scope of the present study, it is essential to discuss the preeminent German theory insofar as it interprets the moral dimensions of literary tragedy.

Hegel: The Conflict and Resolution of Ethical Claims

Hegel initiates the modern discussion of tragedy in connection with philosophical issues such as the relationship between freedom and necessity, universality and individuality, and the meaning and direction of history.[42] He conceives of tragic action as *a conflict between ethical claims*, which are "supplied by the world of those forces which carry in themselves their own justification, and are realized substantively in the volitional activity of mankind."[43] Such ethical forces include the love between husband and wife, and between parent and child, the patriotism of citizens, and the will of the leaders of a state. Expressed concretely in the particular actions of human agents, these abstract ethical claims clash with other equally valid forces. Then their ideal "concordancy is cancelled, and they are asserted in contrast to each other in interchangeable succession."[44] Each side of such a moral contradiction is justified in itself, yet because it tends towards the negation and violation of the other, each claim also falls under ethical condemnation. Hegel's

---

[40] A. W. Schlegel, *Lectures on Dramatic Art and Literature*, trans. John Black, in Clark, *Theories of Drama*, p. 344.

[41] S. T. Coleridge, "Greek Drama," in Clark, *Theories of Drama*, p. 425.

[42] Hegel discussed tragedy in a number of his works: *The Philosophy of Fine Art, The Phenomenology of Mind, Lectures on the Philosophy of Religion*, and *Lectures on the Philosophy of History*. These writings have been collected in *Hegel on Tragedy*, ed. with an introduction by Anne and Henry Paolucci (New York: Harper and Row, 1962).

[43] *Hegel on Tragedy*, p. 46.

[44] Ibid., p. 48.

conception of the tragic *reconciliation* or resolution of this ethical conflict involves the claim that tragedy vindicates "eternal justice":

> Eternal Justice is operative in such aims and individuals under a mode whereby it restores the ethical substance and unity in and along with the downfall of the individuality which disturbs its repose. For, despite the fact that individual characters propose that which is itself essentially valid, yet they are only able to carry it out under the tragic demand in a manner that implies contradiction and with a one-sidedness which is injurious. . . . That which is abrogated in the tragic issue is merely the *one-sided* particularity which was unable to accommodate itself to this harmony.[45]

Tragedy shows that the world cannot tolerate conflict and opposition between ethical forces which should be harmonious. What is "eternally substantive" is vindicated, while "false one-sidedness" is overthrown. The best and purest example of tragedy is Sophocles' *Antigone*: the opposition of Creon and Antigone represents a collision between the values of the state and those of the family, "that is, between ethical life in its social universality and the family as the natural ground of moral relations."[46]

Hegel's is the most fully developed of the romantic attempts to distinguish the characteristics of ancient and modern or romantic tragedy. Romantic tragedy, for Hegel, included contemporary plays by Schiller and others and, above all, the works of Shakespeare; *Hamlet* was the masterpiece of romantic literature. Hegel thought that modern romantic tragedy differed from Greek tragedy in three ways: with regard to the *ends* which characters pursue, the mode of the central *conflict*, and the nature of the final *reconciliation*. In modern literature the content of the ethical ends for which characters strive is no longer "universal and essential," but "individual passion, the satisfaction of which can only be relative to a wholly personal end, generally speaking the destiny of some particular person. . . . It is not therefore the ethical vindication and necessity, but rather the isolated individual and his conditions to which our interest is directed."[47] The dominating content of modern drama is "the right of subjectivity" in its collision with external circumstances. A second difference is that the conflict in modern tragedies is usually an internal one, owing to the divided character of a protagonist's ends and passions. In contrast, the heroes of ancient tragedy unyieldingly adhere to and identify their fate with one ethical demand. Finally, the nature of

---

[45] Ibid., p. 49.

[46] Ibid., p. 68. Many critics have taken issue with Hegel's interpretation of *Antigone*. See Albin Lesky, *A History of Greek Literature*, trans. James Willis and Cornelis de Heer, (New York: Thomas Crowell, 1966), p. 280: "As applied to the *Antigone* the theory of equal but opposed schemes of values is a misinterpretation." Lesky sees Antigone's claims vindicated over Creon's.

[47] *Hegel on Tragedy*, pp. 60–61.

the tragic reconciliation in modern tragedy is not the Greek restoration of eternal justice, but what is for Hegel a comparatively meaningless emotional "commiseration" with "the contingency of the earthly state" reflected in the fate of the hero.[48]

In all of these respects Hegel thought that romantic literature (the first signs of which began as early as Euripedes) represented a falling-off from its great classical stage in the plays of Aeschylus and Sophocles. The reasons behind Hegel's negative evaluation of modern tragedy indicate a problematic aspect of his theory. Hegel disliked the internal conflicts of modern "subjectivity" because his theory of tragedy cannot account for the self-division of morally autonomous characters. Given his view that universal forces are realized in individuals, Hegel has difficulty explaining the internal ambiguities of the human will. His overall philosophical approach requires that human character be essentially and actually unified, so that its "one-sidedness" conflicts with the demands of absolute justice. "The universal inherent in these powers must in particular individuals acquire the concentrated unity and concreteness of a *whole*, and a *single whole* . . . the entire self-contained human individuality which we designate as character."[49] Because of his requirement that tragic characters be undivided in their advocacy of some moral claim, Hegel denigrated the ethical significance of the internalized moral struggles dramatized in many modern works. One has to take issue with his contention (as in his analysis of *Hamlet*) that modern representations of a character's moral struggles show merely pointless vacilation and the weakness of indecision. However, if we disregard Hegel's demand that individuals be the undivided embodiments of abstract ethical claims, his general approach to tragedy is illuminating. The insights made possible by focusing on how ethical demands conflict within one character can be seen in A. C. Bradley's Shakespearean criticism—though it will be shown below that internalizing the ethical conflict creates other problems for criticism.

Another contribution of Hegel's theory of tragedy is his emphasis on the *consciousness* of the tragic protagonist as a condition of the most significant moral action. Hegel thought that tragedy is only fully realized when the hero realizes before he acts that his actions may lead to his destruction. The crucial choice of *Antigone* as the paradigm case of tragedy breaks with the Aristotelian tradition focusing on *Oedipus Rex*. Hegel even questioned whether *Oedipus Rex* could be understood as a tragedy from the perspective of a modern ethical sensibility: "The point of view of our profounder modern consciousness of right and wrong would be to recognize that crimes of this description, inasmuch as they

[48] Ibid., p. 90.
[49] Ibid., p. 152.

were neither referable to a personal knowledge or volition, were not deeds for which the true personality of the perpetrator was responsible."[50] Some critics have made this aspect of Hegel's theory an indispensable requirement for tragedy: "The protagonist of tragedy caught in an inescapable conflict must be *fully aware of his situation*: he must suffer knowingly."[51] But rather than being formulated as a critical dogma, Hegel's position suggests the need to investigate in particular works the effect of a protagonist's consciousness and moral awareness.

One of Hegel's most influential ideas is his formulation of the concept of *tragic guilt*. Tragic guilt unites the elements of innocence and culpability involved in the hero's self-destruction: "We must above all place on one side the false notion of *guilt* or *innocence*. The heroes of tragedy are quite as much under one category as the other."[52] Hegel rejects disdainfully the neoclassical theory of poetic justice: "We have to guard ourselves therefore from concluding that a denouement of this type is merely a moral issue conformably to which evil is punished and virtue rewarded."[53] The concept of tragic guilt represents a new way of accounting for the moral ambiguity of tragic action. Instead of the traditional interpretations of the protagonist's *hamartia*—whether understood in terms of a flaw, passion, or an erring will—Hegel sees the source of catastrophe in the hero's moral one-sidedness, in a goodness which is too pure to exist in the world without conflict.

Hegel's notion of tragic guilt is less a moral concept, however, than a metaphysical or ontological one; the concept is based on a philosophical theory of individuation rather than the analysis of particular actions. Tragic guilt arises necessarily when the abstract ethical unity on the ideal level realizes itself in concrete existence. In *The Phenomenology of Mind* Hegel explains why all human action involves the guilt of "one-sidedness":

> The essential ethical reality has split asunder into two laws, and consciousness, taking up an undivided single attitude towards law, is assigned only to one. . . . By the act it gives up the specific character of the ethical life, that of being pure and simple certainty of immediate truth, and sets up the division of itself into self as active and reality over against it, and for it, therefore, negative. By the act it thus becomes *Guilt*.[54]

The individual is guilty because his acts do not conform to the Absolute Idea, but his guilt is tragic because he does not intend evil, but only acts in accord with the necessary demands of his personal being. Thus guilt becomes coextensive with life itself. As it has been used in literary criticism,

---

[50] Ibid., p. 69.
[51] Lesky, *Greek Tragedy*, p. 10.
[52] *Hegel on Tragedy*, p. 70.
[53] Ibid., p. 71.
[54] Ibid., p. 271.

the idea of tragic guilt has often resulted in failure to discriminate the precise causes of tragic actions. When guilt is seen as an innate and inevitable quality of human life, it blinds the critic to important differences between particular tragic actions, and between tragic actions and other human actions. Yet despite its inherent ambiguity as a concept and the dangers of applying it indiscriminately to all human action, Hegel's idea of tragic guilt is the first significant attempt to account philosophically for both the free choices and the determining conditions which lead a protagonist to his downfall, and for the copresence of moral guilt and innocence in tragedy.

For Aristotle and most of the critical tradition until Hegel, tragedy was a genre of literary art defined by formal considerations. For Hegel, and consequently for Schopenhauer, Nietzsche, and a succession of other philosophers and literary theorists, tragic art exists because there is a tragic dimension or aspect of the world. The object of a theory of tragedy therefore becomes a matter of describing the essence, vision, spirit, or view of life implied by a recognition of the tragic character of existence. For Hegel the meaning of the tragic is bound up with the question of the meaning of history in light of the problem of evil and suffering. His theory transforms the resolution of tragedy into a secular theodicy, a vision of "ewige Gerechtigkeit" and "vernüftiges Schiksal." "Eternal justice" is vindicated by the downfall of one-sided claims of absoluteness; the final annulment of contradictions in the course of the world's evolution proves that fate is not unintelligible or blind but an affirmation of "the rationality of destiny."[55] The phenomenon of tragic conflict and resolution reveals history's "rational necessity," which requires and justifies the finite individual's suffering and destruction. In tragedy we come to recognize and accept the meaningful course of history in spite of the "sacrifice" of individuals.

The optimism and confidence implied in Hegel's progressive view of history are reflected in the definition of the tragic as the *resolution* of conflict rather than the *fact* of conflict itself. To some extent Hegel's theory falsifies the genuine insight that "pity and terror" lie at the center of the experience of tragedy (though Hegel's idea of reconciliation can be seen as a modification of the notion of catharsis as the final effect of tragedy). Hegel passes quickly over the disturbing aspects of tragedy in stressing the spectator's sense of reconciliation and acquiescence. In fact, though, spectators admire a hero's assertion of deeply-felt, though "one-sided" values, and they are horrified by his downfall. A. C. Bradley rightly argues that "not to mention the suffering and death we have witnessed, the very existence of the conflict, even if a supreme ethical power is felt to be asserted in its close, remains a painful fact, and, in

---

[55] Ibid., p. 71.

large measure, a fact not understood."[56] Hegel's view of eternal justice removes all the pain from the collision of Antigone and Creon, all the suffering from Oedipus's calamity. An "eternal justice" which so flagrantly violates the normal human sense of justice is not accepted quite so easily, if at all. Hegel's view of the reconciliation involved in tragedy should be tested against a comparison of the specific effects of particular works.

Hegel's theory of the tragic had a profound influence in two ways. It led to a virtual explosion of philosophical theories of tragedy in the nineteenth and twentieth centuries by such writers as Schopenhauer, Kierkegaard, Nietzsche, Unamuno, Scheler, Reinhold Niebuhr, Jaspers, and Malraux. And second, it created the theoretical basis for the study of "the tragic" in other literary forms, specifically in the novel. The latter development will be discussed in the last part of this chapter. We turn now to Hegel's influence on the tragic theories of Schopenhauer and Nietzsche and the criticism of A. C. Bradley.

Like Hegel, Schopenhauer and Nietzsche understood the tragic as essentially a matter of conflict. But they completely rejected Hegel's optimistic version of an evolutionary process ending in reconciliation. From either of their perspectives, Hegel's stress on the rational necessity for the removal of "one-sidedness" appears reminiscent of the neoclassical theory's ideal of poetic justice. In *The World as Will and Idea* (1818), Schopenhauer interpreted tragedy as a vision, not of the rational unfolding of the World Spirit, but of the eternal, aimless conflict of the ultimate Will with itself: "The end of this highest poetical achievement is the representation of the terrible side of life. The unspeakable pain, the wail of humanity, the triumph of evil, the scornful mastery of chance, and the irretrievable fall of the just and innocent, is here presented to us; and in this lies a significant hint of the nature of the world and of existence. It is the strife of the will with itself . . . visible in the suffering of men."[57] Tragedy mirrors not the actual sins of one person but the original sin of being born, "the crime of existence itself." Tragedy gives man an insight into the blind energy of the will. In the aesthetic encounter with this form of art the spectator can free himself of the futile desire to struggle and instead learn to live in resignation, serenely contemplating the clash of forces in the phenomenal world.

Nietzsche's *The Birth of Tragedy* (1872) also understood the tragic as a conflict which is essentially blind and irrational. However, Nietzsche repudiated Schopenhauer's belief that tragedy teaches resignation and withdrawal from life. For Nietzsche, tragedy was an aesthetic transfiguration of suffering and a test of man's capacity to affirm life in spite of evil:

---

[56] A. C. Bradley, "Hegel's Theory of Tragedy," in *Hegel on Tragedy*, p. 378.
[57] Schopenhauer's *The World as Will and Idea*, trans. R. B. Haldane and John Kemp, in Adams, *Critical Theory since Plato*, p. 448.

> That life is really so tragic would least of all explain the origin of an art
> form—assuming that art is not merely imitation of the reality of nature but
> rather a metaphysical supplement of the reality of nature, placed beside it
> for its overcoming. The tragic myth, too, insofar as it belongs to art at all,
> participates fully in this metaphysical intention of art to transfigure.[58]

Art is the "truly metaphysical activity of men" in that only through art
can man "justify his existence": only from an aesthetic, rather than a
moral standpoint, can existence be justified. From the aesthetic point of
view, tragedy shows us that "even the ugly and the disharmonic are part
of an artistic game that the will in the eternal amplitude of its pleasure
plays with itself."[59] Nietzsche likened the beauty of tragedy to that of
musical dissonance. Through the "Dionysian wisdom" embodied in the
"Apollonian form" of tragedy, man is shown that the construction and
destruction of the phenomenal world represents "the overflow of a pri-
mordial delight."[60] Nietzsche's understanding of the essence of tragic
wisdom culminates in his conception of "the mystery doctrine of tragedy": "the fundamental knowledge of the oneness of everything existent,
the conception of individuation as the primal cause of evil, and of art as
the joyous hope that the spell of individuation may be broken in augury
of a restored oneness."[61]

In their stress upon the terrible aspects of life represented in tragedy,
Schopenhauer and Nietzsche have had a more powerful impact on modern
theories of tragedy than has Hegel (except by way of Marxist theory). Schopenhauer thought that tragedy leads us to resignation and detachment
from existence; Nietzsche held that tragedy is the greatest affirmation of
life, because it is made in the face of the most horrible pain. Both thinkers
stressed tragedy's focus on evil and "the terrible side of life": they saw not a
dialectical movement towards resolution, but the bare fact of suffering
itself. This shift of emphasis from Hegel's perspective expresses a radically
differing interpretation of the ultimate vision of human moral existence
implied by tragedy. Tragedy reveals not the guilt of a particular individual, but that of the universe itself: the "guilt" of placing man in an intolerable position. But do particular literary works actually imply either of
these visions? Is suffering presented in a work as the result of human errors
or "one-sidedness" or is it portrayed as an inevitable aspect of human existence? Is tragic conflict presented as aimless, repetitive, or meaningful only
from a supra-historical perspective (as in the views of Schopenhauer and
Nietzsche)? Or is the conflict shown as leading to the restoration or realization of historical moral values? In the present study these questions about

---

58 Nietzsche's *The Birth of Tragedy*, in *Basic Writings of Nietzsche*, trans. and ed., with
commentaries by Walter Kaufmann (New York: Modern Library, 1966), p. 140.
59 Ibid., p. 141.
60 Ibid., p. 142.
61 Ibid., p. 74.

the ways evil is presented cannot be answered *a priori* in terms of a philosophy of the tragic, but rather suggest perspectives on the particular literary works we will examine.

A. C. Bradley: Tragedy as the Self-Waste of Spirit

The criticism of A. C. Bradley exemplifies nineteenth century theory's interest in the philosophical implications of "the tragic," its emphasis on complexities of character, and the shift from a didactic view of literature to one stressing its humanistic glorification of man's spiritual powers. Bradley's debt to and his modifications of Hegel's ideas about the tragic are revealed in his essay "Hegel's Theory of Tragedy." Bradley accepts Hegel's idea that tragedy involves a conflict of ethical claims, but he relocates the essential conflict *within* characters: "tragedy portrays a self-division and self-waste of spirit."[62] Tragedy shows a character's goodness wasted—yet in the events which destroy him the hero's vitality and spiritual value as a human being are realized. Somewhat inconclusively, Bradley takes issue with Hegel's view of the element of reconciliation in the tragic catastrophe, asserting that Hegel "sometimes exaggerates it, and at other times rates it too low . . . [Hegel] does not notice that in the conclusion of not a few tragedies pain is mingled not merely with acquiescence, but with something like exultation . . . connected with our sense that the hero has never shown himself so great or noble as in the death which seals his failure."[63] The conflict, waste, and emerging value disclosed in the fate of the protagonist mirror a similar process in the overall development of the world. Like Hegel, Bradley thinks that tragedy raises the issue of whether the universe's order is ultimately moral or not. But in Bradley's view tragic conflict is a morally ambiguous process, not a vision of the triumph of "eternal justice." Tragedy is painful to us because the catastrophe—"the violent self-restitution of the divided spiritual unity"—involves the waste of a marvelous human life. Yet the world's order also appears as sympathetic to human values, in that it reacts violently to expel the evil engendered by a tragic conflict: "Our sense that the ultimate power cannot endure the presence of such evil is implicitly the sense that this power is at least more closely allied with good."[64] Thus the ultimate power at work in the tragic process of conflict and waste appears both as a hostile fate and as a just moral order.

Bradley's view of tragedy is more fully developed in *Shakespearean Tragedy* (1904), especially the first chapter's account of "the substance of Shakespearean tragedy." His primary interest centers on the characters of tragedy. The story or action of a Shakespearean tragedy consists of deeds which issue from character: "actions in the full sense of the word . . . acts

---

[62] Bradley, "Hegel's Theory of Tragedy," p. 381.
[63] Ibid., p. 379.
[64] Ibid., p. 380.

or omissions thoroughly expressive of the doer—characteristic deeds."[65] The influence of Hegel's "one-sidedness" can be detected in Bradley's view of the tragic hero as an exceptional individual with "a fatal tendency to identify the whole being with one interest, object, passion, or habit of mind."[66] This tragic trait lies at the root of both the hero's "greatness of soul" and the fatal error which destroys him. Bradley argues that the hero's greatness need not be strictly moral in order for his downfall to reveal the waste of human excellence. For example, in spite of Macbeth's moral corruption and the crimes to which this leads him, Shakespeare gives this character "a power which excites astonishment, and a courage which extorts admiration . . . and adds to it a conscience so terrifying in its warnings and so maddening in its reproaches that the spectacle of inward torment compels a horrified sympathy and awe which balance, at the least, the desire for the hero's ruin."[67] The tragic hero need not be "good" in all his actions, but "it is necessary that he should have so much of greatness that in his error and fall we may be vividly conscious of the possibilities of human nature."[68] The tragic hero's greatness is the basis of "the center of the tragic impression," our sense of the waste of human goodness. Yet this waste is not merely depressing for the spectator, for Shakespeare "makes us realize so vividly the worth of that which is wasted that we cannot possibly seek comfort in the reflection that all is vanity."[69] Bradley's perceptive interpretations of the central characters evaluate the virtues and fallibility of each protagonist without becoming moralistic. Following Bradley, my own analyses of tragedies will assume that a character's virtue (as I prefer to call it) is a particular form of human excellence rather than strictly moral conduct. However, in contrast with Bradley's notion of "greatness of soul," the particular form of virtue at stake in each tragic novel and the literary techniques by which it is portrayed need to be more carefully delineated.

Bradley's analysis of the ambiguous "moral order" implied by Shakespeare's plays anticipates Ricoeur's account of the central tragic vision. Bradley argues that "the ultimate power in the tragic world is not adequately described as a law or order which we can see to be just and benevolent—as, in that sense, a 'moral order': for in that case the spectacle of suffering and waste could not seem to us so fearful and mysterious as it does."[70] But if characters in Shakespeare's tragic world do not appear simply as sinners against a moral order, neither do they appear as mere victims of a hostile power; they have some responsibility for their

[65] A. C. Bradley, *Shakespearean Tragedy* (1904; Greenwich, CT: Fawcett, n.d.), p. 20.
[66] Ibid., p. 27.
[67] Ibid., p. 28.
[68] Ibid., p. 28.
[69] Ibid., p. 29.
[70] Ibid., p. 31.

own fates. One has to account for both the "negative" aspect of fatality in the world order and for the "positive" aspect by which its working appears as morally justified. Bradley thinks that only the spectator's sense that the universe is ruled by a force which is at least partly in accord with human standards of justice can explain the affirmative aspects of our imaginative experience of tragedy, though he takes care to distinguish his idea of justice from the didactic notion of poetic justice: "Let us put aside the ideas of justice and merit, and speak simply of good and evil. . . . Let us understand the statement that the ultimate power is 'moral' to mean that it does not show itself indifferent to good and evil."[71] Tragedy is the exhibition of a "convulsive reaction" by which the world expels an evil. On the other hand, the world order does not simply defend itself against a poison, but "poisons itself." This mysterious process of self-waste is the ultimate cause of tragedy, for "there is no tragedy in its expulsion of evil: the tragedy is that this involves the waste of good."[72] Thus tragedy portrays two sides of both human character and the world order: their animation by a drive towards perfection and their generation of evil within themselves. The whole process of tragic action is "no solution of the riddle of life," but rather a "painful mystery." Shakespeare did not attempt to justify the ways of God to men, but dramatized inexplicable facts of human experience: "We remain confronted with the inexplicable fact, or the no less inexplicable appearance, of a world travailing for perfection, but bringing to birth, together with glorious good, an evil which it is able to overcome only by self-torture and self-waste. And this fact or appearance is tragedy."[73]

Explained in these general terms, Bradley's theory of tragedy as a conflict and self-wasting of human goodness appears abstract—perhaps a typical nineteenth century view of Creative Evolution.[74] But Bradley's sensitive and perceptive interpretations of *Hamlet*, *Macbeth*, *Othello*, and *King Lear* show his creative use of the theory, which guides his analysis without imposing a mechanical scheme on the plays. Bradley's theory is, with Ricoeur's, the best account of the ethical structure of tragedy: its balance of fate and human responsibility, its depiction of suffering linked to moral agency, of a person's own virtues helping to destroy him, and of the intertwining of a character's defects with his most admirable qualities. However, for Bradley the question of the nature of the

---

[71] Ibid., p. 37.

[72] Ibid., p. 40.

[73] Ibid., p. 41.

[74] George Eastman, in *A Short History of Shakespearean Criticism*, p. 193, expresses doubts especially about Bradley's emphasis on the impression of waste, "for not only do the characters not speak about it, but waste is, ultimately, a mechanical concept related to efficiency and deriving from a nineteenth century secularism that fits Shakespeare's universe somewhat doubtfully."

ultimate power in the tragic universe "must not be answered in 'religious' language," for he thinks Shakespeare attempted to describe the mystery of life entirely in the secular terms of the Elizabethan age.[75] It seems puzzling that Bradley arbitrarily bars the critic from using religious terms to describe the ultimate powers in the cosmos; here one must agree with Ricoeur that it may be appropriate to use religious language to describe the tragic vision of a particular author. In any case, Bradley is extremely perceptive about the ways in which tragedy's ethical structure engages the spectator's affective responses, and about the close connections between emotional, moral, and aesthetic aspects of the imaginative experience of tragedy.

The main problem with Bradley's theory is that it is exclusively concerned with the central protagonist in each play. His approach psychologizes the entire tragic action into a play of forces within the hero's soul. "In this essentially 'lyric' definition, the tragic becomes a personal and subjective quality."[76] As the culmination of romantic literary theory, Bradley's work reveals the limitations as well as the strengths of this tradition as an approach to tragedy. In stressing the greatness of the individual soul, whether the tragic hero torn asunder by spiritual conflict or the tragic author who unites in his soul the antagonistic values of human life, romantic criticism typically displays a drastic loss of awareness of the *social context* of tragic action. Bradley shows little concern with the social and political situation within which a protagonist's actions are shaped, and scant interest in the cultural values which formed Shakespeare's conception of moral conflict. Twentieth century literary theories have sought in a number of ways to understand tragedy in terms of an individual's being caught between conflicting forces in his society.

III. *Modern Tragic Theory*

Evil in the Individual and in the Social Group

Partly through the influences of Freud and Marx, many twentieth century discussions of tragedy have been set in terms of the dynamic processes of social groups. Both Freudian and Marxist interpretations of tragedy locate the causes of the protagonist's downfall in social processes lying beyond his control. They tend to see the hero's destruction as the culmination of increasing tensions between a society's professed moral values and other forces in human motivation. This shift of emphasis to the group involves describing tragedy in social scientific rather than moral terms. Yet it has implications for an ethical understanding of tragedy. As it

[75] Bradley, *Shakespearean Tragedy*, p. 30.
[76] Wimsatt and Brooks, *Literary Criticism*, p. 559.

has influenced literary criticism the focus on group dynamics has meant a reversal of the classical humanist emphasis on the protagonist's moral guilt. The "guilty" hero of tragedy is exculpated as an innocent victim, and in his place is indicted the hypocritical society which accuses him.

Freud's theory of tragedy in the final pages of *Totem and Taboo* attributes the supposed guilt of the tragic hero to the projection of a repressed sense of guilt by the members of his society. *Oedipus Rex* is one of the "ineradicable traces in the history of humanity" of the murder of a primal father by his sons and the origin of guilt in "deferred obedience" to the dead father. The significance of "tragic guilt" is its indication of the sons' ambivalent relationship with a father-figure:

> Why had the Hero of tragedy to suffer? and what was the meaning of his "tragic guilt"?. . . . He had to suffer because he was the primal father, the Hero of the great primaeval tragedy which was being re-enacted with a tendentious twist; and the tragic guilt was the guilt which he had to take on himself in order to relieve the chorus from theirs. The scene upon the stage was derived from the historical scene through a process of systematic distortion—one might even say, as the product of a refined hypocrisy. In the remote reality it had actually been the members of the Chorus who caused the Hero's suffering; now, however, they exhausted themselves with sympathy and regret and it was the Hero himself who was responsible for his own sufferings. The crime which was thrown on to his shoulders, presumptuousness and rebelliousness against a great authority, was precisely the crime for which the members of the Chorus, the company of brothers, were responsible. Thus the tragic Hero became, though it might be against his will, the redeemer of the Chorus.[77]

The reversal involved in Freud's demystification of the supposed moral guilt of the hero is revealed in his comment that tragedy represents "systematic distortion" and "refined hypocrisy" about the real responsibility for the death of the disguised father-figure. The hero's "tragic guilt" is projected onto him by the Chorus, representing the primitive "band of brothers," because of their remorse for the primaeval deeds of murder and incest. Whether or not an actual historical deed lies at the origin of the Oedipus complex, tragedy symbolizes feelings of guilt which all persons feel as a result of desires for what is forbidden by parental authority and power. Of course, the psychological feeling of guiltiness for an imagined crime is not genuine moral guilt, but simply a phenomenon of human psychic behavior. However, Freud's whole therapeutic purpose assumes that individuals are not only mentally unhealthy but morally wrong when they avoid facing their own sense of guilt by projecting it in moral terms onto others—as does the society of the tragic hero.

Freud's influence has led to many critical interpretations of literature

---

[77] Sigmund Freud, *Totem and Taboo*, trans. James Strachey (New York: Norton & Co., 1950), p. 156.

in terms of the decisive role of unconscious forces in directing human actions, and in producing conflicts between sexual and aggressive desires and the prohibitions of social morality. As does Freud, Kenneth Burke sees a scapegoating process as central in tragedy. Tragedy is a form of symbolic transformation by which dangerous and immoral tendencies in the author of a work—and its audience—are sloughed off by being identified with a character who is killed or sacrificed. The tragic hero functions as a scapegoat figure who is representative of certain unwanted evils in society. By the literary depiction of the hero's death in a wider context of symbolic action, criminal tendencies are transformed and transcended. Society's ambiguous sacrifice/killing of the hero involves its members' unconscious and imaginative participation in the crimes of the hero, and thus a "socialization of a loss" of certain tendencies in human nature. "The delegation of one's burden to the sacrificial vessel of the scapegoat is a giving, a socialization, albeit the socialization of a loss, a transference of something deeply within, devoutly a part of one's own self. . . . It delegates the personal burden to an external bearer, yet the receiver of this burden possesses consubstantiality with the giver, a pontification that is contrived (where the scapegoat is the 'bad' father) by objectively attributing one's own vices or temptations to the delegated vessel."[78] In Burke's view of tragedy, the transformations of character structure achieved through identification with or rejection of certain symbolic forms are in large part shaped by a society's view of certain tendencies in human nature as moral or immoral.

René Girard, too, has followed Freud in interpreting tragedy as a portrayal of a society making a scapegoat-figure suffer to relieve its members' own unresolved anxieties and sense of guilt. But while Girard sees the hero's guilt as projected by his society, his theory "involves rejecting the role of the father, transcending the family framework and the dogma of psychoanalysis." And for Girard aggression is a more fundamental human instinct than sexuality. The fact that the "sacrificial victim" of his community's aggression happens to be a father in some tragedies is irrelevant to the real causes of collective violence. "The enormous impression made on the community by the collective murder is not due to the victim's identity per se, but to his role as unifying agent."[79] For Girard, tragedy exemplifies the universal social process by which a community's origin is established and its stability preserved by unanimous collective violence directed at an arbitrary victim. The tragic hero, like sacrificial religious figures and cult objects, fulfills the need for an

[78] Kenneth Burke, *The Philosophy of Literary Form: Studies in Symbolic Action*, third edition (Berkeley: University of California Press, 1973), p. 45.
[79] René Girard, *Violence and the Sacred*, trans. Patrick Gregory (Baltimore: Johns Hopkins University Press, 1972), p. 214.

outlet for the human aggression that always threatens a society's fragile order. Girard asserts that, unlike Freud, he does not simply reverse the locus of guilt from the hero to the chorus, from the surrogate victim to the crowd: "This concept of a simple one-way projection of guilt seems to me inadequate. . . . The surrogate victim, even when falsely accused, may be as guilty as the others. . . . The Freudian interpretation is thoroughly modern in its inversion of the mythical content."[80] But though Girard tries to avoid a moral interpretation and claims simply to expose the pattern of violence underlying all human culture, his theory, too, involves a clear position with regard to the moral conflicts of a tragic plot. All moral claims are understood in terms of their function in the process by which a society preserves itself from self-destruction. In a sense Girard reverses Freud's condemnation of society, because he thinks that only by the periodical repetition of the act of sacrificing a scapegoat can human culture be maintained. For tragedy this means that the hero's death, despite his innocence, is justified by the necessity of his society's deflecting violence outside itself onto a surrogate victim. As in Freud's theory, though, the reason for which a society professes to punish a hero's actions—its moral rationale—is largely irrelevant to the real sources of the tragic situation.

Marxist critics, too, usually interpret tragedy's moral conflicts in terms of an underlying social process: the class struggle. The Marxist view of tragedy shows the influence of Hegel, but the "conflict of ethical forces" is seen in historical terms. Gyorgy Lukacs claims that "it is no accident that the great periods of tragedy coincide with the great, world-historical changes in human society."[81] The rise of the Greek polis, the "birth pangs" of new social classes during the Renaissance, and the rise of the proletariat in the nineteenth century are reflected in the tragic literature of each of these eras. Lukacs sees a vital connection between dramatic conflict and historical transformations in the author's society. From such a perspective, the tragic hero is the "world-historical individual" whose life embodies the conflicting forces of a decisive moment of history: "The social collision as the centre of drama, round which everything revolves and to which all components of the 'totality of movement' refer, requires the portrayal of individuals, who in their personal passions directly represent those forces whose clash forms the material content of the 'collision.'"[82] For Lukacs tragedy represents a critical or subversive view of society even when the author does not suggest an alternative form of social organization. Shakespeare, for example, showed the bloody conflicts and irresolvable problems

---

[80] Ibid., p. 203.
[81] Gyorgy Lukacs, *The Historical Novel*, trans. Hannah and Stanley Mitchell (Boston: Beacon Press, 1962), p. 97.
[82] Ibid., p. 104.

of the feudal order and thus pointed to its eventual dissolution. Similarly, Lucien Goldmann derives Racine's tragic perspective primarily from the discontent of a particular social class of nobles.[83] For a Marxist critic, tragedy's depiction of a person at odds with his environment can be attributed to the author's dissatisfaction with the structure of his society's economic and political relationships. The moral issues at stake in the plot of a tragedy are deemed to be only "surface" phenomena which disguise the real source of contention. However, as in the case of Freud's unmasking of the "hypocrisy" of the "band of brothers," a Marxist approach involves not an end of the critic's moral concerns but their radical displacement: from the self-understanding of individual characters in a work to the validity of a society's basic patterns of organization and loyalty. Tragedy's moral significance lies in its depiction of the evolution of the class struggle and its presentation of the world's historical movement as essentially justified. At the very least, a tragic author shows the injustice and oppressive force of particular historical institutions; at the most he calls prophetically for the revolution that will establish a more just society. For Marxist critics, too, tragedy has an ethical dimension which depends less upon its portrayal of individual characters than on its depiction of the dynamic relationships within social groups.

In contrast to these approaches to tragedy in terms of the processes of group behavior, a number of modern literary critics reassert the classical humanistic perspective on tragedy as a study of moral evil in particular individuals. There are several forms of this general approach. Tragedy has been seen as a recognition of the ways man engenders evil, and the tragic flaw correlated with the Christian idea of sin.[84] Robert Heilman understands tragedy's basic moral structure in contrast with that of melodrama. Melodrama locates the basic conflict between wholly good characters and external antagonists, which may be physical obstacles or characters who are wholly evil. In tragedy conflict is centered within the main character: "the heart of the tragic is the divided personality."[85] Tragedy shows a character destroyed by his own nature rather than the conqueror or victim of some external power. "In tragedy we find responsibility and guilt; it is

[83] Lucien Goldmann, The Hidden God, trans. Philip Thody (New York: Humanities Press, 1964).

[84] T. R. Henn, in The Harvest of Tragedy (London: Methuen & Co., 1956), pp. 289–90: "A return to the doctrine of Original Sin . . . affords both an explanation of the tragic flaw, and, in conjunction with the sin of pride, the emergence of evil upon the tragic world. . . . It is the recognition of this sin, and of its illimitable consequences, which I see as the root of the tree of tragedy."

[85] Robert B. Heilman, Tragedy and Melodrama (Seattle: University of Washington Press, 1968), p. 291.

there that we discover the source of evil, not in things, not in others, but in ourselves."[86]

Many critics have argued that tragedy must focus on the inevitability of evil within human nature and within the universe as a whole, but not on the specifically social causes of suffering. The reason given for this view is that, where a disaster could have been avoided with some other form of social organization, the sense of tragic inevitability and fate is dissipated. In "the drama of social protest," the evils depicted "are largely external, identifiable, and, with certain recommended changes in the social order, remediable"; in contrast, the forces which destroy a tragic hero are "fate, the gods, chance, the power of his own or the race's past working through his soul."[87] From this point of view, a protagonist is destroyed because of the author's conception of the permanent nature of things; evil is the inevitable consequence of the hero's violation of the world's order. Tragedy does not question a particular society's values, but sees them as an aspect of the permanent structure of the world.

Locating the responsibility for evil exclusively in either the tragic hero or in his society oversimplifies the structure of tragedy. We need to understand both the significance of the protagonist's moral guilt and the way external pressures shape his or her fate. Here we may appropriate Northrop Frye's helpful explanation of how each of two reductive formulas distorts tragedy. The theory that tragedy exhibits the omnipotence of an external fate fails to distinguish tragic action from irony because it does not acknowledge the genuine heroic qualities of the protagonist. This view corresponds to theories of tragedy which locate the source of evil and suffering in the "hypocrisy" or "contradictions" of the hero's society, thus making the hero a helpless victim. "The other reductive theory of tragedy is that the act which sets the tragic process going must be primarily a violation of *moral* law, whether human or divine; in short Aristotle's *hamartia* or 'flaw' must have an essential connection with sin or wrongdoing."[88] Here Frye is referring to the moralistic theory, which locates the origin of all evil in the individual protagonist and fails to account for the way that tragedy depicts an individual's life caught up in a much larger series of events and presents the "theme of narrowing a comparatively free life into a process of causation."[89] In order to explain how tragedy eludes these two reductive theories, Frye appropriates a line from *Paradise Lost* in which Milton describes God's relation to Adam. Just as God made man "sufficient to have stood, though free to

[86] Ibid., p. 38.
[87] Richard Sewall, "Tragedy," in *The Encyclopedia Britannica*, 15th edition, volume 18, p. 587.
[88] Northrop Frye, *The Anatomy of Criticism: Four Essays* (Princeton: Princeton University Press, 1957), p. 210.
[89] Ibid., p. 212.

fall," so Frye's tragic "mode" demands of its central figures a qualified degree of moral accountability. For "if the hero was not sufficient to have stood, the mode is purely ironic; if he was not free to fall, the mode is purely romantic."[90] This synopsis of the nature of tragic responsibility concurs with the positions of Bradley and Ricoeur.

Most critics would agree that tragic responsibility lies somewhere between the extremes of a character's complete moral culpability and his utter innocence when he is violently rejected by his community. But this area of consensus remains rough and general because the ethical dimensions of tragedy have rarely been thoroughly explored. Most approaches have conceived of "virtue" as a vague quality of goodness inherent in an isolated character, rather than as the form of a particular culture's ideal of moral excellence, expressed in concrete actions in a social context. Because the meaning of virtue is not defined or seen in its social contexts, critics have not advanced beyond calling its crucial role in the tragic action "ironic" or "paradoxical" or "ambiguous." What is needed is an exploration in specific instances of the precise nature of this ethical irony, ambiguity, or paradox at the heart of tragedy. This can only be done by defining the moral virtues of tragic protagonists in terms of specific values of the author's culture, and by analyzing the connections between virtue and tragic action. By interpreting a character's virtue in terms of broader cultural values, we will understand tragedy as both an exploration of a character's moral development and an investigation of the implications of a society's fundamental beliefs about what is normative or desirable in human life. Such an approach overcomes the dichotomy between individualistic and collective-oriented perspectives on tragedy.

Our approach presumes no strict conception of the tragic writer's attitude towards his culture's values. It does not assume with a Marxist critic that the tragic poet's depiction of human suffering is based on a subversive and revolutionary perspective on a disintegrating pattern of social values. Nor does it assume with Geoffrey Brereton that the tragedian is essentially supportive of a healthy community's beliefs, and provides by means of his art a cathartic outlet for occasional misgivings and anxieties.[91] The nature of the author's attitude to his society's values needs to be investigated in each particular work. What is essential for

---

[90] Ibid., p. 38.

[91] Geoffrey Brereton, in *Principles of Tragedy* (Coral Gables, FL: University of Miami Press, 1968), p. 73: "A confident society can afford to tolerate subversion when presented to it in established art-forms. . . . Tragedy then serves, to borrow Aristotle's invaluable theory of catharsis, as a purge for its fears of real subversion—which must always be present. It expends its tragic heroes as insurance premiums, and goes home relieved and fortified by the spectacle of dreadful happenings which it feels secure enough to contemplate. . . . On the other hand, a precarious society will not dare to ask questions for fear of the possible answers."

tragedy is not an author's conservative or radical attitude to his society, but a commitment to artistic exploration of the implications of his culture's moral notions in a conflict situation. Raymond Williams asserts that the historical context of great tragedy is usually neither a period of open revolution nor an era of confidence in established norms, but rather a time when inherited beliefs are critically questioned:

> [Tragedy seems] to depend more on an extreme tension between belief and experience than on an extreme correspondance. Important tragedy seems to occur neither in periods of real stability, nor in periods of open and decisive conflict. Its most common historical setting is the period preceding the substantial breakdown and transformation of an important culture. Its condition is the real tension between old and new: between received beliefs, embodied in institutions and responses, and newly and vividly experienced contradictions and possibilities. . . . Beliefs can be both active and deeply questioned, not so much by other beliefs as by insistent immediate experience. In such situations, the common process of dramatizing and resolving disorder and suffering is intensified to the level which can be most readily recognized as tragedy.[92]

If tragedy is an active questioning of received beliefs by the "insistent immediate experience" dramatized in literary art, we can assume neither the author's defense nor his rejection of established values, but only radical testing of their implications in a crisis. The author explores how much of human experience his culture's moral beliefs make sense of by confronting the most difficult moral situations. The tragic writer does this by showing how the particular forms of virtue a society fosters can bring about moral evil and suffering, or can conflict with other essential virtues.

This approach to tragedy suggests a new perspective on the question of the "death" of tragedy in the modern world. In 1929 Joseph Wood Krutch asserted that tragedy could no longer be written because of a general loss of confidence in the greatness of human nature, a universal modern incapacity to conceive of man as noble. "A tragic writer does not have to believe in God, but he must believe in man."[93] More recently, George Steiner has accounted for "the death of tragedy" after "the great divide" of the seventeenth century in terms of the "triumph of rationalism and secular metaphysics." According to Steiner, tragedy depends on a community's conception of a hierarchical world order and supernatural powers. Tragedy is written "only if there is some context of belief and convention which the author shares with his audience; in short, only

---

[92] Raymond Williams, *Modern Tragedy*, (Stanford: Stanford University Press, 1966), p. 54.
[93] Joseph Wood Krutch, "The Tragic Fallacy," in *Tragedy: Vision and Form*, ed. Robert Corrigan (San Francisco: Chandler Publishing Co., 1965), p. 276.

if there is in live force what I have called a mythology."[94] However, if tragedy does depend on values shared by the author and his audience, these values need not be a particular mythology or religious position, but rather may be a set of deeply-rooted beliefs about the nature of moral goodness in conduct and character. The works at the center of this study depend on such cultural ideals of virtue. Our approach to the tragic novels, therefore, will not ask whether they presuppose some abstract faith, whether in "man" or in "gods" or in God. We will rather explore what the novels show about one aspect of a culture's style of faith: its conceptions of the ways individuals achieve moral excellence. For "faith in man" or in God is always expressed in terms of the validity and limitations of specific cultural forms, particular concrete images of what persons are and should be. Tragedy is still "possible" not because of some enduring religious myth, but because certain modern writers, as much as Shakespeare or Sophocles, feel the need to explore the implications of their culture's ideas about virtue, and to do this by telling the story of a good man who dies partly because of his very goodness.

Tragedy and the Tragic Vision in the Novel

The assertion that novels may be tragedies or contain tragic elements raises the issue of what tragedy is as a genre. There have been three general approaches to this complicated issue: attempts to define tragedy, descriptions of elements in tragedy, and interpretations of the "tragic vision" or view of existence taken as the essence of tragedy. While the purpose of this study is not to define the genre, but to explore a theme in tragedy, these three types of approach need to be discussed in so far as they influence my perspective.

Most critics prefer to avoid the difficulties involved in trying to define the vast number of works which have been interpreted as tragedy. Definitions almost inevitably seem so vague and all-encompassing that they include every serious work of literature, or else so specific as to disqualify arbitrarily many works which are commonly accepted as tragedies.[95] The

---

[94] George Steiner, *The Death of Tragedy* (London: Faber & Faber, 1961), pp. 193, 318. The discussion of the possibility of modern tragedy is somewhat amusing because other critics argue that tragedy is "dead" because contemporary audiences have too *much* "faith in man." Stanley Edgar Hyman, in "Psychoanalysis and the Climate of Tragedy," in *Tragedy: Vision and Form*, pp. 287–301, has pointed to the confidence of recent revisionist psychoanalysts that man is fundamentally good if only his neurotic traits are scientifically treated. Orrin E. Klapp, in "Tragedy and the American Climate of Opinion," in *Tragedy: Vision and Form*, pp. 302–14, has lamented that peculiarly American way of looking at life which includes the elements of optimism, naturalism, and other-directedness, all of which he takes to be antithetical to a tragic view of things.

[95] Elder Olson, *Tragedy and the Theory of Drama* (Detroit: Wayne State University Press, 1966), p. 169, says that "tragedy is drama which proposes the exhibition of an action of the utmost seriousness and the utmost significance." Tragedy is defined as "an

validity of a definitional approach to the genre of tragedy has therefore been attacked by many critics in recent years. Clayton Koelb argues that it is impossible to devise a definition of tragedy that will apply even to all the works of the Greek dramatists, and concludes that "'tragedy' carries so much meaning that it actually communicates nothing. Better, then, to resist the temptation and keep to critical terms which, while more modest, are more precise."[96] Raymond Williams points out the ways that "liberal" thought's definition of tragedy, like all definitions, reflects ideological beliefs and excludes many important works from consideration. (However, like all theorists of tragedy, Williams cannot avoid some kind of working definition of his subject: "all that is common, in the works we call tragedies, is the dramatisation of a particular and grievous disorder and its resolution."[97]) Many critics hold that genre-based definitions are abstract and inflexible and lead to static classifications rather than important insights into literary works.

A second approach to tragedy involves description and generalization about elements found in a number of works. While definitions specify elements which are necessary and sufficient for a thing to be a member of a certain class, the descriptive approach cites common features of numerous works but does not absolutely require the presence of any one pattern or element. For example, Geoffrey Brereton lists a number of "constants of dramatic tragedy," including conflict, irony, retribution, and recognition. He claims that, while tragedy need not contain any given one of these factors, some of them are always present, because "without any of them it would seem impossible to construct a story bearing on the serious exploration of power"[98] (his conception of tragedy's central preoccupation). Dorothea Krook's *Elements of Tragedy* also describes tragedy's general form, though Krook sometimes appears to define the genre as well. She finds four "common elements which may properly be called the universal elements of tragedy; . . . they form, and can be used as, criteria of tragedy which are universally valid—criteria of *recognition*, that is, of the tragic wherever the tragic has occurred."[99] The four elements are an act of shame or horror, suffering, knowledge gained about the fundamental human condition, and affirmation of "the dignity of the human spirit and the worthwhileness of

investigation of the possibilities of human *freedom*" by Walter Kerr, *Tragedy and Comedy* (New York: Simon & Schuster, 1967), p. 121; and as "fiction inspired by a serious concern with the problem of man's fate" by Herbert J. Muller, *The Spirit of Tragedy* (New York: Knopf, 1956), p. 11. Oscar Mandel's *A Definition of Tragedy* (New York: New York University Press, 1961) is an insightful exception to the general uselessness of "definitions."

96 Clayton Koelb, "The Problem of 'Tragedy' as a Genre," *Genre* 8 (1975), 264.

97 Williams, *Modern Tragedy*, p. 53.

98 Brereton, *Principles of Tragedy*, pp. 116, 126.

99 Dorothea Krook, *Elements of Tragedy*, (New Haven: Yale University Press, 1969), p. 2.

human life."[100] The conjunction of these elements forms a basic model which can be used to illuminate similarities and differences among particular works of tragedy.

As do these works, the present study attempts to describe variations in a general pattern of elements found in a number of works, rather than to define the genre. Our focus is not on whether the elements (which will be summarized in chapter VI) are necessary or sufficient for a work to be a tragedy, but rather on the way each specific work reveals the moral implications of some ideal of human excellence. This is a thematic study, not a definition of a genre.

Many discussions of tragedy, including most approaches to tragic novels, involve an attempt to characterize the "vision," the philosophical perspective, or the view of life implicit in tragedy. Simplifying only a little, one can divide these studies quite naturally into "optimistic" and "pessimistic" interpretations of the tragic vision. Theories of the essential vision of tragedy nearly always culminate in either of two general claims. Either it is asserted that tragedy's depiction of the human response to suffering and evil elicits a mysterious but deeply-felt sense of the universe's ultimate meaningfulness and coherence, or it is argued that so much purposeless suffering reveals man's final homelessness and alienation within a cosmos which so often frustrates his deepest aspirations and hopes.

Krook's final element of "affirmation" and the connection that she finds between her four elements and "an objective order of values which incorporates the human and transcends it" aligns her with the "positive" humanistic idea of the tragic vision. As Krook understands the tragic pattern of elements, the primary "act of shame" is a violation of an objective moral order, the hero's suffering is expiatory, the knowledge which issues from tragedy "renders intelligible . . . the necessity of the suffering, as expiatory," and the final affirmation of tragedy validates the "supremacy of the universal moral order."[101] This account of the elements of tragedy resembles Richard Sewall's description of the main components of the tragic vision: *evil* ("all the forces, within and without, that make for man's destruction, all that afflicts, mystifies, and bears him down"[102]); a protagonist's conscious *suffering* in the face of the evil; and, simply, *values* which give the suffering meaning. In tragedy, "suffering has been given a structure and set in a viable relationship; a structure which shows progression towards value, rather than the denial of it, and a relationship between the inner life of the sufferer and the world of

---

[100] Ibid., p. 8.
[101] Ibid., p. 17.
[102] Richard Sewall, *The Vision of Tragedy* (New Haven: Yale University Press, 1959), p. 47.

values about him."[103] Krook and Sewall, and Brereton, Krutch, Steiner, and Myers—and the substantial majority of critics—believe that tragedy depends on a vision of an ordered and meaningful universe, however mysterious the working of that order, and however painful for humans the consequences of violations of that order. Without some such sense of cosmic order and value, they would all say, a spectacle of evil and suffering is merely depressing. Unless there is at the core of the tragic vision an intuition of enduring values, one cannot account for the deep sense of liberation and understanding that arises from reading or viewing a tragic work of art.

Another group of critics sees tragedy's essential vision as an expression of nihilism and despair at man's subjection to the chaotic and "Manichean" dissonances of the universe. Murray Krieger's *The Tragic Vision* first distinguished the radical pessimism of the tragic vision from the "superficial affirmations" of the literary form "tragedy." The tragic vision was once "contained" within the aesthetic form of tragedy:

> The tragic vision was born *inside* tragedy, as a part of it: as a possession of the tragic hero, the vision was a reflection in the realm of thematics of the fully fashioned aesthetic totality which was tragedy. But fearful and even demoniac in its revelations, the vision needed the ultimate soothing power of the aesthetic form which contained it—of tragedy itself—in order to preserve for the world a sanity which the vision itself denied.[104]

Here Krieger shows his debt to Nietzsche's ideas about Dionysian wisdom and Apollonian form. But according to Krieger, in modern literature the tragic vision's pessimism and its apprehension of the demonic have burst the bounds of the "assurances of form" which once seemed to "guarantee the cosmic order beyond the turbulence."[105] Krieger finds a basic pattern of experience in modern tragedy: a protagonist realizes the ultimate arbitrariness and futility of inherited and socially approved values and is destroyed when he confronts the unresolvable ethical ambiguities of an extreme crisis situation. Tracing this theme through novels by Gide, Malraux, Mann, Kafka, Conrad, and others, Krieger claims to "demonstrate that all moral action authentically undertaken—from the worst to the best intended, undertaken in pride and humility alike—is for these authors doomed not only to destroy the agent but to damn him as well."[106] Similarly, for Laurence Michel the tragic vision is the nihilistic "thing" contained with difficulty within the aesthetic form of tragedy. The critic's task is "saving the tale" from attempts to deny the full horror

---

[103] Ibid., p. 48.
[104] Murray Krieger, *The Tragic Vision* (Chicago: University of Chicago Press, 1960), p. 3.
[105] Ibid., p. 4.
[106] Ibid., p. x.

of tragedy's apprehension of the demonic aspects of life.[107] And William Brashear finds the inspiration for tragic art in "the power of negative thinking."[108] According to these three critics, then, the tragic vision perceives with horror the futility of all moral activity and expresses humankind's despair over a world without ultimate purpose, order, or enduring value.

The assumption that there exists a single tragic vision seems to me to distort many interpretations of particular works. One sees the "optimists" founder as they try to redeem Conrad's blackest works, while those who understand the tragic vision in terms of nihilism and despair neglect affirmative elements in works by Melville or Mann. Dubious marginal categories such as "tragedy manquée" or "pseudotragedy" are devised to dispose of difficult cases. The complexity and subtlety of literary works are neglected by sweeping generalizations such as "a vision of despair" or "an affirmation of the nobility of man." For this reader, it should be asked of each literary work, not simply whether it is ultimately hopeful or pessimistic about life, but how much of and what aspects of human experience its "vision" encompasses and interprets. It needs to be stressed, too, that tragedy is not a flat assertion about the nature of the world, but an author's interpretation and assessment of his characters' ways of viewing the world.[109]

My approach here differs from these conceptions of the tragic vision in two ways. First, it does not assume that there is a single tragic vision of

---

[107] Laurence Michel, *The Thing Contained: Theory of the Tragic* (Bloomington, IN: Indiana University Press, 1970), p. 10: "It is a meretricious softening when the critic gives in to the desire to solve, explain, or be reassured or comforted or cheered up. . . . Even the tragedians themselves, under the terrific stress of their intuitions, more often than not succumb to the demands and blandishments of religious or ethical direction, heroic humanism, or the satisfying rigors of conventional aesthetics."

[108] William Brashear, *The Gorgon's Head: A Study in Tragedy and Despair* (Athens, GA: University of Georgia Press, 1977), p. 5: "The tragic vision, by which I mean that ultimate dimension of consciousness, the mind as universal solvent, is the *sine qua non* ingredient of all true tragedy. . . . It directs our eyes on the Gorgon's head without danger of petrifaction. For tragedy is an aesthetic mastery by the enlarged consciousness of the inevitable and chaotic forces of the infinite."

[109] Certain studies of the tragic dimensions of particular authors' works avoid the sweeping generalizations of the "tragic vision" approach; I am thinking specifically of F. O. Matthiessen's work on Hawthorne and Melville in *American Renaissance* (Oxford: Oxford University Press, 1941); George Steiner's *Tolstoy or Dostoevsky* (Harmondsworth, Enland: Penguin Books, 1959); Dorothy Van Ghent on Conrad and James in *The English Novel: Form and Function* (New York: Harper and Row, 1953); and Jeannette King on Hardy, Eliot, and James in *Tragedy in the Victorian Novel* (Cambridge: Cambridge University Press, 1978). Two anthologies have focused on a broad range of tragic works in the modern period: Cleanth Brooks, ed., *Tragic Themes in Western Literature* (New Haven: Yale University Press, 1955); and Nathan A. Scott, Jr., ed., *The Tragic Vision and the Christian Faith* (New York: Association Press, 1957).

human existence which is basically optimistic or pessimistic. And secondly, the present study focuses primarily on the affirmation or disparagement of more limited—but more concrete and critically negotiable—values, rather than "human existence." It focuses specifically on the validity and limitations of particular styles of moral action and character. In assessing cultural ideas of virtue, it may be discovered that an author's work implies a broad statement of hope or despair about the human condition. An author may show that the failure of virtue is not only a possibility for one type of moral excellence, but an inevitable fact of human life, and this realization may provide the grounds for radical pessimism or for renewed confidence about moral action. But this aspect of a work's vision will be approached indirectly in the present study, as one dimension of the primary theme of the work's critique of a particular style of virtue.

A word needs to be said in defense of an ethical approach to tragedy. Many critics have objected to attempts to make tragedy morally explicable. Northrop Frye does not think that tragedy depends on the moral status of the protagonist's acts: "The tragedy is in the inevitability of the consequences of the act, not in its moral significance as an act."[110] Frye criticizes moral interpretations of tragedy because he thinks that they tend to produce a desperate search for moral flaws in even relatively innocent sufferers such as Cordelia or Iphigenia. "Here we are getting away from tragedy, and close to a kind of insane cautionary tale, like Mrs. Pipchin's little boy who was gored to death by a bull for asking inconvenient questions."[111] Similarly, Lionel Trilling argues that moral "pedagogy" and tragedy are antagonistic:

> Tragedy, for its part, invites us to find in it some pedagogic purpose, but the invitation cannot really be thought to be made in good faith. We cannot convince ourselves that the two Oedipus tragedies teach us anything, or show the hero as learning anything. It is true that tragedies are often about knowing and not knowing, and they range themselves on the side of knowing. But this partisanship must be approached warily lest we find ourselves in the unhappy situation of those critics who tell us that Lear and Gloucester suffered to good purpose because their pain "educated" them before they died. When, as with *Oedipus Rex*, a great tragedy is made to yield such conclusions as that fate is inscrutable and that it is a wise child who knows his own father, or as with *King Lear*, that the universe is uncomfortable and its governance morally incomprehensible, we decide that tragedy has indeed nothing to do with the practical conduct of life except as it transcends and negates it, that it celebrates a mystery debarred to reason, prudence, and morality.[112]

---

[110] Frye, *Anatomy*, p. 38.
[111] Ibid., p. 211.
[112] Lionel Trilling, *Sincerity and Authenticity* (Cambridge, MA: Harvard University Press, 1971), pp. 83–84.

Tragedy is especially prone to silly moralizing because of the history of the tragic flaw theory, against which Frye and Trilling take exaggerated precaution. However, the issue goes much deeper, to the very validity of an ethical approach to literature. Ethical criticism is a way of engaging literature which now lacks a critical theory and a methodology and hence scholarly respectability. But while there is a real danger that an ethical approach to literature will reduce it to a tool of propaganda or social reform, there is also a danger of divorcing literature from broader human values and meanings, including moral ones. Trilling's own work, in fact, provides several suggestions about how to conceptualize the moral dimensions of literature. In "Manner, Morals, and the Novel," Trilling wrote that the "moral realism" of the great novelists involves "the perception of the dangers of the moral life itself," the recognition that "the moral passions are even more wilful and imperious and impatient than the self-seeking passions."[113] The novel has been "the most effective agent of the moral imagination" for the last two hundred years because of its invitation to readers to put their own most generous wishes under examination and its suggestion that conventional education may not provide adequate preparation for reality. In *Beyond Culture*, Trilling hinted at the connections between literature and the critical assessment of cultural values, viewing "literary situations as cultural situations, and cultural situations as great elaborate fights about moral issues, and moral issues as having something to do with gratuitously chosen images of personal being, and images of personal being as having something to do with literary style."[114] He found deep moral significance in such images of personal being as "sincerity" and "authenticity," and in his book of that title described an important instance of "the moral life in process of revising itself, perhaps by reducing the emphasis it formerly placed upon one or another of its elements, perhaps by inventing and adding to itself a new element, some mode of conduct or of feeling which hitherto it had not regarded as essential to virtue."[115]

This study will explore in some detail the ways authors have showed "the moral life in process of revising itself" as characters discover unsuspected practical implications of their culture's paradigms of virtue. In the process, it is hoped that the value of an ethical criticism of literature will be demonstrated.

---

[113] Lionel Trilling, "Manners, Morals, and the Novel," in *The Liberal Imagination* (Harmondsworth, England: Penguin Books, 1948), pp. 221, 222.
[114] Lionel Trilling, "On the Teaching of Modern Literature," in *Beyond Culture* (New York: Viking Press, 1968), p. 13.
[115] Trilling, *Sincerity and Authenticity*, p. 1.

2

The *Princess Casamassima* as Tragedy:
The Bewilderment of
"A Youth on Whom Nothing Was Lost"

The character and the virtues of *The Princess Casamassima*'s protagonist are suggested by Henry James's description of Hyacinth Robinson as "a youth on whom nothing was lost" (I, 169).[1] The novel's first presentation of the boy Hyacinth intimates both an advantage and a potential danger in being this sort of person: the child's expression "showed a quick perception as well as great credulity" (I, 18). From the beginning, James links the fine sensibility and capacity for appreciation in the "remarkably organized youth" with the possibility of his being quite bewildered or overwhelmed by his impressions of life. In his depiction of Hyacinth's tragedy, James undertook an exploration of the potential dangers and weaknesses inherent in some of the qualities of character he most admired. In *The Princess Casamassima* James showed how it is Hyacinth Robinson's virtues—the best aspects of his character—that bring about his moral dilemma and downfall.

I. *Hyacinth's Character and Tragic Error*

Two groups of character traits that are essential aspects of Hyacinth's complex personality comprise the main features of James's conception of moral goodness. The kind of person "on whom nothing is lost" has both an unusual sense of personal responsibility to his or her self, and a distinctive style of moral relationship to other persons. First, Hyacinth's fine consciousness makes him particularly qualified to understand and appreciate the value of his experience, especially artistic and cultural experience. Hyacinth's yearning for rich "impressions" is not simply a hedonistic wish for ease and self-indulgence; his fundamental desire is for knowledge and experience of the artistic heritage of European civilization: "It was not so much that he wanted to enjoy as that he

---

[1] *The Princess Casamassima* (New York: Scribner's, 1908). All references to the novel and to the preface are to the two volumes of the New York Edition and are cited parenthetically in the text.

wanted to know; his desire wasn't to be pampered but to be initiated . . . his personal discomfort was the result of an intense admiration for what he had missed" (I, 170). Hyacinth has the sensibility and "penetrating imagination" of the natural artist. Like Anastasius Vetch, he knows and appreciates "the difference between the common and the rare" (I, 94). The young man's essentially disinterested aspiration to experience his society's finest art and culture, and to know other persons who share these values, contrasts sharply with the other working-class characters of London and with the discontented political radicals at the "Sun and Moon" tavern, who are motivated simply by material greed and envy of the rich—the Jamesian version of *ressentiment*. Hyacinth's intelligence, sensitivity, and deep love for art and beauty are the marks of a person who recognizes and appreciates cultural value for its own intrinsic worth. For James, this capacity for rich imaginative experience represents a kind of human excellence which has a moral dimension based ultimately on a person's responsibility to the self.

While James considered them indispensable attributes of a morally mature self, a person's aesthetic capacity and desire to seek cultural experience are not a sufficient criterion for virtue. A second group of character traits distinguishes Hyacinth as a person of unusual moral goodness: his sensitivity and deep feeling for other persons, his desire to alleviate suffering, his loyalty to his friends, and his "good faith" with others. Hyacinth resembles Ralph Touchett of *The Portrait of a Lady* in his capacity for loving other persons and desiring their happiness while remaining largely free of possessiveness or jealousy. This deep concern for other persons prompts Hyacinth's involvement with a group of political revolutionaries. Whereas the other radicals are animated by motives ranging from Paul Muniment's personal ambition to the Poupins' enjoyment of their role as persecuted exiles to the Princess's urge to "get out of herself," Hyacinth can honestly claim, "All I pretend to is my good faith and a great desire that justice shall be done" (I, 216–17). While the political actions of other characters are motivated primarily by ideological or selfish considerations, Hyacinth's political commitments spring mainly from his sensitivity to human suffering and from his loyalties to particular persons. For Hyacinth is unusually devoted to his friends. No one could "cultivate with more art the intimate personal relation" than he, for Hyacinth "had dreamed of the religion of friendship" (I, 228; II, 141). The moral worth of Hyacinth's fidelity to the values of "the personal" emerges more and more clearly as his friends fail or betray him in various ways.

James valued the virtues of a character like Hyacinth Robinson for aesthetic as well as moral reasons. In his Preface to *The Princess Casamassima*, James explained the artistic considerations that shaped his conception of Hyacinth. He claimed that the characters in a literary work are "interesting only in proportion as they feel their respective situations," and that it is those characters who have "the power to be finely aware and richly responsible" who enable us as readers to "'get most' out of all that happens to them" (I, vii–viii). Explicitly calling attention to Hyacinth's tragic role, James compared his protagonist with Hamlet and King Lear. James spoke of his hero's "consciousness . . . subject to fine intensification and wide enlargement" and his "passion of intelligence," and placed him in the company of the heroes and heroines of his other major works: "intense *perceivers*, all, of their respective predicaments" (I, xii, xiv, xvi). Hyacinth's character reflects James's developing artistic theories about the functions of a highly conscious central figure through whose point of view the reader will appreciate the story.[2]

Because of his social background, Hyacinth is condemned initially to see the world of culture and art only from the outside. He longs for the refinements and pleasures of the aristocracy, but is constantly reminded of "the high human walls, the deep gulfs of tradition, the steep embankments of privilege and dense layers of stupidity fencing the 'likes' of him off from social recognition" (I, 133). His sense of exclusion and injustice impel him to a growing involvement with a group of political radicals and anarchists. Yet at the same time that Hyacinth feels more and more the need for a radical political solution to Britain's social inequities, he unexpectedly establishes "a social—not less than a socialist—connexion" (I, xvii). As James puts it in his Preface, his hero comes to "fall in love with the beauty of the world, actual order and all, at the moment of his most feeling and most hating the famous 'iniquity of its social arrangements'" (I, xvii). His new social connection with Princess Casamassima sharpens Hyacinth's long-standing sense of conflict between being drawn to "the people" and to the privileged class which he sees as "the flower of a high civilization": "It made him even rather faint to think that he must choose: that he couldn't (with any respect for his own consistency) work underground for the enthronement of the democracy and yet continue to enjoy in however platonic a manner a spectacle which rested on a hideous social inequality. He must either suffer with the people as he had suffered before, or he must apologize to others, as he sometimes came so near doing to himself, for the rich" (I, 171). Hyacinth's "social" and "socialist" sympathies, then, draw him to antagonistic social classes. Lady Aurora, the Princess, Paul, and the other characters all strive to break out of the stifling expectations and conventions of their own class,

---

[2] Hyacinth embodies, too, some of the virtues James admired in novelists. The description of Hyacinth as "a youth on whom nothing was lost" echoes James's advice to aspiring novelists in "The Art of Fiction," in *Theory of Fiction: Henry James*, ed. with an introduction by James E. Miller, Jr. (Lincoln, NE: University of Nebraska Press, 1972), pp. 27–44. James refers twice to persons "on whom nothing is lost" as he explains what it means to "write from experience."

and yearn for experiences denied them by their backgrounds. But while the other characters are essentially single-minded, Hyacinth is torn between two equally strong loyalties: to the political cause of London's masses of suffering poor and to the world of those "happy few" individuals lucky enough to enjoy art and leisure and culture.

His attractions to Princess Casamassima and Millicent Henning involve both Hyacinth's social and socialist sympathies and his need for personal relationships. Hyacinth has a highly developed "sense of the beauty of women" (II, 14), and this property of his nature contributes not a little to his fate. Though the Princess becomes more and more engaged in revolutionary politics and disparages her former way of life, it is as "the revelation of what he supposed to be society" (I, 216) that she mainly strikes Hyacinth; she epitomizes his conception of a union of personal beauty, intelligence, and appreciation for the artistic glories of European civilization. For Hyacinth, "magnificently plebian" Milly embodies the strengths and the crudities of "the people"; he imagines her on the barricades with "a red cap of liberty on her head" (I, 164). With characteristic irony, and the suggestion that Hyacinth's vivid imagination colors his perception of his friend, James notes that Milly herself, coming from a more impoverished background than Hyacinth, "had no theories about redeeming or uplifting the people; she simply loathed them, for being so dirty" (I, 163).

James links his protagonist's virtues with his bewilderment and tragic errors. In his Preface, he argues that "bewilderment" is a necessary element in any story, as a crucial source of the reader's interest in a fictional character. If James had stressed the value of an intelligent and perceptive hero, he was aware, too, of "the danger of filling too full any supposed and above all any obviously limited vessel of consciousness" (I, ix). He therefore insisted on the importance of his protagonist's "remaining 'natural' and typical, . . . having the needful communities with our own precious liability to fall into traps and be bewildered. It seems probable that if we were never bewildered there would never be a story to tell about us; we should partake of the superior nature of the all knowing immortals whose annals are dreadfully dull as long as flurried humans are not, for the positive relief of bored Olympians, mixed up with them" (I, ix). In short, a hero should be fallible enough to be bewildered and therefore commit an error, but also intelligent and perceptive enough to recognize the nature of his dilemma.

The impetus for the train of events which culminates in Hyacinth's suicide is his "giving himself away" twice, to both his "social" and "socialist" allegiances. First, in the final chapter of Book II, Hyacinth impulsively makes a vow to an anarchist group to perform an unspecified act of violence in the distant future. The second event which brings about his moral dilemma is his repeatedly-prolonged visit to Medley, the

Princess's country estate. Though each of his allegiances expresses a morally admirable quality of his character, each is also a tragic error: in conjunction they lead to his death. For Hyacinth is confounded by the fatal combination of his political vow to overthrow an unjust social system and his deepening sense of loyalty to his society's artistic and cultural achievements. His double commitment to the political revolution and to "civilization as we know it" results in the "bewilderment" that precipitates the final catastrophe.

Hyacinth's vow to the anarchist Hoffendahl commits him to perform on command some unspecified act of violence. This vow, made with courage and the best of intentions, is clearly a tragic error: a choice made without knowledge of all it would entail, and which leads directly to Hyacinth's death. Chapter 21 portrays the circumstances that prompt and make credible the fatal oath. The occasion is a gathering of discontented workers in the "Sun and Moon" on a gloomy winter's evening. The meeting gives rise to "crude fatuity and flat-faced vanity," empty rhetoric and endless ineffectual speculation about the means to a more just society. James emphasizes Hyacinth's sense of futility and frustration and his deep desire that "the good they were striving for, blindly, obstructedly, in a kind of eternal dirty intellectual fog, would pass from the stage of crude discussion and mere sore, sharp, tantalizing desireableness into that of solid, seated reality" (I, 340). In this discouraging situation, Hyacinth yearns to offer an example of serious commitment or self-sacrifice. His outburst in the pub so impresses Muniment, Poupin, and Schinkel that they take him to see "the real thing": Diedrich Hoffendahl, mastermind of a terrorist conspiracy to bring down the governments of Europe. Several chapters later, Hyacinth confides to the Princess that, on that night, "I pledged myself by everything that's sacred. . . . I gave my life away" (II, 45). He promised to commit an act of terrorism that would probably cost him his life. Furthermore, Hyacinth agreed not to judge the merits or probable efficacy of the act; he took "a vow of blind obedience, the vow as of the Jesuit fathers to the head of their order" (II, 54).

There is a striking hiatus of three months between chapter 21 and the account of Hyacinth's stay at Medley at the start of Book III. The juxtaposition of these widely-separated experiences suggests that Hyacinth's initiation into the world of art and culture and the growth of his intimacy with the Princess represent a commitment as binding, and as compromising, as his vow to the revolution. Hyacinth is warned pointedly by everyone—by Vetch, Paul, Milly, and Sholto—that the Princess and her way of life threaten his integrity and his identity. He is admonished repeatedly by Madame Grandoni, the Princess's elderly attendant and confidante: "Don't give up yourself," "Remain faithful," for the Princess is a *capricciosa* (I, 282; II, 10). But Hyacinth cannot resist this rare opportunity to know better a gracious and charming lady and her aristocratic way of life. The extent to which Hyacinth's intimacy with her has compromised his freedom is revealed by his decision not to return to his employment at Crookendon's, and instead to extend his stay at Medley to three weeks. Hyacinth senses his liberty is lost, and wonders uneasily "what would become of him if he should add another servitude to the one he had undertaken at the end of that long, anxious cab-drive through the rain" (II, 22). James shows how difficult it would be for Hyacinth to refuse the offer of "the wine of romance, of reality, of civilization." At the same time, he points out Hyacinth's "forgetfulness of what he had most said to himself": that he should "insist at every step on knowing what he was in for" (II, 41). At Medley, Hyacinth both fulfills his deepest desires and aspirations—above all, for "the pleasure of conversation, the greatest he knew" (II, 60)—and forfeits his independence and his resolution not to forget his origins.

Both Hyacinth's involvement in the revolutionary underground and his initiation into the privileges of the upper classes result as much from his unusual susceptibility to the influence of strong personalities as from his political and cultural loyalties. Hyacinth is an impressionable young man, candid with other persons, trusting in their good faith, and rather malleable under their influence. He arouses in other persons both an impulse to protect him and a desire to possess him. When she first sees him as an adult, Milly cries, "I could swallow him at a single bite" (I, 72). Paul laughs at Hyacinth's suggestion of a stroll together and offers to "carry" him (I, 118). Just as Hyacinth's deepening loyalty to the world of culture depended on his fascination with the person of Princess Casamassima, so it is the charisma of the man Hoffendahl as much as his vague political program that inspires Hyacinth to make his vow. He confesses to the Princess that Hoffendahl was "the very incarnation of a strong plan"; "He made me see, he made me feel, he made me do, everything he wanted . . . I simply couldn't help myself" (II, 47; 50). That "nothing is lost" on Hyacinth in his personal relationships is a mark of the virtues for which we like and admire him: his sensitivity, good faith, loyalty. But these same qualities of his character make him highly susceptible to the powerful wills of other characters. In committing himself unreservedly to persons more single-minded and unscrupulous than himself, Hyacinth does exactly what he has been warned against: he "gives himself away"—not just once, but two times.

The commitments Hyacinth makes lead also to his incurring a certain amount of moral guilt. At Medley he begins to understand that his vow to bring down the ruling classes will involve destroying a world he has learned to love, as well as living human beings. Certain that the aristocracy is ultimately doomed, Hyacinth realizes that "the people I find myself pitying now are the rich, the happy" (II, 58). At the same time, Hyacinth feels that his initiation into the world of the aristocracy is a betrayal of his working-class values and the persons who nurtured him. Hyacinth feels not only grief, but a sickly shame when, returning home to Lomax Place after his stay with the Princess, he finds Pinnie on her deathbed. And he is conscious of an act of self-betrayal in having abandoned the tools of his trade to cultivate his new connections with the nobility. Furthermore, in spite of all his intelligence and self-scrutiny, some of Hyacinth's outbursts indicate that his moral integrity has been compromised to a greater degree than he realizes, as when he tells Captain Sholto, "If I were you, I shouldn't care tuppence for the sort of person I happen to be" (II, 69). Hyacinth appears somewhat startlingly callous when he brashly offers to spare the Princess the occasional discomfort given her by Sholto: "I shall have to kill someone, you know. Why not him while I'm about it if he troubles you" (II, 84).

As the novel approaches its climax, Hyacinth feels a steadily increasing sense of bewilderment in both his political loyalties and his personal relationships. He feels tortured by the conflict between his yearning for a more just society and his horror of betraying the precious "fabric of civilization" he has learned to know. During his visit to Paris and Venice, Hyacinth begins to realize that the idea of a general political rectification raises a number of troubling questions he had not foreseen when he made his oath to the anarchists. In Paris, at once the "most brilliant" and "most blood-stained" of cities, he finds that "what was supreme in his mind was not the idea of how the society that surrounded him should be destroyed; it was much more the sense of the wonderful precious things it had produced, of the fabric of beauty and power it had raised" (II, 125). From Venice, Hyacinth writes the Princess a long letter which is the central statement of his understanding of his moral dilemma. The letter expresses his continued awareness of "the miserable many" alongside his increased appreciation for the achievements of "the happier few," Hyacinth's fear that Hoffendahl's proposed revolution will entail the destruction of the treasures of civilization, and his resolution never to be motivated by jealousy or envy of persons more fortunate than himself:

> The monuments and treasures of art, the great palaces and properties, the conquests of learning and taste, the general fabric of civilization as we know it, based if you will upon the despotism, the cruelties, the exclusions, the monopolies and the rapacities of the past, but thanks to which, all the same, the world is less of a "bloody sell" and life more of a lark—our friend Hoffendahl seems to me to hold them too cheap and to wish to substitute for them something in which I can't somehow believe as I do in things which the yearnings and the tears of generations have been mixed . . . Hoffendahl wouldn't have the least feeling for this incomparable old Venice. He would cut up the ceilings of the Veronese into strips, so that everyone might have a little piece. I don't want everyone to have a little piece of anything and I've a great horror of that kind of invidious jealousy which is at the bottom of the idea of a redistribution. (II, 145–46)

When he returns to London Hyacinth discerns how much "the general fabric of civilization as we know it" is built on past injustices, the extent to which the world of art and culture is bound up with social power. The comprehensive scope of Hyacinth's imagination contrasts with the "healthy singleness" (II, 218) of Paul Muniment's vision. Hyacinth recognizes the iniquity of present political conditions, but "whatever he saw, he saw—and this was always the case—so many other things besides. He saw the immeasurable misery of the people, and yet he saw all that had been, as it were, rescued and redeemed from it: the treasures, the splendours, the successes of the world" (II, 217). James stresses the roots of Hyacinth's conflict in his very being, in the struggle between his plebian mother and his aristocratic father. The thought of deserting either of his parents fills Hyacinth with shame. Tossed between the pulls of antagonistic loyalties, he feels "the perpetual sore shock of the rebound. There was no peace for him between the two currents that flowed in his nature" (II, 264). This deep division between antithetical sympathies and irreconcilable loyalties is Hyacinth's state of mind when his "call" comes, requiring that he fulfill his pledge to the anarchists by murdering a duke.

In addition to his sense of the impossibility of resolving the conflict between his political and cultural loyalties, Hyacinth's final act of despair is motivated by his feeling of being abandoned and betrayed by his friends, especially the Princess, Paul, and Milly. The Princess loses interest in Hyacinth when she becomes involved with Muniment, a figure more masculine, willful, and single-minded in his dedication to the revolution. Hyacinth's sense of exclusion and exile culminates in one of the great Jamesian betrayal scenes in which a protagonist (compare Hyacinth with Isabel Archer, Strether, and Maggie Verver) glimpses some intimate scene or gesture from which he or she is excluded. At the end of chapter 40, Hyacinth and Prince Casamassima watch impotently as the Princess and Paul enter her house together. Hyacinth finds himself spying on them, and feels his heart beat "insanely, ignobly" (II, 324). He realizes that he has lost the Princess, and, after his last interview with her, feels himself truly "extinct." Hyacinth feels abandoned, too, by Paul and by Milly. Though he forbids himself to be jealous or to resent his friends, Hyacinth's sense that they have deserted him just when he needs them contributes greatly to the bewilderment that prevents him from finding a way out of his impasse.

Hyacinth refuses simply to disregard his past commitment. Though the other conspirators might have killed him as a traitor, the primary factor which binds Hyacinth to his vow is not fear but his own honor. When Poupin tries to persuade him that he is released from his oath because his convictions have changed, Hyacinth returns, "Does it alter my sacred vow? There are some things in which one can't change. I didn't promise to believe; I promised to obey" (II, 371). Yet if he cannot disregard his vow, neither can he fulfill it, for he now esteems the values of the aristocratic world he pledged to destroy. Understanding the seriousness with which Hyacinth takes his obligation, but not realizing that in fact the call to act on it has been made, the Princess imagines herself to be speaking only hypothetically of his actual grim situation: "I pity you, my poor friend . . . for I can imagine nothing more terrible than to find yourself face to face with your obligation and to feel at the same time the spirit originally prompting it dead within you" (II, 403). Hyacinth's moral impasse arises from the demand that he fulfill a sacred vow when his sense of what is sacred has changed radically. He has not ceased to value the original purpose of the vow, but a new-found and equally deep sense of obligation to other values prevents him from discharging his appointed duty. Hyacinth fears, too, that to murder a nobleman would re-enact his own mother's crime against his father. He is horrified by the dishonor this public spectacle would bring upon his mother, and sickened by the thought of the indelible "personal stain" this act would give his own character forever. This new scruple and his "loathing the idea of a *repetition*" (II, 419) weigh heavily on Hyacinth's mind in the novel's final presentation of his deliberations. Torn between belief in the revolution's justice and admiration for his culture's artistic treasures, between the desire to honor a sacred pledge and his scruples about acting from hidden motives of envy or revenge, between the conflicting elements of his own nature bequeathed him by "the blood of his passionate plebian mother and that of his long-descended supercivilized sire" (II, 264)—torn between all these irreconcilable elements and loyalties, and feeling abandoned by the persons he most loves and needs, Hyacinth decides to take his own life. Wishing to atone for the guilt he has incurred already and to avoid even greater guilt, he sacrifices himself rather than any of the values he holds sacred.

II. *Hyacinth as Tragic Hero:*
Consciousness that "Surveys the Whole Field"

Much of the critical discussion of *The Princess Casamassima* has centered on the issue of whether or not Hyacinth has the attributes of a tragic hero. Lionel Trilling argued that Hyacinth dies as a tragic hero who takes upon himself both the guilt of European civilization's history of injustice and the guilt of revolutionary political movements which would destroy the past's cultural glories along with established social power: "Hyacinth's death, then, is not his way of escaping from irresolution. It is truly a sacrifice, an act of heroism. He is a hero of civilization because he dares do more than civilization does: embodying two ideals at once, he takes upon himself, in full consciousness, the guilt of each. He acknowledges both his parents. By his death he instructs us in the nature

of civilized life and by his consciousness he transcends it."[3] Most critics
have claimed that Trilling's view makes Hyacinth too heroic, that in
fact, as F. W. Dupee puts it, Hyacinth is "a case merely of unrequited
sensibility, of the man who is too good for this world."[4] Interpreters of
the novel have usually thought that Hyacinth's final bewilderment indicates that his suicide represents an evasion of the issues confronting him
rather than a conscious moral decision. Thus one critic asserts that to
speak of Hyacinth assuming the guilt of the worlds of the rich and the
poor "is to go beyond what is offered us of his actual consciousness."[5] But
while Trilling did not account adequately for Hyacinth's bewilderment
and confused state of mind, he was essentially correct to interpret Hyacinth as a tragic figure. However, Trilling's focus on the moral ambiguities of European civilization accounts for some of James's interests, but
does not adequately formulate the organizing principle of this novel.
James's primary concern in *The Princess Casamassima* is his exploration
of the strengths and the tragic liabilities of Hyacinth's virtues of consciousness and imaginative sensibility.

One must not claim too much for "our little hero," as James refers to
Hyacinth at several points. James's impressionable protagonist can be com-
pared not only with Hamlet and Lear, but with "innocents" such as Verena
Tarrant of *The Bostonians* and child heroes and heroines like little Morgan
Moreen in "The Pupil" or Maisie. In his Preface to *What Maisie Knew*,
James emphasizes the breakdown of Hyacinth's character rather than its
strengths when he compares Maisie and Morgan to "our portentous little
Hyacinth of *The Princess Casamassima*, tainted to the core, as we have
seen him, with the trick of mental reaction on the things about him and
fairly staggering under the appropriations, as I have called them, that he
owes to the critical spirit. He collapses, poor Hyacinth, like a thief at
night, overcharged with treasures of reflexion and spoils of passion of
which he can give, in his poverty and obscurity, no honest account."[6] In
The Princess itself, numerous characterizations of Hyacinth are far from
flattering. Vetch tells Pinnie that the lad is "a thin-skinned, morbid,
mooning, introspective little beggar, with a good deal of imagination and

[3] Lionel Trilling, "*The Princess Casamassima*," in *The Liberal Imagination* (Harmondsworth, England: Penguin Books, 1948), p. 95.

[4] F. W. Dupee, *Henry James* (New York: Wm. Morrow & Co., 1951), p. 136.

[5] Terry Comito, "Introduction" to the Apollo edition of *The Princess Casamassima*
(New York: Thomas Crowell, 1976), p. xiv. Other critics who share this view of Hyacinth
include Mildred Hartsock, "*The Princess Casamassima*: The Politics of Power," *Studies
in the Novel* 1 (1969), 297–309; Irving Howe, *Politics and the Novel* (New York: Avon
Books, 1957); and Jane M. Luecke, "*The Princess Casamassima*: Hyacinth's Fallible Consciousness," in *Henry James: Modern Judgments*, ed. Tony Tanner (Nashville: Aurora
Publishers, 1970), pp. 184–93.

[6] Preface to *What Maisie Knew*, in *The Art of the Novel: Critical Prefaces by Henry
James*, ed. Richard P. Blackmur (New York: Scribner's Sons, 1934), p. 156.

not much perseverance, who'll expect a good deal more of life than he'll find in it" (I, 32). All the other characters in the novel offer ironic views of Hyacinth that undercut his own high view of his abilities. But with all his limitations, it is the strengths and the moral virtues of Hyacinth's character more than his weaknesses which lead to his undeserved suffering and destruction. More precisely, it is the dangers and liabilities inherent in his very virtues which prove Hyacinth's undoing.

Because *The Princess Casamassima* develops a political theme far more than most of James's work, the majority of critics have emphasized the novel's portrayal of the conflict between the revolutionary goal of social justice and the dependence of artistic values upon established power.[7] Several critics, though, have emphasized the "personal" theme: Hyacinth's disappointment and frustration in his search for meaningful personal relationships. Often the latter group of critics has seen as a major flaw the novel's shift of focus from the political to the personal issue.[8] However, the political and the personal dimensions of the novel can be understood as two sides of James's study of the various hazards to which "a youth on whom nothing was lost" would be susceptible. These two dimensions of the novel reveal distinct attributes of Hyacinth's unusual character and contrasting aspects of his fatal "bewilderment." The novel's unity and its significance, according to this interpretation, lie in James's depiction of the way that Hyacinth's capacity to perceive and experience intensely in both the political and personal spheres brings about his moral predicament and his final catastrophe.

James shows the reader what his protagonist's virtue entails in experience by suggesting comparisons with other, less perspicacious characters—the "fools" that James claimed were necessary for any story (I, xii). We see

[7] This political theme has been explored most thoroughly by Trilling, *Liberal Imagination*; Howe, *Politics and the Novel*; Leon Edel, *Henry James: The Middle Years: 1882–95* (New York: Avon Books, 1962); W. W. Tilley, *The Background of "The Princess Casamassima"* (Gainesville, FL: University of Florida Press, 1961); George Woodcock, "Henry James and the Conspirators," *Sewanee Review* 60 (1952), 219–29; and John Kimmery, "*The Bostonians* and *The Princess Casamassima*," *Texas Studies in Literature and Language* 9 (1968), 537–46.

[8] See J. A. Ward, *The Search for Form: Studies in the Structure of James's Fiction* (Chapel Hill, NC: University of North Carolina Press, 1967), p. 124: "In effect the novel changes direction in its final movement. The great 'political' issue that has troubled Hyacinth and engaged nearly everyone is certainly redefined and perhaps even transcended. The social question counts far less than the question of whether Hyacinth's few friends will offer him the loyalty and compassion that he is shown to require . . . The structural flaw: Hyacinth's tragic dilemma has been too soon formed." The theme of Hyacinth's search for personal relationships is also treated by John Kimmery, "*The Princess Casamassima* and the Quality of Bewilderment," *Nineteenth Century Fiction* 22 (1967), 47–62; Thomas Hubert, "*The Princess Casamassima*: Ideas Against Persons," *Arizona Quarterly* 32 (1976), 341–52; and John O'Neill, *Workable Design* (Fort Washington, NY: Kennikat Press, 1973).

Hyacinth's virtues clearly when he confronts characters who either can not or will not "appreciate" all that he does. His bewilderment results from his apprehension of, and his taking seriously, so much that other characters neglect or overlook, given their mental limitations or their "healthy single-mindedness." Even the Princess, though certainly no "fool" in the gross sense, has a "faculty of completely ignoring things of which she wished to take no account" (I, 211). Hyacinth has no such convenient mental lapses; "nothing is lost" on him.

In contrast to the other characters, Hyacinth recognizes the moral culpability of both the underground political movement and the established social powers that make possible "civilization as we know it." Hyacinth's divided political consciousness depends on his intelligence, sense of aesthetic beauty, and moral conscience. These virtues are all required for him to feel keenly both the intrinsic values of culture and the urgency of the problems of massive suffering and social injustice. Furthermore, his sensitivity both to beauty and to human suffering augment each other, so that his tormented self-division increases dialectically. His sense of the misery of the people makes him value even more highly the precious things that help make "the world . . . less of a 'bloody sell' and life more of a lark" (II, 145). He feels that "in this world of effort and suffering life was endurable, the spirit able to expand, only in the best conditions" (I, 168). At the same time, his growing appreciation for the opportunities of "the happier few" only intensifies his conviction that some radical step must be taken to make life more tolerable for "the miserable many." Hyacinth's virtues of consciousness and sensibility lead him to the tragic realization that the world of aesthetic beauty is bound up with the world of coercive political power, and that either to support or to challenge this alliance of art and power must involve some degree of moral guilt. James once formulated a concise definition of "moral energy"; "The essence of moral energy is to survey the whole field."[9] In its penetrating discernment of the moral ambiguities of both high culture and political revolution, Hyacinth's comprehensive vision embodies this primary Jamesian virtue.

Hyacinth's intense loyalty to his friends is equally responsible for his unusual fate. Hyacinth's devotion to Paul and the Princess contrasts sharply with their willingness to sacrifice him for an ideological scheme. Hyacinth's trust and his dream of "the religion of friendship" forbid him to criticize their failure to reciprocate his warmth and honesty. During a Sunday outing at Greenwich, Hyacinth seems both an unusually loyal friend and something of a dupe when he tries to persuade himself that he is not disappointed by Paul's failure to perceive and meet his need for sympathy. Hyacinth excuses his friend's coldness in a way that reveals his own blindness as well as a generous wish to make allowances for

---

9 James, "The Art of Fiction," in Miller, *Theory of Fiction*, p. 43.

Paul's different conception of their relationship: "Hyacinth didn't make the reflection that he [Paul] was infernally literal; he dismissed the sentimental problem that had worried him; he condoned, excused, admired—he merged himself, resting happy for the time, in the consciousness that Paul was a grand person, that friendship was a purer feeling than love and that there was an immense deal of affection between them" (II, 219). Hyacinth admires Paul for the very qualities which the reader perceives to be Paul's weaknesses in comparison with Hyacinth. Though vaguely troubled by the role Paul had taken in inducing him to make the vow to Hoffendahl, Hyacinth feels that "he himself could never have risen so high" (II, 136). Of the attributes which Hyacinth reveres in his friend, "most enviable of all was the force that enabled him to sink personal sentiment where a great public good was to be attempted and yet keep up the form of caring for that minor interest" (II, 138). This passage shows one of James's distinctive methods for ironically revealing a person's moral nature: one character praises another for some minor virtue in a context that raises questions about a far more essential or inclusive virtue. The reader compares Paul's "sinking personal sentiment" in the revolution with Hyacinth's deep affection and trust in his friends; the hollowness of Paul's caring only for the "form" of friendship is evident. Hyacinth's "good faith" in other persons, while it blinds him to some of the less admirable qualities of his friends, stands out prominently as a virtue against James's depiction of other characters' calculations and duplicities. His candor and trust in others can be abused but, even when leading to mishap, they remain morally superior to Paul's cold-blooded practical efficiency and ideological detachment.

If *The Princess Casamassima* has any chief weakness, it is probably Hyacinth's continuing worship of the Princess, even after she has abandoned him. W. J. Harvey has claimed that James too thoroughly subverts the value of the Princess through continual ironic qualification of her pretenses. The reader is left wondering whether Hyacinth's estimation of her character isn't wildly exaggerated.[10] Hyacinth is warned over and over again that the Princess shifts her allegiances and commitments rather casually. As James mentions in his Preface, her "prime note" is simply "an aversion to the *banal*" (I, xix). Hyacinth's repeated failure to judge the Princess's character as harshly as does the reader threatens to establish him as a pathetic simpleton deluded by others rather than a heroic figure torn

---

[10] W. J. Harvey, *Character and the Novel* (Ithaca: Cornell University Press, 1965), pp. 82, 85: "James's predicament is that on the one hand he must show the Princess, not merely as superficially attractive, but as possessing a genuine value; to do otherwise would be to coarsen the quality of Hyacinth's response where the whole novel assumes his sensitivity and fineness of perception. On the other hand James must, by ironic qualification, pare away and subvert the value of the Princess; . . . . one must ask whether James has not made the process of ironic qualification too effective, whether it doesn't subvert her status entirely?"

between his own divided sympathies. Some critics have claimed that the novel suffers—and fails to be tragic—because the several betrayals of Hyacinth at the end of the book rob him of dignity and make him a passive victim.[11] If the Princess's basically shallow character completely deceived Hyacinth, the novel would probably fail as tragedy. But the Princess's character is somewhat redeemed for the reader by several factors. One crucial element in our final judgment of her is her effort to release Hyacinth from his vow and her desperate attempt to rescue him in the last chapter. Her grief when she finds his body shows that she recognizes, if too late, Hyacinth's true worth as a person and friend. And, though she is somewhat self-deceived about her motives for concern for the poor—for "her behavior, after all, was more addressed to relieving herself than to relieving others" (II, 260–61)—the Princess is sincerely, if in an ill-conceived way, attempting to atone for many years of self-indulgence. "She regarded her other years, with their idleness and waste, their merely personal motives, as a long, stupid, sleep of the conscience" (II, 261). In addition, even though Madame Grandoni finally leaves the Princess, we cannot doubt this wise and just lady's attestation of the basic integrity of Christina's character. Though her behavior is sometimes absurd, Christina has an underlying sincerity and goodness, as well as embodying the grandness, mystery, and romance of the civilization that Hyacinth treasures.

More importantly, Hyacinth is not as blind to the faults of his friends as has usually been claimed. He is quite aware of many of the Princess's failings: "among this lady's faults (he was destined to learn they were numerous) not the least eminent was an exaggerated fear of the commonplace" (I, 209). But her foibles simply don't detract from Christina's positive power of attraction for him. When Hyacinth is inspired at the very end by "the great union of her beauty, her sincerity, and her energy" (II, 405), we feel that his love for her encompasses her confusion and mistakes. In this respect James contrasts him sharply with most of the other characters. When her money will have run out, Paul will have no more use for the Princess than for "the washed-out tea-leaves in that pot" (I, 413). Hyacinth knows that Milly's friendship, too, is capricious and fitful: he is well aware that "they were a pair of very fallible creatures, united much more by their weaknesses than by any consistency or fidelity they might pretend to practice toward each other" (II, 330). Hyacinth recognizes most of his friends' inconsistencies, yet loves them none the less.

---

11 See O'Neill, *Workable Design*, p. 68: "Hyacinth the victim, innocent, affectionate, mildly reproachful, staunchly determined not to release himself from a now meaningless vow—this is not a character of tragic self-contradiction, but rather the emblematic Jamesian observer betrayed by ideology and narrow morality. As James lays more and more stress on the betrayal of Hyacinth, he undercuts the basis of our former respect. . . . He becomes merely a pathetically muddled young man."

James's use of motifs of sacrifice and payment in *The Princess* reveals the ambiguity of Hyacinth's suicide because of the mixture of sharp perception and bewilderment in his consciousness. One can choose to make a sacrifice or be sacrificed; one can pay or be made to pay. Within the novel, Hyacinth's suicide is construed in both of these ways. He is referred to by Muniment as a "lamb of sacrifice" (I, 362), implying that he will be put to death by others without understanding or sharing their purpose. Yet Hyacinth consciously desires to make a sacrifice and thereby to resolve the "question of paying for the lot" (I, 355). He finds "an indelicacy in not being ready to pay" for his vow (II, 54). Paul, by contrast, "would make society bankrupt, but he would be paid" (I, 113). James establishes the measure of sincerity and commitment, to one's friends and to one's beliefs, as "what one will give up." Hyacinth's conversations with the Princess, and with others about the Princess, constantly raise the question of whether in fact she would be willing to make "the last sacrifice" for the revolution, as she avows. To Hyacinth's firm conviction that "when the day comes for my friend to give up— you'll see," Mr. Vetch retorts: "Yes, I've no doubt there are things she'll bring herself to sacrifice" (II, 100). In fact, the Princess sacrifices not herself but Hyacinth. James's use of the double meaning of sacrifice, then, brings out the significance of Hyacinth's death. He has been sacrificed *by* his friends, abandoned or subordinated to their ends. Yet he also *chooses* to sacrifice his own rather than another life or any of his deepest values. His suicide reflects the extent to which he has allowed himself to be deceived and exploited by others; thus he appears as their unwitting sacrificial victim—a mere "lamb" rather than a tragic hero. On the other hand, James emphasizes, even in our last view of him, Hyacinth's conscious intent to undergo "a tremendous risk and an unregarded sacrifice" (II, 405). This capacity for offered sacrifice comes as the final mark of the heroism and virtue that establish Hyacinth as a tragic figure.

Hyacinth's consciousness is both "fine" and "bewildered." Trilling claims too much when he asserts, without acknowledging the element of bewilderment, that Hyacinth takes upon himself, "in full consciousness," the guilt of those around him. Yet those critics who refuse to recognize the tragic dimensions of Hyacinth's fate because of his restricted perceptions and his fallible consciousness wrongly assume that the protagonist of a tragedy must fully share our own understanding of his situation. If this were the case, James held in his Preface, there would be no story to tell in the first place, since "bewilderment" is a necessary element in any credible character's story. James depicted Hyacinth's virtues of consciousness and sensibility and the good faith that can be abused, and he showed the combination of circumstances in which these virtues can lead to self-destructive bewilderment.

III. The Princess *as Social Criticism and as Tragedy*

James's tragedy is firmly rooted in a particular historical setting. Many passages in *The Princess Casamassima* reveal James's awareness of the misery of London's poor, the decadence of the aristocracy, and the pressing need for social justice. But the index that marks his society's failure is not so much physical hardship, as the lack of opportunities provided for the life of the imagination in "an age that had lost the sense of fineness" (I, 167). Against this background of material and spiritual poverty, the world of wealth and leisure is presented as both an oppressive political power and as the only escape from deprivation. James satirizes the jaded smugness of such unsavory aristocrats as Sholto, "a cumberer of the earth . . . [who] was nothing whatever in himself and had no character or merit save by tradition, reflection, imitation, superstition" (II, 82). But though the aristocracy's style of life depends on vast social inequalities, for Hyacinth it also represents the only vision of a life worth living, and even a form of victory over suffering: "The poverty and ignorance of the multitude seemed so vast and preponderant, and so much the law of life, that those who had managed to escape from the black gulf were only the happy few, spirits of resource as well as children of luck; they inspired in some degree the interest and sympathy that one should feel for survivors and victors, those who have come safely out of a shipwreck or a battle" (II, 262).

James's presentation of Hyacinth's social position and political consciousness is complex and subtle. Compared with Milly, Hyacinth is "a regular little swell" (I, 164) who has never experienced the most brutal suffering of the London slums. James indicates that a certain degree of material comfort and leisure are necessary before one can begin to form schemes for revolution, since the most degrading and humiliating suffering leaves a person no time or energy for any activity beyond bare survival. Hyacinth is sometimes unappreciative of the comparative advantages he has enjoyed and dramatically enhances his own personal "case" against society. On the other hand, his fine consciousness alerts him to aspects of degradation and misery to which the most desperately poor inhabitants of the urban slums are quite oblivious: "he was aware the people were direfully wretched—more aware, it often seemed to him, than they themselves were; so frequently was he struck with their brutal insensibility, a grossness proof against the taste of better things and against any desire for them" (II, 262). James depicts suffering less often in terms of physical pain or hardship than as an utterly benighted style of living, a complete lack of capacity or desire for aesthetic pleasure or conversation.[12] However, James

---

12 See Comito, "Introduction" to *Princess*, pp. vii–viii: "The grievance registered most feelingly against English society is an 'anguish of exasperated taste,' for which a soiled shirt front or a vulgar intonation speaks more tellingly of dilapidations of the spirit than the rather abstract miseries sometimes evoked. This blighting of style, a pervasive

clearly recognized, too, the comparative luxury of so refined and rarefied a sense of suffering; this awareness is expressed in his satiric reference to the Princess's "theory that the right way to acquaint one's self with the sensations of the wretched was to suffer the anguish of exasperated taste" (II, 182).

Hyacinth articulates the two reasons why James was critical of political radicalism: because so much of the radicals' motivation was due to hypocritical self-righteousness, self-delusion, and envy, and because of the revolution's threat to the cultural treasures he cherished. Like *The Bostonians*, *The Princess* explores the unacknowledged self-interested motivations that sometimes prompt the actions of political radicals. In contrast with Poupin, Muniment, and the Princess, much of Hyacinth's difficulty in committing himself to the revolution derives from his scrupulosity about being free of poses of superior virtue, implicit self-deception, and hidden motives of envy or revenge. Hyacinth's fear that the revolution's success would entail the destruction of civilization's artistic heritage reveals James's deepest loyalty to the established powers. Still, James is remarkably circumspect in his treatment of the revolutionists, and his refusal simply to denounce them as enemies of society is probably one reason for his novel's failure with the public.[13]

James's refusal to resolve these complex political and social recognitions into a simple position for or against either the revolution or the established powers is reflected in Hyacinth's troubled consciousness of the insolubility and the vast scope of the problem of art's dependence on established power in any society. Certain passages in *The Princess* express Hyacinth's sense that it is not only the decadence of the wealthy or the "present arrangement of things" in England or Europe that brings about his impasse, but the very nature of human life in civilization or the fault of "the terrestrial globe" itself: "If it was the fault of the rich, as Paul Muniment held, the selfish congested rich who allowed such abominations to flourish, that made no difference and only shifted the shame; since the terrestrial globe, a visible failure, produced the cause as well as the effect" (II, 268). Though Hyacinth's sense of futility and powerlessness partly reflects his bewilderment, it also expresses James's awareness that the problems Hyacinth finds insoluble are universal in scope. For James recognized that "civilization has a price," as Trilling so concisely put it; this price is the acceptance or toleration of a certain amount of suffering in the course of pursuing its cultural ideals: "If the revolutionary passion

---

'resigned seediness,' is for James, much more than any actual suffering, the measure of his culture's failure and guilt, a failure to provide, except sporadically and for 'the happier few,' the fulfillment of those human capacities it has been its particular glory to envision."

[13] See Tilley, *Background*, p. 59. Tilley judges that James's political views were less conservative towards social reform than those expressed in the mouthpiece of Britain's upper classes, the London *Times*.

thus has its guilt, Hyacinth's passion for life at its richest and noblest is no less guilty. It leads him to consent to the established coercive power of the world, and this can never be innocent. One cannot 'accept' the suffering of others, no matter for what ideal, no matter if one's own suffering be also accepted, without incurring guilt. It is the guilt in which every civilization is implicated."[14]

Most of a society's greatest achievements of art and culture are closely associated with its centers of power. One sees this in the construction of the Pyramids, in the dramatic festivals of ancient Athens, in the churches of the Italian Renaissance, in the establishment of Europe's national museums during the nineteenth century, and in the dependence of much modern art (and academic life) on the philanthropy of business corporations or government foundations. James shows that there is considerable resistance to recognizing all the implications of this association of art and power. Political radicals devoted to establishing a more just society at any price fail to acknowledge the value of their culture's artistic heritage. Established power, on the other hand, often denies its complicity in accepting suffering when it allocates resources to artistic achievements that will be enjoyed only by a small portion of society. But the significance of the association of art and power may be recognized by a certain kind of consciousness, one sensitive both to the cultural values of civilization and to a society's spiritual and material deprivation. His experiences in Paris, Venice, and London reveal to Hyacinth the universality of this situation, the inevitability with which "the monuments and treasures of art, the great palaces and properties, the conquests of learning and taste are . . . based if you will upon all the despotisms, the cruelties, the exclusions, the monopolies and the rapacities of the past" (II, 145). Art and political power are subtly but inextricably linked, and either defending or attacking this alliance involves one in a certain amount of moral guilt. Understanding and sharing the values of both the revolutionaries and the world of art and power, Hyacinth Robinson "gives himself away" twice, and eventually finds himself in a moral impasse. The tragic vision of *The Princess Casamassima* lies in its presentation of the situation that destroys Hyacinth as a fundamental and enduring fact with roots in the very nature of human civilization, and not simply a matter of coincidence or circumstance (though these factors are necessary to realize Hyacinth's tragedy).

Yet if in this respect *The Princess* suggests a tragic vision of human civilization, we should note two crucial aspects of James's sense of tragedy, which is distinctly different from that of Hardy or Conrad. First, James suggests that, while Hyacinth's fate is tragic, it also has comic and pathetic dimensions. James saw "the tragedy and comedy of life" as

[14] Trilling, *Liberal Imagination*, p. 95.

indissolubly connnected (I, v).[15] *The Princess* presents many humorous and wry insights into the confusions and entanglements of the various characters. James presents the inconsistencies and contradictions of all his characters, including Hyacinth, as a source of comic incongruity as well as of tragic pathos.[16] Besides the comic perspectives of other characters in *The Princess*, especially Madame Grandoni and Mr. Vetch, there are several suggestions that Hyacinth himself realizes that his dilemma need not have been as agonizing as he made it. At one point, reflecting on the depth of his affections for both the Princess and Millicent, Hyacinth is "obliged to recognize the liberality of a fate that had sometimes appeared invidious. He had been provided with the best opportunities for choosing between the beauty of the original and the beauty of the conventional" (II, 329). And Poupin, the Princess, Lady Aurora, and Vetch all give Hyacinth examples of "the reconcilement of the disparities" (II, 263) that he feels to be absolutely antithetical. Had Hyacinth greater maturity and a more detached and ironical perspective on his plight, he might have been able to see his situation as an "embroilment" with implications equally comic and tragic. By the end of the novel, though, there is little humor in Hyacinth's situation; his limitations make him seem more a pathetic than a comic figure.

In this regard, a significant comparison can be made between *The Princess Casamassima* and other of James's works in which protagonists find themselves morally compromised but are able not only to survive their ordeal, but to grow in maturity and self-knowledge. Lambert Strether of *The Ambassadors* and Maggie Verver of *The Golden Bowl* both discover that their naiveté and innocence have helped to precipitate a situation in which other characters manipulate and exploit each other. They, too, must recognize their own well-intentioned errors of judgment and a certain amount of moral responsibility for evil. Yet Maggie and Strether are able to reach an accord with themselves and with life through their sacrifice or renunciation of something less than life itself; Maggie relinquishes the closeness of her relationship with her father, and Strether gives up the

---

[15] James implies that Hyacinth's bewilderment is *primarily* tragic, though, when he contrasts his protagonist with Fielding's Tom Jones: "Fielding's hero in *Tom Jones* is but as 'finely,' that is but as intimately, bewildered as a young man of great health and spirits may be when he hasn't a grain of imagination: the point to be made is, at all events, that his sense of bewilderment obtains altogether on the comic, never on the tragic plane" (I, xiii–xiv).

[16] One of the clearest statements of James's sense of the fusion of life's comedy with its tragedy is his formulation of the image of the "strange alloy" of life in the Preface of *What Maisie Knew*, in *Art of the Novel*, p. 143: "No themes are so human as those that reflect for us, out of the confusion of life, the close connexion of bliss and bale, of the things that help with the things that hurt, so dangling before us for ever that bright hard metal, of so strange an alloy, one face of which is somebody's right and ease and the other somebody's pain and wrong."

opportunity to continue to "profit" by his experience of Europe. (In other cases, such as that of John Marcher in "The Beast in the Jungle," James's treatment of the tragedy of an "unlived life" culminates in an unmitigated sense of loss and deprivation.) Hyacinth is a more naive and less resilient version of the Jamesian "innocent" who, rudely awakened to the existence of evil, must establish his own identity and integrity through an act of renunciation. Lacking Strether's detached, ironic perspective on himself or Maggie's or Isabel Archer's energy and resourcefulness in coping with their discovery of evil, Hyacinth feels he can only renounce his own life. Comparison with these characters thus suggests other important Jamesian virtues that Hyacinth lacks. But it is certainly unreasonable to moralistically condemn Hyacinth's suicide on the grounds that other Jamesian protagonists are not driven to this extreme.[17] Hyacinth's tragic division mirrors an immense political problem, while the typical Jamesian protagonist's moral dilemma is limited to establishing a right relationship with a small circle of intimate friends and family members. In any case, many of his works reflect James's sense of tragedy, but that sense is only one of the many elements shaping all his fictions, including *The Princess.*

A second distinctive aspect of James's sense of tragedy is its intimate connection with his affirmations of value. Though *The Princess* has been interpreted as "Schopenhauerian," this adjective is misleading in that it implies that James's sense of tragedy led him to metaphysical pessimism and the wish to withdraw from life.[18] Such an interpretation does not account for the increased appreciation for certain values which arises, even in Hyacinth's own troubled consciousness, from recognizing the insoluble moral dilemma at the heart of civilization. Hyacinth's knowledge that his political commitment may cost him his life determines him to live in conformity with "the great religious rule—to live each hour as if it were to be one's last . . . simply in extreme thankfulness for every good minute that's added" (II, 57). Hyacinth abides to the end by this rule, which anticipates Strether's advice to Little Bilham in *The Ambassadors.* His unusual sensitivities to both beauty and suffering bring about his impasse, but they also aid his effort to live with grace and gratefulness. In Paris Hyacinth is filled with "a sense of everything that might hold one to the world, of the sweetness of not dying, the fascination of great cities, the charm of travel and discovery, the generosity of admiration" (II, 141). Hyacinth appreciates the preciousness and beauty of life,

---

17 This is the argument of Luecke, "*The Princess Casamassima*: Hyacinth's Fallible Consciousness."

18 See Joseph J. Firebaugh, "A Schopenhauerian Novel: James's *The Princess Casamassima*," *Nineteenth Century Fiction* 13 (1958), 177–97. Another interpretation which underestimates the affirmative dimensions of James's tragic works is John R. Dove, "The Tragic Sense in Henry James," *Texas Studies in Literature and Language* 2 (1960), 303–14.

not in spite of, but as a direct result of the conflicts of his anguished consciousness. His fate is poignant and disturbing, but it also discloses Hyacinth's, and James's, deep convictions about life's positive values. James's sense of tragedy, then, does not suggest disgust with existence or a feeling that life is futile, but rather a determination to hold the more firmly and thankfully to the values a fine consciousness finds in experience.[19] Even though Hyacinth finally found it impossible to maintain this attitude, the overall effect of his fate on the reader is not a sense of embittered hopelessness about the fate of consciousness in the modern world, but rather an increased sense of the beauty of the world Hyacinth believes he must sacrifice, and of sadness over the waste of this life with such a capacity for rich personal experience.

The Princess Casamassima involves a critique of the Jamesian virtues of consciousness and sensibility by inducing us to respect and admire "a youth on whom nothing was lost" and yet understand how his own character brings about his moral impasse and the "bewilderment" that leads him to kill himself. The novel reveals James's loyalty to the cultural achievements of European "civilization as we know it" despite his awareness of its moral ambiguity in resting upon a history of past violence and present social injustice. While *The Princess* shows the universal scope of the problem that baffles Hyacinth, it also expresses James's sense of the intermixture of tragedy with life's comedy, irony, and pathos. And the fate of James's young hero, while fully tragic, stresses appreciation for "a sense of everything that might hold one to the world" (II, 141).

[19] Several of James's non-fictional writings bear witness to and illumine this view that even tragedy can enrich consciousness: the passage on Turgenev's "total view of the world," which sees life as a battle, but an experience to be welcomed so long as it helps to "swell the volume of consciousness," in James's "Ivan Turgenieff" (sic) in Miller, *Theory of Fiction*, p. 301; James's "voice of stoicism" letter of 1883 to Grace Norton, in Morton D. Zabel, ed., *The Portable Henry James*, revised by Lyell H. Powers (New York: Viking, 1968), p. 645; his letter of 1914 to Henry Adams describing his art as an "act of life" performed with a "ghastly grin," in Zabel, *Portable James*, pp. 671–72; and James's late essay "Is There a Life After Death?" in F. O. Matthiessen, ed., *The James Family* (New York: Knopf, 1948), pp. 602–14, in which James finds the hope for immortality dependent on the accumulation of personal impressions on a consciousness.

3

Prudence in *Billy Budd*:
An Equivocal Virtue in a "Man-of-War" World

Prudence implies the ability to exercise sound judgment and discretion in the pursuit of one's goals, and caution or circumspection as to possible dangers. Prudence requires both skill in discerning the most suitable course of action in given circumstances and facility in implementing one's intentions. Without prudence, the best intentions cannot be realized in action.

Though prudence is a central moral virtue, it has come to have some negative and some morally ambiguous connotations. There are two reasons for this. First, prudence alone is not sufficient to make a person morally good. Its moral status depends on the ends which prudence serves; a prudent thief carefully and shrewdly pursues his end of robbery. Secondly, prudence often seems to involve excessive cautiousness and concern to protect either one's own safety or certain institutional forms. Prudence is a "worldly wisdom" that can entail a refusal to take risks for another person. Prudential self-concern, a necessary if subsidiary aspect of moral life, can be opposed to the Christian imperative to put the neighbor's good before one's own. It can also conflict with the other-regarding injunctions of a secular morality—perhaps even with a military officer's duties to his subordinates.

The virtue of prudence has a long and refined history of use in philosophical and theological ethics; Aristotle and Aquinas, in particular, give it extended analysis. The concrete significance of prudence in the moral life can also be understood by focusing on the way in which literary works explore its ambiguities. The works of Herman Melville, especially *Billy Budd*, explore both the essential necessity of this virtue in experience and also the negative implications prudence can take on in particular individuals in certain circumstances: its possible subversion in a person whose will is evil, its potential conflict with the rights of other persons, and its sometimes excessive concern with the stability of institutional forms.

I. *Prudence in Melville's Earlier Works*

Melville had begun to explore the implications of prudence in his works prior to *Billy Budd*. It is the fact of evil in the natural world that makes prudence necessary. As central to *Moby-Dick* as Ishmael's moments of visionary insight into Nature are his reflections on the necessity of a practical, worldly, and common-sense view of her dangers. "The Mast-Head" (chapter 35) describes a sublime trance induced in a meditative sailor assigned a watch in the crow's nest. The narrator concludes with a warning about—and to—romantic and melancholy young men who offer "to ship with the Phaedon instead of Bowditch." Ship captains can have little use for an enthusiastic Platonist, who will sight no whales. To the meditating dreamer himself, as his spirit ebbs away in pantheistic identification with nature, the narrator warns: "While this sleep, this dream is on ye, move your foot or hand an inch; slip your hold at all; and your identity comes back in horror. Over Descartian vortices you hover. And perhaps, at mid-day, in the fairest weather, with one half-throttled shriek you drop through that transparent air into the summer sea, no more to rise for ever. Heed it well, ye Pantheists!" Ishmael's meditations on natural phenomena, especially on the great white whale itself, reveal an oscillation between moments of lyrical effusion over its beauty and cautious drawing back from nature's hidden dangers, because he shares "the instinct of the knowledge of the demonism in the world." Moby-Dick's "gentle joyousness" and "enticing calm" as he majestically glides through the sea conceal his deadly power: "No wonder there had been some among the hunters who namelessly transported and allured by all that serenity, had ventured to assail it; but had fatally found that quietude but the vesture of tornadoes" (chapter 133). Melville's descriptions of the natural world show a tension between the impulse towards mystical identification and the prudent avoidance of danger. His sketches of "The Encantadas," too, reveal this rhythm of attraction and guarded reserve. The necessity of prudence is somewhat comically brought out in an observation on the Galapagos tortoise in "Sketch Second." For these massive turtles, who will not turn aside in their crawlings, but only plod directly forwards, the world is full of insurmountable, immovable obstacles. "Their crowning curse is their drudging impulse to straightforwardness in a belittered world." Prudence is necessary in the natural world because of its various threats and obstacles to the unwary.

Human society, too, requires a cautious apprehension of possible dangers. In "Benito Cereno," Captain Delano is "a person of singularly good nature, not liable, except on extraordinary and repeated incentives, and hardly then, to indulge in personal alarms, any way involving the imputation of malign evil in man." Delano's unsuspicious character prevents him from realizing the imminent peril to both Don Benito's and his own ship from the rebellious slaves. The disaster which is narrowly averted leaves little doubt as to the negative judgment that must answer the narrator's initial query about Delano's obliviousness to the presence of evil: "Whether, in view of what humanity is capable, such a trait implies, along with a benevolent heart, more than ordinary quickness and accuracy of intellectual perception, may be left to the wise to determine." In *Pierre*, too, the main character cannot comprehend the theory of "virtuous expediency" expounded in the strange pamphlet by Plotinus Plinlimmon. Plinlimmon compares the absolute morality of the Sermon on the Mount to the "chronometrical" time kept by a ship on its voyages. Absolute morality is as impractical in human society as would be the attempt to live by Greenwich time rather than "horological" (local) time when the ship docks in China. Plinlimmon defends "what the best mortal men do daily practice," and presents "consolation to the earnest man, who, among all his human frailties, is still agonizingly conscious of the beauty of chronological excellence." That Pierre cannot understand the pamphlet symbolizes the blindness of the idealistic love which eventually leads to his downfall. Pierre's and Delano's lack of apprehension of evil in human nature is as potentially tragic as Billy Budd's similar naiveté and lack of prudence.

If Melville repeatedly stressed the need for prudence, though, his works prior to *Billy Budd* also reveal intimations of what will be a central theme in his last work: the limitations and possible inadequacies of prudence. In introducing the Plinlimmon pamphlet, the narrator of *Pierre* says that "to me it seems more the excellently illustrated restatement of a problem, than the solution of the problem itself." The "problem" is the moral mediocrity, the self-concern and limited vision of the merely prudent man, who conforms to social practices rather than commit "suicide to the practical things of this world." In the pamphlet itself, "horological" virtue is presented as the right moral pattern for the good man to follow, though the "chronometrical" model of perfection revealed in Jesus should not be forgotten. But no real example of such "virtuous expediency" appears in the novel. The "worldly" characters— such as Falsgrave, who carries a brooch representing "the allegorical union of the serpent and the dove"—appear merely self-serving and hypocritical. Indeed, Melville's use of the term "prudence" throughout his works is often pejorative, implying a lack of spontaneity or courage or fellow-feeling. Yet prudence is indeed a virtue in Melville's moral vision, if we consider not just his explicit references to this term, but the characters who display what most translations of Aristotle call "practical wisdom": skill in making and acting on judgments about the good in particular circumstances.

In "Bartleby the Scrivener," the lawyer who narrates the story displays a limited degree of this practical judgment and prudence. The lawyer is somewhat comically baffled at how to help Bartleby, a lost soul who appears from nowhere as mysteriously as does Billy Budd. Like Captain Vere, the lawyer is loyal to the institutions of the temporal world, but is a basically humane man who does what he can for poor Bartleby. Though some critics have seen the lawyer (as they have seen Vere) as the incarnation of the bureaucratic functionary, he is a better man than he professes to be in his repeatedly frustrated attempts to make a place for Bartleby in the world of Wall Street. What can he do for a soul who would "prefer not to" do anything, and finally prefers not to live? At first Melville presents mainly the humorous aspects of the lawyer's attempts to be practical and efficient in dealing with the obstinately passive Bartleby, as when he moves his entire office rather than have the police take the scrivener away. But we increasingly sense the anguish the lawyer feels at his inability to remedy the nameless malaise that makes Bartleby an "isolato." The lawyer is a sort of comical Vere, helplessly and futilely trying to reconcile the demands of institutional forms with an individual who, like Billy, seems to have descended from another world. In "Bartleby," though, the scrivener is a victim of some deep inner anomie, not the perpetrator of a murder. His poignant and pathetic fate brings out both the humanity and the impotence of the lawyer's earnest and exasperated practicality. In *Billy Budd*, the tragic choice Vere faces reveals a quite different sense of the limitations of prudence in reconciling the fate of an ethereal soul with the prerequisites of collective social life.

In Melville's last prose work before *Billy Budd*, *The Confidence-Man: His Masquerade*, the ambiguities inherent in prudence are explored in greater depth. This satiric novel depicts a series of encounters between the Confidence-Man in his various disguises and the characters from whom he solicits money. When a stranger asks a character whether he or she "has confidence," the typical reaction is "a natural struggle between charity and prudence," (38).[1] In the first half of the book, until the introduction of Pitch, Melville stresses the need for prudence on a Mississippi steamboat, where one's casual acquaintance may be a gambler, imposter, or the very devil in one of his masquerades. The Confidence-Man tries to disarm the cautious reserve of his victims by doubting "the existence of unmerited misery" (55) and of anything else that might undermine confidence in the final benignity of the world and of human nature. After showing the man who lacks prudence as an easy prey for the Confidence-Man, Melville begins to explore the morally questionable aspects of prudence. Though he, too, is finally persuaded to

---

[1] Herman Melville, *The Confidence-Man: His Masquerade*, edited by Hershel Parker (New York: Norton, 1971). All quotations refer to this edition and are cited parenthetically in the text.

give three dollars to the Confidence-Man, the "Missouri bachelor," Pitch, is the only character to penetrate the devil's deceptive optimism; he at least realizes he has been fleeced, and rebuts him in his next masquerade as the cosmopolitan (chapter 24). But Pitch's experiences make him not only prudent but misanthropic; his knowledge of evil embitters him. Pitch applies to humanity in general the animosity that the "Indian-hater" focuses on one object. Melville poses but two alternatives: believe in the innate goodness of the universe, and be duped; or acknowledge the evil at the heart of things, and risk estrangement from your fellow humanity. The prudence learned through painful experience is not a joyful wisdom.

Hawthorne had said that Melville "can neither believe, nor be comfortable in his disbelief, and he is too honest and courageous not to try to do one or the other." The emotional tension between these two attitudes underlies the structure and the narrative rhythms of much of Melville's work—including the *Confidence-Man*, which many critics have seen only as a relapse into complete disbelief and skepticism. For in this novel, Melville shows not only the blindness of several varieties of nineteenth-century American optimism, but also the dangers of prudent guardedness about evil. Melville uses sources in the Bible and in Shakespeare's works to develop the thematic tension between the need to believe, to have confidence, and the need to doubt. Melville's ideas about prudence have their deepest roots not in Aristotle's ethics, but in the wisdom literature of the Old Testament: in the books of Ecclesiastes and Job and Proverbs.[2] The "sober philosophy of Solomon the wise," as China Aster's epitaph puts it (189), contrasts sharply with Jesus' advice in the Gospel of Matthew to "sell all thou hast, and give to the poor" (148). Melville's many Biblical allusions pose the issue of how to reconcile the prudential counsels of the wisdom tradition with Christian injunctions to give up worldly concerns.

Shakespeare's works, too, function as a literary source for the conflict between prudent worldly wisdom and a more heroic form of virtue. Chapter 30 involves a long discussion between the cosmopolitan and "Charlie Noble" over how to characterize Polonius's advice to Laertes in *Hamlet*. Charlie says the father's prudential maxims to his son are "false, fatal, and calumnious" (148). The cosmopolitan ironically defends Polonius on the grounds of charity, but admits that his words involve "an unhandsome sort of reflection upon human nature." "Prudent minds," he asserts, will not articulate their deeper thoughts about this "queer man," Shakespeare, who could create a character such as Autolycus in *The Winter's*

[2] On Melville's treatment of themes in the Old Testament wisdom literature, see Nathalia Wright, *Melville's Use of the Bible* (Durham, NC: Duke University Press, 1949), pp. 93–112.

Tale. By this rogue, "trust, that is, confidence—that is, the thing in the universe the sacredest—is rattlingly pronounced just the simplest" (150). The cosmopolitan goads Charlie into a vehement attack on Polonius, especially the latter's warning against financially aiding unfortunate friends. When the cosmopolitan tells Charlie he is in urgent want of money, Charlie's outraged refusal reveals the hypocrisy of his having so righteously rejected the prudential counsels of Polonius. Charlie is exposed as a "genial misanthrope" (154) whose philosophy of benevolence and philanthropy hides his underlying refusal to sacrifice for another person. Though everyone pays lip service to the Bible's Christian virtues and Shakespeare's heroic virtues, both of which require courage and sacrifice for others, in practice prudential self-concern intervenes to limit charity and trust. Prudence seems both despicable and yet the inevitable way of the world. The result is a society of solitary selves, either hypocritical confidence-men, disillusioned victims, or crazed Indian-haters.

In his satire of Emerson and Thoreau in the characters of the "mystical master" Mark Winsome and his "practical disciple" Egbert, Melville exposes the coldness and selfishness of the New England mercantile attitude that underlies the lofty philosophy of "Self-Reliance." The Emersonian doctrines are totally unrealistic and unworkable in practice. In his essay on "Prudence," Emerson wrote: "Trust men, and they will be true to you; treat them greatly, and they will show themselves great." Melville's marginal comment on this: "God help the poor fellow who squares his life according to this."[3] Melville saw that the metaphysical confidence of the Emersonian was usually combined with practical shrewdness and wariness. But, as an "innocent" question of the Confidence-Man suggests, Egbert's philosophical position is unnecessary or pointless if it merely "tends to the same formation of character with the experience of the world" (170). When Egbert claims that his refusal to help a needy friend does not express "vile prudence" but a noble Platonic conception of friendship, Melville shows how the doctrine of self-reliance tends in practice towards a self-concern that contradicts Christ's command to look after the neighbor. The Emersonian philosophy leads to an atomistic society of distrustful Yankees, prudently calculating their own best advantage and disdaining to help each other.

The thrust of Melville's satire here, however, is not to attack the need for prudence, but to point out discrepancies and illusions in the transcendentalist philosophy. Prudence remains indispensable for coping with the wiles of the Confidence-Man. Yet Melville points out problems which result from learning the necessity of prudence: Pitch's misanthropic distrust of mankind, the Indian-hater's violent paranoia, and the tightfisted, hardhearted coldness to a needy person displayed by Charlie and Egbert.

3 Quoted in the Norton Critical Edition of *The Confidence-Man*, p. 262.

Still another danger in prudence is its tendency to produce an accommodationist stance towards existing social institutions. Pitch accurately diagnoses and denounces this consequence of prudent self-concern when he attacks the cautious evasions of an abolitionist: "Picked and prudent sentiments. You are the moderate man, the invaluable understrapper of the wicked man. You, the moderate man, may be used for wrong, but are useless for right" (97).

In sum, Melville satirizes the types of nineteenth century optimism that deny the reality of evil and the consequent need for prudence. But he also shows the moral cowardice, the lack of charity, and the selfishness of the cynics and pragmatists who simply conform to the way of the world. Prudence is shown to be necessary, and then called in question, though not completely undermined. As we shall see, Melville's treatment of prudence in *Billy Budd* is similar to the attitude revealed in *The Confidence-Man*. But in the latter work, the issue involves only a few dollars more or less, and the treatment of the many stock characters is directed towards morose satire of the clichés of American positive thinking. In *Billy Budd*, Melville focuses on the dilemma of one character whose tragic choice between a prudent course of action and a riskier one involves the fate of many lives.

II. *Varieties of Prudence on the* Bellipotent

In Melville's last work, Billy Budd is falsely accused of mutiny by the master of arms, John Claggart. Billy strikes him dead, and, after a trial on the ship, is hung at the insistence of Captain Vere. Billy Budd has the guileless and naive moral sensibility of a child. It is in the characters of Claggart and Captain Vere that Melville develops the theme of the equivocal nature of the virtue of prudence in the world of a "man-of-war" battleship.

Before Melville introduces Vere, he sets up a standard against which we are to measure him: the British commander Lord Nelson. The narrator first states several criticisms of Nelson by what he calls "martial utilitarians." These detractors hold that "Nelson's ornate publication of his person in battle was not only unnecessary, but not military, nay, savored of foolhardiness and vanity" (57).[4] At the battle of Trafalgar, where Nelson was fatally wounded, his dying commands to anchor the fleet were overruled by his successor in command, and a great storm destroyed much of the fleet. Nelson is therefore accused of a lack of prudence that results in catastrophe for himself and his ships. The narrator rebuts this criticism by "the Benthamites of war," insisting that "the *might-have-been* is but boggy

---

[4] Herman Melville, *Billy Budd, Sailor: (An Inside Narrative)*, edited by Harrison Hayford and Merton M. Sealts, Jr. (Chicago: University of Chicago Press, 1962). All quotations refer to this edition and are cited parenthetically in the text.

ground to build on." In fact, Nelson showed great prudence in his concern *for the fleet*: "Certainly, in foresight as to the larger issue of an encounter, and anxious preparations for it—buoying the deadly way and mapping it out, as at Copenhagen—few commanders have been so painstakingly circumspect as this same reckless declarer of his person in fight" (57–58). The narrator distinguishes prudential considerations as applied to Nelson's naval duties from prudence applied to his own personal safety: "Personal prudence, even when dictated by quite other than selfish considerations, surely is no special virtue in a military man; while an excessive love of glory, impassioning a less burning impulse, the honest sense of duty, is the first" (58). Nelson, then, displays both prudence for his fleet and a magnificent heroism in times of crisis.

Captain Vere is "a sailor of distinction even in a time prolific of renowned seamen" (60). While not a great hero like Nelson, he is a first-rate captain with solid achievements. Many critics have compared Vere unfavorably to Nelson, and indeed, Melville draws a contrast between the two men.[5] Vere is "intrepid to the verge of temerity, though never injudiciously so" (60). Though superior to the average captain, he is not a Nelson: "whatever his sterling qualities, he was without any brilliant ones" (61). But this comparison hardly reflects discredit on Vere. Nelson is after all "the greatest sailor since the world began" (58); Vere only a good one. Vere stands in relation to the legendary figure of Nelson much as does Billy Budd to the archetype of the "Handsome Sailor" Melville describes in the first chapter. The characters in *Billy Budd* have affinities with the heroes of myth and legend, but they are realistically portrayed human agents who differ from their mythic counterparts in significant and instructive ways.

Vere's prudential virtues are delineated by means of accounts of his political beliefs and his relationship with the crew. He is a conservative who admires "unconventional writers like Montaigne, who, free from cant and convention, philosophize upon realities. . . . In this line of reasoning, he found confirmation of his own more reserved thoughts" (62). The reasons for Vere's political conservativism foreshadow an important theme Melville develops at the end of the novella: the merits and possible limitations of prudent concern for existing social forms.[6] Melville's setting of

<hr>

[5] For Rowland Sherrill, *The Prophetic Melville: Experience, Transcendence, and Tragedy* (Athens, GA: University of Georgia Press, 1979), p. 232, the digression on Nelson functions "to point out the personal prudence, regardless of its motive, which Vere will interpose between himself and his experience of Billy Budd and, therefore, to explain Vere's failure." See also Evelyn Schroth, "Melville's Judgment on Captain Vere," *Midwest Quarterly* 10 (1969), 189–200. But Vere's prudence is for his ship, not for himself (personal), and it is one of his virtues as a naval commander.

[6] The political dimensions of Melville's treatment of Vere are the focus of the only full-length scholarly work on *Billy Budd*, Thomas Scorza's *In the Time Before Steamships: "Billy Budd," the Limits of Politics, and Modernity* (De Kalb, IL: Northern Illinois

Billy Budd legitimates Vere's anxieties about disorder. The story takes place just after the French Revolution, and after the Nore mutiny within the English navy, at a time when Britain was threatened with the possibility of violent revolution or social upheaval. Vere's "settled convictions were as a dike against those invading waters of novel opinion social, political, and otherwise" (62). In contrast to other members of the aristocratic classes, who attacked new social theories because of their threat to traditional privileges, "Vere disinterestedly opposed them not alone because they seemed to him insusceptible of embodiment in lasting institutions, but at war with the peace of the world and the true welfare of mankind" (63). Vere wishes to preserve the existing forms of order in his society because he believes they best ensure its lasting security. Melville's political sympathies lie with British law rather than its antagonists; when the Nore mutineers deface the English colors, they transmute "the flag of founded law and freedom defined, into the enemy's red meteor of unbridled and unbounded revolt" (54).

A certain aloofness and distance characterize Vere's relations with his fellow officers and the common sailors. Melville gives his protagonist a "dry and bookish" character and an undemonstrative manner that make him appear remote and pedantic to the other officers. But their failure to understand Vere reflects more on these men than on Vere: in a nature like his, "honesty prescribes . . . directness, sometimes far-reaching like that of a migratory fowl that in its flight never heeds when it crosses a frontier" (63). This point should be kept in mind when we consider the reactions of his fellow officers to his conduct during Billy's trial. All in all, Vere is initially presented as a good sailor and a thoroughly reliable military leader, the kind of man in whose care and safety the good order of a ship can be placed with confidence. Vere is not like Captain Graveling, "'a respectable man'" who displays "much prudence, much conscientiousness" mainly to secure his personal comfort and peace—his "quiet pipe" (45). Vere's prudential virtues—his perspicacity and sound judgment, the knowledge and wisdom that come from years of service, and his "prompt initiative" (90)—define his character as an "exceptional individual" and give him superior merit as a naval officer.[7] However, these admirable qualities provide no guarantee that he will judge rightly in a difficult moral dilemma.

University Press, 1979). Scorza sees Vere as the embodiment of conservative Burkean political virtue, struggling with the increasingly limited possibilities for politics in the modern age. For an antithetical view, which sees Melville attacking Vere's Burkean political opinions, see Ray Browne, "*Billy Budd*: Gospel of Democracy," *Nineteenth Century Fiction* 17 (1963), 321–37.

[7] Werner Berthoff, *The Example of Melville* (Princeton: Princeton University Press, 1962), pp. 194–203, interprets Vere in terms of the Aristotelian and Miltonic virtue of "magnanimity" (pride). Berthoff is not convincing when he goes on to assert that this "greatness of soul" also characterizes Billy.

In delineating Billy Budd's character, Melville explores the virtue of prudence from another perspective. What would a person be like who entirely lacked this quality? Billy is a natural "innocent," amazingly unconscious of the dangers the world may hold for him. He is "one to whom not yet has been proffered the questionable apple of knowledge" (52). Melville hints at the disaster that awaits Billy by presenting the speculations of an old sailor, the Dansker, "as to what might eventually befall a nature like that, dropped into a world not without some man-traps and against whose subtleties simple courage lacking experience and address, and without any touch of defensive ugliness, is of little avail; and where such innocence as man is capable of does yet in a moral emergency not always sharpen the faculties or enlighten the will" (70). Billy lacks "defensive ugliness": prudent wariness about the pitfalls and ambushes lurking behind the benign appearances of the world. Yet Billy is not simply a fool; all the characters in the novella see in him a myste-rious spiritual quality. The sailors instinctively feel that Billy reveals humankind's primeval trust and confidence in life's goodness. Billy shows what "Adam presumably might have been ere the urbane Serpent wriggled himself into his company" (52).

The *urbane* Serpent: Melville links the knowledge of evil with the development of city life. In contrast to the mature sophistication of the urbane, Billy is representative of both the "juvenile race" of sailors and of primitive, pre-civilized human nature. The typical virtues and vices of sailors are contrasted with those of city-dwelling landsmen: "Are sailors, frequenters of fiddlers' greens, without vices? No; but less often than with landsmen do their vices, so called, partake of crookedness of heart, seeming less to proceed from viciousness than exuberance of vitality after long constraint; frank manifestations in accordance with natural law" (52). The sailors' exuberant vitality is a pardonable fault, and the decorum and restraint they lack is presented as a somewhat questionable moral quality. For prudential wariness and discretion are based on an intuition of evil which may indicate the inner bias of a soul. Billy's nature remains "unsophisticated by those moral obliquities which are not in every case incompatible with that manufacturable thing known as respectability" (52). In the following quotation, Melville shifts his anal-ogy from sailors and landsmen to primitive peoples and "citified man," still contrasting essential human innocence with the wariness and caution learned through convention and experience:

> And here be it submitted that apparently going to corroborate the doc-
> trine of man's Fall, a doctrine now popularly ignored, it is observable that
> where certain virtues pristine and unadulterate peculiarly characterize any-
> body in the external uniform of civilization, they will upon scrutiny seem
> not to be derived from custom or convention, but rather to be out of
> keeping with these, as if indeed exceptionally transmitted from a period

prior to Cain's city and citified man. The character marked by such qualities has to an unvitiated taste an untampered-with flavor like that of ber-
ries, while the man thoroughly civilized, even in a fair specimen of the
breed, has to the same moral palate a questionable smack as of a com-
pounded wine. (52–53)

The landsman, especially the city-dweller, has learned to protect himself
by developing a "ruled undemonstrative distrustfulness" (87). But in the
process, he has lost the "virtues pristine and unadulterate" of the sailor or
the primitive innocent like Billy, who remains "a sort of upright barbar-
ian" (52) through all his experiences.

In the third main character in *Billy Budd*, John Claggart, Melville
explores the way that prudence complicates the nature of a person essentially evil. When prudence is present in a character as a secondary virtue
without a basic orientation to good, it makes such a person far more diabolical and efficient in the pursuit of his ends. Claggart has what Aristotle calls
"cleverness," which is not the same as, but is closely related to, practical
wisdom.[8] Claggart rose in the ranks to his position as master-of-arms by
exercising a number of traits essential to this police function: "his constitutional sobriety, an ingratiating deference to superiors, together with a
peculiar ferreting genius manifested on a singular occasion; all this, capped
by a certain austere patriotism, abruptly advanced him to the position of
master-at-arms" (67). The idea that moral corruption is wrought by civilization is further developed as Melville shows how organized life in society
requires the services of "negative virtues" in a character like Claggart:

> Civilization, especially if of the austerer sort, is auspicious to it. It folds
> itself in the mantle of respectability. It has its certain negative virtues serv-
> ing as silent auxiliaries. It never allows wine to get within its guard. It is not
> going too far to say that it is without vices or small sins. There is a phenom-
> enal pride in it that excludes them. It is never mercenary or avaricious. In
> short, the depravity here meant partakes nothing of the sordid or sensual. It
> is serious, but free from acerbity. Though no flatterer of mankind it never
> speaks ill of it. (75–76)

Claggart is but the representative of a basic tendency in the development of civilization, which values and rewards the "negative virtues"
which ensure its stability.

Prudence depends on the ability to calculate means of implementation

---

[8] Aristotle, *Nichomachean Ethics*, IV, 12, trans. W. D. Ross, in *Introduction to Aristotle*, ed. Richard McKeon (New York: Modern Library, 1947), p. 440: "There is a faculty
which is called cleverness; and this is such as to be able to do the things that tend towards
the mark we have set before ourselves, and to hit it. Now if the mark be noble, the cleverness is laudable, but if the mark be bad, the cleverness is mere smartness; hence we call
even men of practical wisdom clever or smart. Practical wisdom is not the faculty, but it
does not exist without this faculty."

and to weigh alternatives: it is an intellectual virtue. Like Hawthorne, Melville was fascinated, all his creative life, with the ways that a brilliant mind can be perverted by an evil heart. Claggart is an example of "Natural Depravity," a nature said to be "invariably . . . dominated by intellectuality" (75). In a passage reminiscent of the characterization of *Moby-Dick*'s Captain Ahab, Melville describes Claggart's cool use of reason to execute his scheme of destroying Billy Budd, for whom he has conceived an insane hatred: "Toward the accomplishment of an aim which in wantonness of atrocity would seem to partake of the insane, he will direct a cool judgment sagacious and sound" (76). Claggart's madness is focused entirely on one object; his outward bearing and his choice of means to achieve his ends are entirely rational. Ahab's words could well apply to Claggart: "All my means are sane, my motive and my object mad."

Closely associated with his prudence is Claggart's scrupulous conscience. The prudent person often keeps a close account of his moral life. One reason for the disesteem in which prudence is sometimes held lies in the excessive scrupulosity which has often characterized religious groups which set a high priority on prudence, including the Pharisees and the Puritans. A scrupulous conscience may be but the means by which a person sets himself in the right against others. Claggart, one of Melville's most purely diabolical characters, displays this intense need to justify to himself his hatred for Billy Budd. His malice takes the form of cynical disdain: "to be nothing more than innocent!" Yet he is drawn to Billy's innocence as a "moral phenomenon": he "fain would have shared it, but he despaired of it" (78). Claggart, the embodiment of the cleverness learned in society, both despises and yearns for the natural virtues of primitive, unsophisticated man. Melville probes the twisted workings of Claggart's conscience in rationalizing his rage when Billy accidently spills some soup in his path. This petty incident is the motive for a plan of revenge and the pretext by which he "justified animosity into a sort of retributive righteousness. The Pharisee is the Guy Fawkes prowling in the hid chambers underlying some natures like Claggart's" (80). Pharisaical scrupulosity gives an additional incentive of moral passion to Claggart's scheme to incriminate Billy. For his conscience is "but the lawyer to his will" (80).

One final aspect of Claggart's nature needs comment—his secrecy:

> An uncommon prudence is habitual with the subtler depravity, for it has everything to hide. And in case of an injury but suspected, its secretiveness voluntarily cuts it off from enlightenment or disillusion; and, not unreluctantly, action is taken upon surmise as upon certainty. And the retaliation is apt to be in monstrous disproportion to the supposed offense; for when in anybody was revenge in its exactions aught else but an inordinate usurer? (80)

The secrecy Claggart requires to pursue his plans means he cannot learn the truth about Billy's total lack of ill will toward him; on some deep level Claggart does not want to know that nothing in Billy could justify his project of revenge. Secrecy ensures that his actions will be taken on dubious grounds. The narrator's reflections on Claggart put Vere's conduct in an unfavorable light, for Vere's secrecy in the disciplinary proceedings is one of the chief aspects of his handling of the case that is criticized. Though Vere's motives for secrecy are quite different from Claggart's, he is equally cut off from the possibility of ascertaining whether his fears have real grounds.

Prudence is also the chief characteristic of the aging sailor known only as the Dansker. "Years, and those experiences which befall certain shrewder men subordinated lifelong to the will of superiors" have developed the Dansker's "pithy guarded cynicism" (71). He correctly surmises that Claggart is scheming for Billy's punishment. Twice when Billy asks him why the master-at-arms is "down on him" the Dansker refuses to elaborate, for "long experience had very likely brought this old man to that bitter prudence which never interferes in aught and never gives advice" (86). The Dansker realizes that Billy is incurably naive, that he cannot even understand, much less heed, a warning about the malice lurking in Claggart. So the aged sailor protects himself from possible repercussions in a fruitless intervention in Billy's plight. His "Delphic deliverances" are those of a detached choral figure who can only observe the oncoming calamity. But the Dansker's guarded refusal to extend himself for Billy when risk is required also suggests a perspective on the actions taken by Vere, whose conduct of Billy's case involves an analogous kind of guardedness.

III. *Vere's Tragic Choice*

Prudential considerations determine Vere's actions in the novella's decisive events. Vere is immediately suspicious when Claggart informs him that Billy is plotting mutiny. "Something exceptional in the moral quality of Captain Vere" that makes him a "veritable touchstone" of another man's nature (96) enables him to detect the hidden malice in the master-at-arms. Vere tests Claggart by making him repeat the charge directly to Billy, who is so shocked by the false accusation that his stutter prevents him from speaking. In his frustration, he lashes out at Claggart, and with one blow kills him. Here is the moment of tragic *peripeteia*—the reversal of everyone's expectations. Claggart is dead, Billy dazed by what he has done, and Vere astounded at this miscarriage of his intentions in bringing together the two men. How could anyone have anticipated such an eruption of violence, so completely contrary to expectation in the young sailor? "Fated boy," says Vere, his fatherly aspect suddenly "replaced by the military disciplinarian" (100). He exclaims to the surgeon who examines Claggart's corpse: "Struck dead by an angel of God! Yet the angel must

hang!" (101). Critics have often seen Vere's instant reaction as a prejudg-
ment that makes a mockery of Billy's trial. Yet it is difficult to see why
these words should be so interpreted. Vere sees at once that, in these wartime circumstances, Billy's act sets in motion a series of legal proceedings
which requires the captain to take an active part. He cannot simply pretend that Claggart's death never happened. He knows the penalty for killing an officer during wartime. Nonetheless, the formal judicial process
must be gone through.

One of the incidents that calls Vere's conduct into question is the
description of the surgeon's reaction to Vere. The chief thing which
disturbs the surgeon is Vere's desire for secrecy: his precautions to prevent the crew from realizing what has taken place. Yet "the prudent
surgeon," who thinks Billy's case should be referred to the admiral rather
than tried on the ship, is later shown to be incapable of assessing Vere's
conduct. His is the sort of prudent mind that refuses to risk judgment in
matters that go beyond strict scientific fact. His limitations are clearly
revealed in chapter 26, where he excuses himself from venturing an
opinion on a matter involving "will power" on the grounds that "I doubt
its authenticity as a scientific term. . . . It is at once imaginative and
metaphysical—in short, Greek" (125). The surgeon raises the issue of
Vere's secrecy, but he hardly provides the definitive judgment.

The period during which the events on board the *Bellipotent* take
place demands "from every English sea commander two qualities not
readily interfusable—prudence and rigor" (103). This statement precedes
the narrator's discussion of why Vere decides to hold a secret drumhead
trial of Billy Budd. Far from indicating a despotically authoritarian use
of power, Vere's attempt to "guard as much as possible against publicity"
until his course is decided upon is based on his belief that "circumspect-
ness not less than promptitude was necessary." "Rigor" would demand an
instant peremptory reaction; Vere, "though in general a man of rapid
decision," opts prudently for restraint while he deliberates. Of Vere's
decision to avoid publicity, the narrator comments non-committally,
"Here he may or may not have erred" (103). Despite this disclaimer, the
narrator clearly disapproves of Vere's maintenance of secrecy insofar as
it resembles "the policy adopted in those tragedies of the palace which
have occurred more than once in the capital founded by Peter the Bar-
barian" (103).[9] But Vere could hardly investigate this delicate matter on

---

[9] Hayford and Sealts, in their "Notes and Commentary," p. 177, assert that "this sen-
tence is nearer than any other in *Billy Budd* to indicating disapproval of Vere's course of
action." Melville *canceled* a passage in his manuscript that showed the surgeon's reflections shifting the blame from Vere's prudent policy to unpredictable twists of fate: the
surgeon "could not help thinking how more than futile the utmost discretion sometimes
proves in this human sphere subject as it is to unfor[e]seeable fatalities: the prudent
method adopted by Captain Vere to obviate publicity and trouble having resulted in an

deck in full view of the entire ship's company. In any case, whether he erred or not in holding the secret drumhead court, as in staging a private confrontation between Billy and Claggart, Vere's procedure reflects his concern to avert a disturbance among the crew. Vere's prudence has inadvertently brought about the death of Claggart; now it will determine his reasoning in demanding Billy's execution.

In his statement to the court, Vere insists that a martial court must confine its attention strictly to certain aspects of this problematic case. He argues that the court can not consider "the essential right and wrong involved in the matter." It must consider only the consequences of Billy's blow, not Billy's intent. Nor can the court ponder Claggart's nature, "a matter for psychologic theologians to discuss." Vere sets out a number of polarities which define and limit the function of the court. Attention must be focused on military duty, not "moral scruple—scruple vitalized by compassion" (110). He contrasts allegiance to Nature with allegiance to the King, holding that in accepting their commissions the officers "ceased to be natural free agents" (110). Martial law, claims Vere, operates through the officers: "For that law and the rigor of it, we are not responsible. Our avowed responsibility is in this: that however pitilessly that law may operate in any instances, we nevertheless adhere to it and administer it" (111). He contrasts heart and head, masculine and feminine elements in human nature, and private conscience with the official code. But the court is still not convinced. Vere's closing appeal is to the court members' "instinct as sea officers." He argues that if clemency is granted, at a moment when the threat of mutiny hangs over the fleet, the crew will think the officers afraid to do their clear duty and execute the law. The decisive argument that sways the court is "the forethought he threw out as to the practical consequences to discipline, considering the unconfirmed tone of the fleet at the time, should a man-of-war's man's violent killing at sea of a superior in grade be allowed to pass for aught else than a capital crime demanding prompt infliction of the penalty" (113). The court convicts Billy and he is hung at the yardarm the next dawn.

The central issue which divides critics of *Billy Budd* is a moral one: whether Vere did the right thing or not. Some critics have seen Melville's last work as his "testament of acceptance," in which he symbolically represented his final reconciliation with the necessities of social existence.[10] They point to the religious imagery which suffuses the last

---

event that necessitated the former, and, under existing circumstances in the navy, indefinit[e]ly magnified the latter" (Hayford and Sealts, "Notes and Commentary," p. 178). This superceded passage emphasizes that the inadequacy of practical wisdom comes through no fault of its own; thus the final text seems to challenge Vere's procedure.

[10] Among the vast critical literature on *Billy Budd*, representative works which defend Vere's conduct are Grant Watson, "Melville's Testament of Acceptance," *New England*

pages of the novella, and to Vere's apparent lack of remorse for his actions, even as he lies dying, wounded after Billy's execution in an encounter with the French fleet. According to this interpretation, Vere has an ideal balance of heart and intellect; he both understands the legal and moral complexity of Billy's case and cares for him as an individual. He does the best that can be done in a desperately perplexing situation. For another group of critics, *Billy Budd* is a bitter attack on the impersonality and brutality of the modern state, and on Vere as its representative. Vere is viewed as an authoritarian tyrant who needlessly executes an "essentially innocent" man and therefore dies at the hands of the French ship *Athée*, which one critic calls "perhaps the least subtle *deus ex machina* in American literature."[11] From this point of view, the novella is seen as Melville's protest against the repressive nature of organized society, the basic moral norms for which are derived from the needs of warmaking.

There is a great deal of textual evidence to support both of these perspectives, and critics will undoubtedly continue to attack or defend Vere.[12] However, a more adequate interpretation would establish a structural *relationship* between the passages that endorse Vere's conduct and the incidents that call it into question. My own understanding of the

Quarterly 6 (1933), 319–27; F. O. Matthiessen, *American Renaissance* (New York: Oxford University Press, 1941), pp. 500–514; Wendell Glick, "Expediency and Absolute Morality in *Billy Budd*," *PMLA* 68 (1953), 103–10; James Miller, *A Reader's Guide to Herman Melville* (New York: Farrer, Strauss, and Giroux, 1962), pp. 218–28; Milton Stern, "Introduction" to *Billy Budd, Sailor: An Inside Narrative* (Indianapolis: Bobbs-Merrill Co., 1975); and Scorza's *In the Time Before Steamships.*

11 Sherrill, *Prophetic Melville*, p. 235. Other critics who either see Melville attacking Vere's course of action or interpret the novella as an ironic protest against the repressive nature of social structures include Joseph Schiffman, "Melville's Final Stage, Irony: A Reexamination of *Billy Budd* Criticism," *American Literature* 22 (1950), 128–36; Karl Zink, "Herman Melville and the Forms—Irony and Social Criticism in *Billy Budd*," *Accent* 12 (1952), 131–39; and Phil Withim, "*Billy Budd*: Testament of Resistance," *Modern Language Quarterly* 20 (1959), 115–27. These critics may stress either Vere's personal inadequacies or the repressive nature of modern society, but they agree that he made the wrong decision.

12 Some interpreters have tried to reconcile these critical positions by holding that the text is hopelessly ambiguous or "incomplete." See Kenneth Ledbetter, "The Ambiguity of *Billy Budd*," *Texas Studies in Literature and Language* 4 (1962), 130–34; and Paul Brodtkorb, Jr., "The Definitive *Billy Budd*: 'But aren't it all sham?'" *PMLA* 82 (1967), 602–12. The "ragged edges" of the work resulting from the confusing state of the manuscript at Melville's death account for some but not all of the critical controversy. Thomas Scorza's "Note on the Text" in *In The Time Before Steamships*, pp. 182–92, while acknowledging textual difficulties, rightly insists on the need to see *Billy Budd* as an artistic whole: "The work may, in the end, be 'ambiguous,' and in a certain sense the work itself asserts that fact explicitly, but it can only be seen as such and retain critical esteem when it is judged as an integral unit. Such 'ambiguity' is the message of a particular artistic and intellectual point of view, rather than the mark of artistic incompleteness or fickleness" (192).

novella is, in brief, that *Billy Budd* shows how a prudent man—Vere—comes to make a tragic choice in a confusing and ambiguous situation. Up to the end of the trial scene, Melville seeks to persuade the reader of the reasonableness of Vere's prudent course of action. But after the trial, the focus shifts to the tragic consequences that he has effected. Such an interpretation puts Vere in a somewhat different light than the usual pro-Vere or anti-Vere views, and seeks to account for all the perspectives on his procedure given within the text. For *Billy Budd* is structured so as neither to defend nor to denounce Vere's conduct, but rather to show it as a prudent and well-intentioned choice that is only in retrospect perceived as a moral tragedy.[13]

Melville depicts a variety of factors influencing Vere's decision to show why the compounding of circumstances and ambiguous evidence persuades him to demand Billy's execution. As was discussed above, it is prudential considerations that determine Captain Vere's proceedings during the trial. His overriding concern is that "the slumbering embers of the Nore" may break into the fires of mutiny. Melville carefully specifies the historical context of the story's central events to give plausability, but not definite certainty, to Vere's fear of mutiny. The narrator particularly stresses the extreme urgency of the situation in which Vere must make a decision: "The unhappy event . . . could not have happened at a worse juncture" (102). His ship is in foreign waters, and a French vessel has just been sighted; an engagement with the enemy may occur at any moment. "A sense of the urgency of the case overruled in Captain Vere every other consideration" (104). The pressing need for a prompt decision is the primary reason the narrator compares Vere's procedure to the infamous events on the American ship *Somers* in 1842. In that incident, not one but three sailors were executed merely for plotting a mutiny—not, as in Billy's case, for having actually killed an officer. Furthermore, the accused men were not present at their own trial, and their execution was carried out immediately "though in a time of peace and within not many days' sail of home" (114). That notorious precedent does not make Vere's conduct right. But in *Billy Budd*, unlike Melville's earlier allusions to the case, the narrator's focus is not on the injustice of the hanging but on the "harassed frame of mind" of the commanding officer.[14] The historical analogy does not justify Vere, but it helps to explain his course of

---

[13] My interpretation of *Billy Budd* should be compared to that of James Miller, in *Reader's Guide*, who uses the Plinlimmon pamphlet to endorse Vere's conduct; and to Wendell Glick, "Expediency and Absolute Morality in Billy Budd." Both of these views emphasize not the positive value of prudence but the impracticality of absolute standards of morality in this "horological" world.

[14] For discussion of the *Somers* case in *White-Jacket* and Melville's war poetry, see the note to leaf 281, pp. 191–93 in Hayford and Sealts' "Notes and Commentary" to *Billy Budd*.

action. The relevance of the *Somers* case is that "the urgency felt, well-warranted or otherwise, was much the same" (114).

Vere's conduct is only explicable in the context of his alternative courses of action. Two other possibilities are suggested: either to turn the case over to the admiral or, as one officer puts it, "to convict and yet mitigate the penalty" (112). But Vere is several days' sail away from the fleet, and the danger of encountering a French ship is imminent. To try Billy on the ship "would not be at variance with usage" (104), and Vere is not one to shirk a painful responsibility. Furthermore, it is quite clear that, were Billy to be referred to the admiral for judgment, the verdict would not be less severe. Critics of Vere have usually assumed that the issue is whether Billy lives or dies. In fact it is really a question of who will make a decision which, "under the law of the Mutiny Act," is a foregone conclusion. Vere's other alternative is to convict Billy and yet mitigate the penalty. Perhaps Vere could have viewed the murder as manslaughter and had Billy imprisoned until the ship's return to Britain. But the possibility of so lenient a course is only suggested within the text, and quickly dismissed. If a mitigated penalty were a realistic alternative, Melville would surely have developed Vere's reasons for rejecting it. But Melville wanted to pose a stark alternative. Vere claims that the law is clear—to the crew as well as the officers—and that the consequences of clemency would be the crew's surmise "that we flinch, that we are afraid of them" (113). This, he believes, can only destroy discipline at a time when the ship's order is a matter with momentous consequences. For Vere, the only two practical alternatives are to "condemn or let go."

During the trial the contrast drawn between Vere and his fellow officers tends to call their criticisms of him into question. Though they are as competent at their duties as the surgeon, Vere doubts whether one of them would "prove altogether reliable in a moral dilemma involving aught of the tragic" (105). Vere is an "exceptional man" who must deliberate as to how to state his views to "well-meaning men not intellectually mature" (109). Melville's persistent attempt during the trial scene to show Vere's superiority "not less . . . in mind than in naval rank" (113) underwrites the captain's view of the best course of action.

During the trial scene, then, Vere is portrayed largely in a favorable light. But those critics who think every detail in the story can be reconciled with a position for or against Vere must simplify Melville's total presentation of the situation. For the whole point of Vere's dilemma is that the case is ambiguous, that "innocence and guilt personified in Claggart and Budd in effect changed places" (103), that no clear moral verdict can be delivered without risk and culpability. At this point, Melville most wants his readers to understand *why* the captain acts as he does, after evaluating all the moral and legal and military considerations that bear on his decision. Though as readers we, too, must weigh the evidence and interpret the relative significance of various aspects of the case, we are not permitted to make a simple moral judgment of Vere. At the end of the chapter (21) dealing with Billy's trial, the narrator directly warns against moralistically condemning Vere's conduct in conditions of extreme peril and solitary responsibility:

> Forty years after a battle it is easy for a noncombatant to reason about how it ought to have been fought. It is another thing personally and under fire to have to direct the fighting while involved in the obscuring smoke of it. Much so with respect to other emergencies involving considerations both practical and moral, and when it is imperative promptly to act. The greater the fog the more it imperils the steamer, and speed is put on though at the hazard of running somebody down. Little ween the snug card players in the cabin of the responsibilities of the sleepless man on the bridge. (114)

After the trial, however, Melville's emphasis undergoes a significant shift from the prudential considerations that influenced Vere's decision to the actual consequences of that decision. Now the narrator stresses not the necessity or inevitability of Vere's actions but the injustice of Billy's execution and its deeper implications. This is in accord with the basic moral structure of tragedy, which explores the disjunction between the good intentions of a character and the disastrous practical results of his actions. Melville's narrative focus turns from Billy's legal guilt to the pointlessness of his punishment. For though he has killed a man, it serves no purpose to put him to death, too. In effect, Vere fulfills Claggart's scheme of calculated violence against simple innocence. The moral principle at stake is no longer Vere's legitimate prudence for the ship's safety and his insistence on the justice of the law, but the limitations of prudence, because of its blindness both to the unique value of a particular individual and to the possibilities of more life-giving forms of human community. After the trial, then, Melville's treatment of prudence is set within the context of a critique of military values and of society's concern with institutional stability.

It is highly ironic that, soon after the trial, Vere and Billy may have embraced "even as Abraham may have caught young Isaac on the brink of resolutely offering him up in obedience to the exacting behest" (115). This passage reveals the deep feeling Vere has to suppress: his underlying fatherly love for Billy. Vere is not simply a cold-blooded bureaucrat who mechanically performs his duties. But the irony is that Abraham finally spared Isaac; he doesn't sacrifice the young one, as does Vere, "the austere devotee of military duty" (115). From this point on, Melville develops two implications of Vere's insistence on Billy's execution. He shows that modern civilization has made war rather than Christianity its religion, and that it values preservation of its own institutional forms more than the lives of its citizens.

As the Abraham and Isaac metaphor makes clear, Vere has made

Billy a sacrifice to the god of war, "a martyr to martial discipline" (121). Throughout *Billy Budd* war is presented as a parody of religion.[15] The ship is said to resemble a floating cathedral, and a military officer is like a monk: "Not with more of self-abnegation will the latter keep his vows of monastic obedience than the former his vows of allegiance to martial duty" (104). The chapters just after the trial show Melville's most explicit criticism of the way societies use religion to bolster military endeavors. The ship's chaplain, who unnecessarily comes to console the serene Billy during the night before the execution, is "the minister of the Prince of Peace serving in the host of the God of War—Mars" (122). Though "as incongruous as a musket would be on the altar at Christmas," the chaplain has a place on the man-of-war because "he lends the sanction of the religion of the meek to that which practically is the abrogation of everything but brute Force" (122). If up to this point we have seen how Vere came to believe that Billy's execution was necessary, these bitter comments on the war industry's perverted use of religion suddenly make us question why the rights of individuals and the life of a Billy Budd should be sacrificed for the sake of military success. (The ship from which Billy was impressed into the *Bellipotent* was named the *Rights-of-Man*.) Vere is seen in a new light as a "martial utilitarian," and Billy, in spite of the fact that he has taken a life, as the victim of a terrible travesty of justice. The narrator speaks of Billy's "essential innocence"; the chaplain feels that "innocence was even a better thing than religion wherewith to go to Judgment" (121).

Yet Vere is presented not as the deliberate perpetrator of injustice, but himself a victim. As he probes the nature of social forms, Melville reveals that both Billy and Vere are sacrificed to their society's need for institutional continuity and order. Melville is not an antinomian: he sees that society, like a ship at sea, requires discipline for its very survival. Human life in society necessarily involves organization into certain definite forms. Churches, educational institutions, and armies and navies are structured by particular roles and rules, by lines of authority, and by the coercive power that ultimately enforces the rules. Society's stability depends on the expectation that individuals will act in accordance with certain forms, prudently obeying the rules. The virtue of prudence necessarily entails a concern for social forms.

---

[15] The political bearing of Melville's war poetry on *Billy Budd* is considered in Milton Stern's "Introduction" to the Bobbs-Merrill edition of *Billy Budd*, and by Jane Donahue, "Melville's Classicism: Law and Order in His Poetry," *Papers on Language and Literature* 5 (1969), 63–72. A sharp disagreement exists between Scorza, *In the Time Before Steamships*, who sees Melville viewing war as a "necessary evil" with which political leaders must come to terms, and Joyce Sparer Adler's *War in Melville's Imagination* (New York: Gotham Library, 1980), which interprets *Billy Budd* in terms of Melville's lifelong attempt to break humankind's habitual acceptance of warfare.

Vere has no doubt but that "With mankind . . . forms, measured forms, are everything; and that is the import couched in the story of Orpheus with his lyre spellbinding the wild denizens of the wood" (128). Without the forms of military duty and discipline, a navy would be impossible: individuals might fight or sail a ship when they felt like it, but there could be no assurance that basic tasks would be performed whether or not individuals were inclined to do them. Melville shows that discipline is not just imposed from above, but actively desired by the crew, who insist that everything be done according to "usage," the traditional customs and rules of seagoing life. "In this proceding as in every public one growing out of the tragedy strict adherence to usage was observed" because "sailors, and more particularly men-of-war's men [are] of all men the greatest sticklers for usage" (117).

If some form is necessary to give structure and identity to a society, any given type of form can become repressive and destructive of essential human concerns and values. Any social form contains the potential for tragedy. This potential becomes realized in *Billy Budd* when the strictest form of naval discipline is adhered to although it may not have been necessary. For in spite of Vere's fear of mutiny there is little evidence that mutiny is a real possibility. Vere's prudent concern for secrecy, like Claggart's, cuts him off from the possibility of ascertaining whether there is any actual basis for fear. Note that the reader does not know for certain that mutiny is *not* a possibility, and that Vere is wrong. Rather, we are as unsure as he is as to the real likelihood of insurrection, and we see how he came to his decision to take no chances and insist on Billy's execution.

But how different Vere's decision appears in the light of hindsight, even to the Captain himself.[16] His concern for discipline leads to the denial of life, not to giving it form. At the hanging, Vere stands "erectly rigid as a musket in the ship-armorer's rack" (124): he seems lifeless, an inflexible shell of a man. He has had to impose a wooden form on his own nature, repressing his love for Billy. Vere stifles the best elements in himself in the service of his conception of duty. He, too, is a victim— though he has made himself one—of the demands made by the forms of martial law. Once set in motion, the machinery of discipline and punishment crushes all human feelings and values. The events on board the *Bellipotent* reveal society's mechanisms for preserving its monopoly on

---

[16] Sherrill's *The Prophetic Melville*, ch. 8 and 9, interprets *Billy Budd* in terms of Vere's refusal to recognize the "portentousness" and "the part of wonder" disclosed in Billy. In my view, this aspect of the story—Vere's rejection of Billy's promise of redemption—is emphasized only *after* the trial. Up until and through the trial scene, the narrator has insistently repudiated the possibility of thwarting a Claggart or negotiating a tragic moral dilemma by simply appealing to "the vision of the wonder-world." Vere's prudence is only called in question when the consequences of his decision are irrevocable.

crime: its formal devices for ensuring that only society has the right to take life, whether *en masse* in war or by executing an individual. The eye-for-an-eye, life-for-a-life accounting method that regulates society's legal code is depicted as blind to the possibility of a higher morality.

In the execution and burial scenes, Melville uses contrasts between sound and silence as well as visual imagery to develop a tension between the crew's inner feelings and its outward observance of the forms of naval discipline. After silently witnessing Billy's execution, the crew gives forth "a sound not easily to be verbally rendered" which is compared to "the freshet wave of showers in the tropical mountains," and "seemed to indicate some capricious revulsion of thought or feeling such as mobs ashore are liable to, in the present instance possibly implying a sullen revocation on the men's part of their involuntary echoing of Billy's benediction" (126). But before this murmur can swell or move the crew to action, it is stifled by the whistles and drumbeats calling the men to their stations. These shrill whistles and thudding drums contrast ironically with Vere's own benign comparison of his ship's "measured forms" to the lyre of Orpheus. The only instruments on board the *Bellipotent* help to make war, not music.

The use of natural imagery in the depiction of Billy's death and burial poses again the contrast between prudence as a virtue of civilized life and the "natural virtues" of the young sailor.[17] The man-made forms that regulate naval life seem rigid and stifling, while the natural world around the ship, to which Billy returns, portends a wilder and freer existence. The seafowl circling Billy's burial spot stir the crew to "an uncertain movement" that is strategically cut short by the "signal peremptoriness" of a military drum. The brittle order of the shipboard society is juxtaposed with the formlessness, the purity, and the promise of the new day: "The circumambient air in the clearness of its serenity was like smooth white marble in the polished block not yet removed from the marble-dealer's yard" (128). This striking image suggests that society has formed the white marble which is nature's gift into a tombstone. Contrasts and conflicts between nature and civilized life were developed earlier in the story: in the comparison between sailors and landsmen; in Vere's address to the "primitive instincts" of his officers and the distinctions he draws between Nature's law and the King's; and in the image of Billy in his soiled white clothes "like a patch of discolored snow" lying amidst the shadows of the metal guns. But by the end of the novella, the natural order and society's law are not merely juxtaposed as two conflicting moral standards; the natural world reveals the immorality of the

[17] Scorza, *In the Time Before Steamships*, and Charles Reich, "The Tragedy of Justice in *Billy Budd*," *Yale Review* 56 (1967), 368–89, interpret the novella as Melville's pessimistic vision of the fate of the "natural" element in humankind in the modern world.

military code and of prudence for the forms of the status quo.

Melville comments obliquely on Vere's ideas about form by means of "digressions" on the problem of truth-telling in literary forms. Explaining why his tale involves so many by-paths and historical anecdotes, the narrator speaks of the limitations of pure literary form for his purposes: "The symmetry of form attainable in pure fiction cannot so readily be achieved in a narration essentially having less to do with fable than with fact. Truth uncompromisingly told will always have its ragged edges; hence the conclusion of such a narration is apt to be less finished than an architectural finial" (128). The novella ends with two versions of the events surrounding Billy's execution. The news report in a "naval chronicle of the time, an authorized weekly publication," calls Claggart a "respectable and discreet" man (which indeed he was, in Melville's ambiguous sense) whom Billy "vindictively stabbed" with a knife. The second account of the events is a poetic ballad circulated among the sailors for some time. As does the news report, the poem "Billy in the Darbies," which was the originating germ for *Billy Budd*, also contradicts what the novella has revealed about Billy's character. For, imagining Billy's thoughts as he lies in chains awaiting execution, the poem gives him qualities of sarcasm, irony, and verbal wit that he entirely lacked. Both forms distort the historical truth, but the newspaper account does so in the interest of bureaucratic censorship and patriotic hypocrisy. The other, the poetic form, attempts to understand and depict the inner life of someone in Billy's position, just as the "inside narrative" of the whole novella explores the thoughts and feelings of Billy, Claggart, and Vere. The poem memorializes Billy to the crew, who venerate everything associated with his primitive good nature. The contrast between the two literary forms brings out another aspect of Vere's insistence on the forms of naval discipline. For Vere had insisted that the military court could not consider the inner life of Claggart or Budd, or their motivation, but only the external form of their deeds. "War looks but to the frontage, the appearance," he had said (112). Vere's claim that only the outward appearance can be judged leads to a denial of an essential aspect of the meaning of human acts: their motivation and intentionality. Form is necessary. Nevertheless, as the contrast of the two literary forms reveals, different forms may be life-denying as they allow or do not allow for the expression of the "inner" dimensions and meanings of life.

Forms being necessary for organized social life, a prudent person will not act as if social institutions have no value, or as if they do not create legitimate moral obligations. The virtue of prudence necessarily involves a concern for the rules, commitments, and obligations inherent in social roles and institutions. Yet it is a dangerous mistake to believe that only a particular social form will always preserve some essential value. As Melville showed in his many views of the anatomy of the whale in *Moby-Dick* and in the "Doubloon" chapter, life has no one fixed form: it appears differently when looked at in its different aspects, and from various perspectives.

The tragedy of *Billy Budd* is that Vere insists on upholding a particular form of naval discipline when it preserves the appearance but not the real substance of justice. Vere's prudential virtues—his foresight and concern for the fleet's discipline and his cautious practicality—dictate his demand for Billy's execution. In a sense Vere is completely justified, for Billy has struck and killed a superior officer. Yet given the "essential innocence" of Billy's nature and the depravity of Claggart, the forms of naval usage thwart the deepest human desires as well as the sense of justice of the crew, the officers, and Vere himself. Legal justice violates the sense of a more basic natural law; the "horological" values dismiss the "chronometrical" ones as totally irrelevant; the military code defies "moral scruple—scruple vitalized by compassion" (110). Vere's prudential concern for the correct "forms, measured forms" is seen in the end to have led to an execution which, while legally proper, tortures his own moral sensitivity. Yet we do not simply denounce Vere as a tyrant, for Melville has carefully controlled our perspective on the captain as he came to his decision under terribly difficult circumstances in an ambiguous case where "the innocence and guilt personified in Claggart and Budd in effect changed places" (103). The reader sees how the decision brings agony to Vere, who in fact suffers more mental anguish than Billy: "The condemned one suffered less than he who mainly had effected the condemnation" (115). In short, we have come to understand how Vere's best qualities both help to bring about the tragedy and require him to feel its bitterness.

Billy Budd explores the ambiguity of prudence, the virtue concerned with social forms. Billy lacks all apprehension of evil and ability to negotiate the conflicts of life in society, and becomes an easy prey for Claggart. In Claggart, Melville showed the way that prudence can help a diabolically evil person to pursue his ends all the more efficiently within the correct social forms. And in the character of Captain Vere, Melville discloses that because of his prudent concern for the maintenance of established social forms, an essentially good and admirable man can deliberately, with the best of intentions, bring about a moral tragedy.

4

Idealism and Skepticism
in Conrad's *Nostromo*:
"The Moral Degradation of the Idea"
in Public Action

Like *The Trojan Women, Antony and Cleopatra,* and *The Brothers Karamazov,* Joseph Conrad's *Nostromo* is a tragedy with several protagonists. There are five central characters in the novel: Nostromo, Charles and Emily Gould, Martin Decoud, and Dr. Monygham. Each of them experiences a divisive tension between moral idealism and skepticism. Each character attempts to realize in action some "idea": some belief, purpose, or vision of life that transcends immediate self-interest. But in the tumultuous events that lead to the establishment of the Republic of Sulaco, all the characters fatally compromise their idea in trying to realize it in society. *Nostromo* is constructed so that the most admirable qualities of each character lead in action to a fate that discloses the fallibility and the external perils to an essential Conradian virtue. Their common tragic fate reveals that "there was something inherent in the necessities of successful action which carried with it the moral degradation of the idea" (521).[1]

I. *Idealism and Skepticism*

Nostromo, the character who gives the novel its somewhat misleading title, is the "Capataz de Cargadores," foreman of the lightermen and dock workers of the Oceanic Steam Navigation Company in the Port of Sulaco. For the first half of the novel, we see Nostromo only from the point of view of other characters. Mention of his name is usually preceded by an adjective calling attention to his reputation for courage and his position of trust: he is the "incorruptible," the "illustrious," the "invaluable" Nostromo, whose services are indispensable to the European community of Sulaco. Conrad attributed the initial inspiration for his novel to a casual anecdote he had heard about a man who had "managed to steal a lighter with silver . . . only because he was implicitly trusted by his employers, who

---

[1] *Nostromo* (London: J. M. Dent, 1957). All references to the novel are to this edition and are cited parenthetically in the text.

must have been singularly poor judges of character."[2] In the original report, the thief was a mean and unscrupulous rascal. The impetus for *Nostromo* came when Conrad realized that the thief "need not necessarily be a confirmed rogue, that he could be even a man of character, an actor, and possibly a victim in the changing scenes of a revolution."[3] Captain Mitchell boasts that he was "a pretty good judge of character" when he hired as foreman Nostromo, "a man absolutely above reproach" (13). Despite Mitchell's comically pompous posture, the reader has good reason to take him at his word. The first mention of Nostromo is Mitchell's account of his foreman's brave rescue of "poor Señor Ribiera," the deposed dictator of Costaguana, from an angry mob. In the first 200 pages of the novel, we see Nostromo protecting the Viola family and overseeing Sir John's dangerous journey to Sulaco. We see his virtues in successful action, and hear other characters express their admiration for his courage, loyalty, and resourcefulness. The reader witnesses the triumphant exploits of a publicly proclaimed hero before being called to question the source of his virtues.

Nostromo's heroic actions determine the fate of everyone in Costaguana, for his daring ride to Cayta to bring back General Barrios's troops results in the establishment of the independent state of Sulaco. Even skeptical Dr. Monygham is forced to admit that only Nostromo could carry off such a feat, that "the fellow was unique. He was not 'one in a thousand.' He was absolutely the only one. . . . There was something in the genius of that Genoese seaman which dominated in the destinies of great enterprises and of many people" (452). Nostromo has all the classic virtues of the warrior: absolute fearlessness, physical prowess, and "resource and ingenuity . . . the gift of evolving safety out of the very danger" (529). He is not reflective or self-critical: his heroic actions are an impulsive, unpremeditated expression of his nature. He instinctively possesses the moral quality that Conrad called "fidelity": steadfastness and unflinching loyalty to his comrades in some common enterprise. His very name symbolizes the trust placed in him: "Nostromo" is an English corruption of "nostro uomo," Italian for "our man." All the Europeans in Sulaco believe that Nostromo is "our man."

Nostromo's "idea" is his conception of himself as a hero of his community. This idea has both positive and negative moral implications. It inspires the actions that save Sulaco. But as the novel unfolds, Nostromo's exploits are gradually revealed as the means by which he secures the admiration necessary to flatter his overweening vanity. From the beginning, it is suggested that the motivation for Nostromo's actions is mainly concern for his reputation: Teresa Viola claims "he thinks of nobody but

---

[2] Joseph Conrad, "Author's Note" to *Nostromo*, p. xvi in Dent Edition.
[3] Ibid., p. xvii.

himself" (20). This opinion is corroborated by other characters and finally confirmed: in the end the narrator states that the "very essence, value, reality" of Nostromo's life "consisted in its reflection from the admiring eyes of men" (525). The supreme test for the "incorruptible" Capataz arises when, cut off from his community, his heroic actions are not rewarded with the praise he has come to expect.

Charles Gould's preeminent characteristic is his all-absorbing dedication to the San Tomé Silver Mine. The mine was forced on Gould's father by one of Costaguana's innumerable corrupt governments in repayment for loans extracted from him, and in order to extort yet more wealth in the form of taxes and royalties. Gould watches the cares associated with the mine slowly destroy his father's health. When he inherits the mine, he determines to redeem it from its "curse": "The mine had been the cause of an absurd moral disaster; its working must be made a serious and moral success" (66). The moral rehabilitation of the mine is the "idea" to which Gould single-mindedly commits himself. He firmly believes that the mine's influence will bring about the justice and order so desperately needed in Costaguana. He reasons that "material interests" demand stability and the rule of law, explaining to his wife:

> What is wanted here is law, good faith, order, security. Anyone can de-claim about these things, but I pin my faith to material interests. Only let the material interests once get a firm footing, and they are bound to impose the conditions on which alone they can continue to exist. That's how your money-making is justified here in the face of lawlessness and disorder. It is justified because the security which it demands must be shared with an oppressed people. A better justice will come afterwards. (84)

Gould's idealistic faith is that material progress will lead to the moral reformation of Costaguana's anarchic political life. He soon discovers the danger inherent in the means he adopts to achieve his goal. In an early scene that delineates his moral dilemma in Costaguana, Gould has a momentary premonition of the threat to his idea of having to "stoop for his weapons": "For a moment he felt as if the silver mine, which had killed his father, had decoyed him further than he meant to go; and with the roundabout logic of emotions, he felt that the worthiness of his life was bound up with success. There was no going back." (85)

Charles's wife Emily Gould shares his faith in the moral effect of the San Tomé Mine. Emily is intelligent, generous, and sympathetic to every-one in Sulaco. Her words have "the value of acts of integrity, tolerance, and compassion" (67). The possibility of redeeming the abandoned mine pre-sents itself to the newly-married Goulds "at the instant when the woman's instinct of devotion and the man's instinct of activity receive from the strongest of illusions their most powerful impulse" (74). Like her husband, Emily justifies her commitment to the mine in terms of an idea: the power of moral principle to redeem the material basis of life. When she lays her "unmercenary hands" on the first silver ingot from the mine, "by her imaginative estimate of its power she endowed that lump of metal with a justificative conception, as though it were not a fact, but something far-reaching and impalpable, like the true expression of an emotion or the emergence of a principle" (107). But, in contrast to her husband, Emily will finally come to a bitter recognition that the outwardly successful realization of their "idea" in action means moral defeat.

In contrast with the idealism that predominates in these three characters, Martin Decoud is a radical skeptic who participates in events with a sense of ironic detachment. The narrator of *Nostromo* denounces Decoud as "an idle boulevardier" and attacks repeatedly his "mere barren indifferentism posing as intellectual superiority" (152). Yet as Albert Guerard has pointed out,

> There is, generally, a marked discrepancy between what Decoud does and says and is, and what the narrator or omniscient author says about him. . . . Conrad may be condemning Decoud for a withdrawal and skepticism more radical than Decoud ever shows; which are, in fact, Conrad's own. . . . Far from believing in or caring about nothing, [Decoud] has an ideal of lucidity and of intellectual honesty, he is very much in love, and he is (quite apart from his love for Antonia or from his attitude toward the current political situation) a patriot.[4]

There seem to be "two Decouds" in the novel. Despite the narrator's denunciations of his character, the Decoud depicted in action is in many ways an admirable figure. His idea of himself as a skeptic is based on the moral demands of lucidity and intellectual honesty. Decoud has more insight into other characters than anyone else; his interpretations of Gould's and Nostromo's characters are penetrating and definitive. And Decoud is not a detached intellectual; his actions have decisive effects. It is Decoud's original idea for Sulaco to secede from Costaguana, and it is his political skills that persuade the Europeans of Sulaco, above all Charles Gould, to commit themselves to the revolution. The irony of Decoud's situation is that he is initially drawn into politics by his love for the beautiful patriot Antonia Avellanos. A "man with no faith in anything except the truth of his own sensations" (229), Decoud is surprised by the extent of his growing involvement in events: "His disdain grew like a reaction of his skepticism against the action into which he was forced by his infatuation for Antonia. He soothed himself by saying he was not a patriot, but a lover" (176).

Conrad seems intimately involved, in some ways even identified, with the character of Decoud. What Guerard calls the "distinctly Conradian rhythm and rhetoric" of Decoud's statements strongly resembles

---

[4] Albert Guerard, *Conrad the Novelist* (New York: Atheneum, 1958), pp. 199–200.

the voice of the omniscient narrator.[5] F. R. Leavis claims that Decoud "remains at the centre of the book, in the sense that his consciousness seems to permeate it, even to dominate it. That consciousness is clearly very closely related to the author's own personal *timbre*."[6] The chief reason for Conrad's close identification with Decoud is his imaginative struggle with the value and the danger of Decoud's skepticism, which so resembles a basic tendency of Conrad's own intellectual stance and emotional temperament. Decoud's views are scarcely distinguishable from those expressed in some of Conrad's letters and essays, for example, his advice to the author John Galsworthy: "The fact is that you want more skepticism at the very foundation of your work. Skepticism, the tonic of minds, the agent of truth,—the way of art and salvation."[7] Many critics of *Nostromo* have claimed that Conrad "repudiates skepticism" through his treatment of Decoud. But in fact, Decoud's skeptical perspective on human affairs represents a primary virtue for Conrad. In contrast with the idealistic characters, Decoud, like Dr. Monygham, has the intelligence and lucidity to recognize the self-deception often involved in the pursuit of an idea, and he scrupulously wishes to avoid delusion about his own motivation for action. He tells Mrs. Gould that he is not afraid of his motives: "I am not a sentimentalist, I cannot endow my personal desires with a shining robe of silk and jewels. Life is not for me a moral romance derived from the tradition of a pretty fairy tale" (218). Decoud's strict refusal to fool others or himself about the real basis for his actions emerges as a crucial moral quality as the reader sees the destructive consequences of self-deceiving idealism.

To the cynical skeptic Decoud, Nostromo's public heroism and the idealism of the Goulds seem false, self-deceptive, hypocritical; to the more idealistic characters, Decoud's stance of scornful aloofness only reveals his superficial involvement in life and his alienation from his fellows. *Nostromo* is structured around a number of scenes of confrontation between contrasted characters who reveal the antagonism and the ironic affinities between idealism and skepticism. For example, an encounter between Father Corbelán and Decoud brings them both to reflect "that a masterful conviction, as well as utter skepticism, may lead a man very far on the bypaths of political action" (200). But both skepticism and conviction may just as easily bring self-destruction. As with the idealistic characters, it is Decoud's most admirable qualities—his critical intelligence and relentlessly probing honesty—that lead to his doom.

[5] Ibid., p. 192.

[6] F. R. Leavis, *The Great Tradition* (New York: New York University Press, 1948), pp. 199–200.

[7] Conrad to John Galsworthy, November 11, 1901, in *Joseph Conrad on Fiction*, ed. with an introduction by Walter Wright (Lincoln, NB: University of Nebraska Press, 1964), p. 27.

Like Decoud, Dr. Monygham is a radical skeptic about the possibilities of moral action, but his skepticism springs from a quite different source than Decoud's intellectual detachment and sense of irony. The origin of the doctor's misanthropy is not revealed until quite late in the novel. At first the reader sees in Monygham's cynical comments on Gould's idealism or Nostromo's vanity or Decoud's political schemes only the doctor's "unbelief in men's motives" and "immense mistrust of mankind" (44). In the last part of the novel, "The Lighthouse," we learn that his spirit was broken under torture during the barbarous regime of Guzman Bento. Monygham has become "the slave of a ghost" (374); he is still haunted by nightmares of Father Beron, a sadistic army chaplain who presided over the "confession" extracted from him. Monygham's shame and rage in having confessed have led him to make "an ideal conception of his disgrace" (375). The memory of his own moral defeat gives Monygham a deep suspicion of the virtuous actions of others. Seeing in everyone else the possibility of his own moral fallibility, he always assumes the worst about others' motives and their capacity to live up to their ideals. When the chief engineer says that Gould "must be extremely sure of himself," Monygham comments: "If that's all he's sure of, then he is sure of nothing" (310).

Despite the "bravado of guilt" (312) that makes the doctor so skeptical about moral commitments, he, too, becomes increasingly dedicated to a moral idea. Because it is only with Mrs. Gould that he feels able to accept himself, the doctor comes to place all his trust and loyalty in her. Thus, in order to protect Emily Gould, Monygham is drawn to act for the interests of the silver mine:

> The doctor was loyal to the mine. It presented itself to his fifty-years-old eyes in the shape of a little woman in a soft dress. . . . As the dangers thickened round the San Tomé mine this illusion acquired force, permanency, and authority. It claimed him at last! This claim, exalted by a spiritual detachment from the usual sanctions of hope and reward, made Dr. Monygham's thinking, acting, individuality, extremely dangerous to himself and to others, all his scruples vanishing in the proud feeling that his devotion was the only thing that stood between an admirable woman and a frightful disaster. (431)

Dr. Monygham is the only major character who is in a better position at the end of the novel than he was at the outset. Though the story of his redemption occupies only a small portion of *Nostromo*, it seems to show the possibility of reconciling in action two essential Conradian moral virtues: commitment to an ideal and skepticism. Yet Dr. Monygham's fanatical devotion to Mrs. Gould is a terribly limited ideal, and produces ironic repercussions in action. If his idea's dangers "to himself and others" are avoided by Monygham himself, the doctor's efforts to ensure Mrs. Gould's safety risk a great deal of suffering for others and lead directly to at least one death.

All of these five characters—Nostromo, Charles and Emily Gould, Decoud, and Monygham—are committed to a moral idea. To various degrees, skepticism enables each one to realize some of the limitations and dangers of their "idea"—though this recognition usually comes at the cost of bitter experience. *Nostromo* explores the difficulty of uniting the two virtues of idealistic commitment and skeptical intelligence. The difficulty arises from the fact that these two qualities seem inimical to each other, but in practice either virtue alone leads to self-destruction. Action and critical thought are inimical because taking action requires a basic "illusion": the belief that one's moral idea can be realized in practical terms. The narrator generalizes from Gould's case: "Action is consolatory. It is the enemy of thought and the friend of flattering illusions. Only in the conduct of our action can we find the sense of mastery over the Fates" (66). Skeptical intelligence disperses the "illusion" of mastery that accompanies action. Conrad consistently associates action and work with idealization and illusion, and contrasts these elements with critical thought. Decoud says that Gould "cannot act or exist without idealizing every simple feeling, desire, or achievement. He could not believe his own motives if he did not make them first a part of some fairy tale. The earth is not quite good enough for him, I fear" (214–15). Decoud, and the narrator whose rhetoric and ironic perspective so resemble his, point out that when action is successful it invites further idealization, creating a still greater "illusion" that hides other motivations for action. Like *Lord Jim's* Stein, or Marlow in *Heart of Darkness*, Decoud functions as a touchstone to reveal the self-deception in other characters. He wants to distinguish his own motivation from "the sentimentalism of the people that will never do anything for the sake of their passionate desire, unless it comes to them clothed in the fair robes of an idea" (239). Dr. Monygham, too, wishes to have no illusions about the idealistic basis of his actions: "I put no spiritual value into my desires, or my opinions, or my actions. They have not enough vastness to give me room for self-flattery" (318). Yet despite their skepticism, Decoud and Monygham, quite as much as the more idealistic characters, find themselves attempting to realize a moral idea in the world of public action.

Though it gives rise to "illusion," an "idea" is the necessary basis for a character's action. The notion of the pragmatic efficacy of an idea is expressed by the chief engineer: "Things seem to be worth nothing by what they are in themselves. I begin to believe that the only solid thing about them is the spiritual value which everyone discovers in his own form of activity" (318). This comment is prompted by a discussion of the millionaire Holroyd, whose financial support of the Gould Concession is the means towards his "idea": "the introduction of a pure form of Christianity" into Costaguana (317). Though ideas have no ultimate or secure foundation in the structure of the world, they are pragmatically necessary to motivate action. Individuals would undertake few efforts or risks without an illusion which, through the power of hope and imaginative aspiration, effectively inspires and sustains human activities. Even Decoud admires the way "those Englishmen live on illusions which somehow help them to get a firm hold on the substance" (239). To be intellectually committed to an idea is not enough; one must be prepared to translate it into feasible terms of action, despite the risk of moral compromise. Conrad's portrayal of Giorgio Viola helps the reader to appreciate the main characters' efforts to realize their ideals concretely, even though compromise is required. For the austere idealism, the "spirit of self-forgetfulness" and "puritanism of conduct" (31) of the aging "Garibaldino" are completely irrelevant to the political realities of Costaguana in the 1880s.

Conrad shows the value of commitment to an idea, and he also reveals its illusory quality. Robert Penn Warren has called this motif in Conrad's work the "true lie": "Values are, to use Conrad's word, 'illusions,' but the last wisdom is for man to realize that though his values are illusions, the illusion is necessary, is infinitely precious, is the mark of his human achievement, and is, in the end, his only truth."[8] Yet, as Guerard has pointed out, the notion of the "true lie" destroys "Conrad's healing lucidity and irony": "Conrad does not limit our choice (as Warren implies) to an inhuman naturalism or a self-deceptive idealism, to animal savagery or 'illusion.' *Nostromo* seems rather to distinguish between the self-deluding, self-flattering victim of his own illusions and the genuine clear-headed idealist; between, say, Charles Gould and his wife."[9] It is by portraying their implications in the world of public action that Conrad tests whether a character's "idea" is only a self-deceptive illusion or whether it provides a meaningful basis for action, even when action ends in defeat. For in fact, all the ideas that the various characters try to realize are fatally compromised in action. "Spiritual value" can only be actualized in what *Lord Jim's* Stein called "the destructive element" of reality.

In *Nostromo*, the silver of the mine is the central symbol of the destructive effects of *the public world* on human moral purposes.[10]

---

[8] Robert Penn Warren, "The Great Mirage: Conrad and *Nostromo*," in *Selected Essays by Robert Penn Warren*, (New York: Vintage Books, 1966), p. 45.

[9] Guerard, *Conrad the Novelist*, p. 193. Guerard's view is more accurately nuanced than Warren's or, on the other extreme, that of J. Hillis Miller in *Poets of Reality: Six Twentieth Century Writers* (New York: Atheneum, 1965). Writing of *Heart of Darkness*, Miller interprets Conrad's basic moral vision in nihilistic and pessimistic terms, neglecting the affirmative elements in his work: "It is a mistake to define Conrad's solution to the ethical problem by the phrase the 'true lie.' There is nothing true about any action or judgment except their relation to the darkness, and the darkness makes any positive action impossible" (p. 35). See also footnote 32 below.

[10] Conrad wrote to Ernest Bendz, a Swede who authored an early study of his novels: "I will take the liberty to point out that Nostromo has never been intended for the hero of the Tale of the Seaboard. Silver is the pivot of the moral and material events, affecting

Critics who see the novel's central theme as an opposition between idealism and materialism miss the deepest design of *Nostromo*.[11] It is not just
as an illustration of the corrosive power of materialism that the San
Tomé Mine's silver functions. For Conrad shows the mine's genuine
moral value, too: "The San Tomé Mine was to become an institution, a
rallying point for everything in the province that needed order and
stability to live" (110). Because the mine does have this positive value,
the reader does not immediately lose sympathy for the characters who
make moral compromises for the sake of the mine's security. Early in
the novel, we are prevented from simply condemning Charles Gould's
dedication to the mine when the narrator contrasts his realistic attitude
with that of his wife: "Even the most legitimate touch of materialism
was wanting in Mrs. Gould's character" (75).

That the effects of every character's commitment to the silver prove
so universally destructive indicates that Conrad did not just want to
expose the self-deception of those who place their faith in "material
interests," though this was part of his purpose. The silver should be seen
not so much as a symbol of economic wealth, but as the symbol of the
one universal currency. Silver is the generally accepted medium of
exchange of the public world, the most basic agency of power with
which all persons, whatever their loyalties or ideals, must come to terms.
Each character projects his or her deepest values outward onto the silver,
the means to power in society. But the common effect of translating
personal hopes and ideals into the terms of public exchange is the dehu-
manization and distortion of purpose. Seen in this light, the corrosive
power of the silver symbolizes not only the moral contamination of economic wealth, but, more broadly, the *resistance of the social world* to
moral purpose, and the self-defeating effects of action in the public
arena. The treasure accounts directly only for the fates of Nostromo and
Gould, "the two racially and socially contrasted men, both captured by
the silver of the San Tomé Mine."[12] But Emily Gould, Decoud, and
Monygham also find their fates firmly linked to the mine's. Their devotion to persons they love forces them into the political struggles that

---

the lives of everybody in the tale." Quoted in Jocelyn Baines, *Joseph Conrad: A Critical
Biography* (New York: McGraw-Hill, 1960), p. 301.

[11] See Leavis, *Great Tradition*, p. 191: "*Nostromo* has a main political, or public, theme,
the relation between moral idealism and 'material interests.' . . . This public theme is presented in terms of a number of personal histories." See also Christopher Cooper, *Conrad
and the Human Dilemma* (New York: Barnes & Noble, 1970), p. 148: "The spirit of
materialism which has pervaded the whole book has power even over those of exemplary
goodness. . . . For materialism is the reality of our age. This is Conrad's warning. None
can escape. Partial exemption only can be found by the guiding principles arising from
spiritual values." This view does not account for the ironic effects of the "spiritual values"
so crudely contrasted with materialism.

[12] Conrad, "Author's Note" to *Nostromo*, p. xix.

center on the mine, and these political involvements bring about their own doom or that of other characters. For all these characters, silver is the visible embodiment of the collective destiny that thwarts their love, the general fate that engulfs and destroys private individuals. Without forcing the development of the five main characters into a rigid pattern, it can be shown that, in each of their fates, Conrad explored a basic moral problem. My interpretation of Conrad's critique of virtue in *Nostromo* will take the form of an analysis of the reasons why idealism and skepticism alike lead to the corruption of moral "ideas" in public action. The central moral dilemma Conrad probes in the fates of his protagonists is the difficulty of combining two virtues—fidelity to a moral idea and intellectual skepticism—in action in the "destructive element" of society.

II. *The Fallibility and Vulnerability of the Hero*

There are four aspects of *Nostromo*'s exploration of the dangers to idealism and skepticism in public action: (1) Conrad shows how *self-interest* underlies and can come to undermine moral action. (2) He shows that virtue is partly a public status and a *social role* that can disintegrate apart from "the eyes of others." (3) *Nostromo* depicts the ways a willful *blindness* can accompany moral commitment and lead to a tragic error that destroys the self and others. (4) Conrad's critique of virtue shows how each character's attempt to realize an ideal results in the betrayal and *corruption* of the ideal: "the moral degradation of the idea" in action. The fates of the five main characters in *Nostromo* will be interpreted in terms of these dangers to idealism and skepticism.

It is most often through the ironic comments of Decoud or Monygham that self-interested motives underlying idealistic actions are suggested. Decoud points out that for Father Corbelán, an "avenging spirit" fearlessly devoted to the Church, "the idea of political honour, justice, and honesty . . . consists in the restitution of the confiscated Church property" (188–89). The example of Corbelán illustrates Decoud's general claim that a conviction is basically "a particular view of our personal advantage either practical or emotional. No one is a patriot for nothing" (189). Decoud takes great pleasure in scornfully pointing out the incredible variety of motives that induce persons to try to realize a moral idea. But in addition to relishing the privileged role of a fastidious dilettante, Decoud shows keen moral discernment in exposing the hypocrisy and pretension of others. For example, an early scene in the novel shows Decoud's insight into the real basis of foreign interest in preserving Costaguana's Ribierist government from the Monterist insurrection. The young English engineer Scarfe has innocently disclosed his own stake in the government: the completion of the railway project "would give him the pull over a lot of chaps all through life, he asserted, 'Therefore—down with Montero!'" (169). Decoud comments sarcastically to Mrs. Gould and Don José that such "enlightened" foreign interest in the Ribierist cause is gratifying. He goes on to arraign the "curse of futility" attached to the Costaguanan national character, whose mixture of motives makes it the easy mark of profiteers and criminals:

> It is pleasant to think that the prosperity of Costaguana is of some use to the world. . . . But here we have the naked truth from the mouth of that child. . . . The natural treasures of Costaguana are of importance to the progressive Europe represented by this youth, just as three hundred years ago the wealth of our Spanish fathers was a serious object to the rest of Europe—as represented by the bold buccaneers. There is a curse of futility upon our character: Don Quixote and Sancho Panza, chivalry and materialism, high-sounding sentiments and a supine morality, violent efforts for an idea and a sullen acquiescence in every form of corruption. We convulsed a continent for our independence only to become the passive prey of a democratic parody, the helpless victims of scoundrels and cut-throats, our institutions a mockery, our laws a farce. (170–71)

The actions of all the characters in the novel converge on the "one ever-present aim to preserve the inviolable character of the mine at every cost" (112). In the first two of the novel's three parts, Conrad uses the silver as a touchstone to reveal the variety of human aims and purposes possible and likely in a common enterprise. It is love for another person that provides the essential motivation for three of the main characters: Decoud's love for Antonia Avellanos, Dr. Monygham's for Mrs. Gould, and Mrs. Gould's for her husband. Dedication to a loved one leads these characters, as much as Charles Gould and Nostromo, to make extensive moral compromises to protect the mine. Their originally disinterested motives become linked to their efforts to establish the conditions necessary for their love, and increasingly questionable as they require the sacrifice of other values. The "indestructible," "incorruptible" silver of the mine, which comes to be sought as the means to every private end, symbolizes the resistance of the world—especially the public, political world—to human intentions. And it reveals the various forms of self-interest in all attempts to realize a moral idea in action.

Not only idealism masks hidden motives. Decoud's ironic perspective on the world is partly a pose he strikes to justify his wish to remain aloof from human folly. Similarly, until he becomes attached to Mrs. Gould, Monygham's general cynicism about life serves to protect him from having to risk his integrity again by committing himself to a moral idea. Both Decoud and Monygham are skeptics about human conduct, but their skepticism springs from quite different sources, and functions defensively in contrasting ways. Unlike Decoud, Monygham's skeptical view of human moral conduct is based not on a theoretical rejection of idealism as self-deceptive, but rather on the knowledge of his own moral failure. Monygham's despair about human moral capacities is the fruit of bitter experience, and the reader respects it more than Decoud's youthful, somewhat abstract, and untested cynicism.[13] "There could be no doubt of [Monygham's] intelligence; and as he had lived for over twenty years in the country, the pessimism of his outlook could not be altogether ignored" (311). In the episode of torture that still haunts his dreams, Monygham's integrity was shattered not by selfish motives, but by unbearable "pain which makes truth, honour, self-respect, and life itself matters of little moment" (373). Unable to forgive himself for falsely incriminating others to save himself, he believes that everyone must have a point at which their fidelity and courage become vulnerable. His awareness of the potential weakness of virtue in an extreme test leads Monygham to doubt the reality of human moral goodness. The skepticism of Decoud and Monygham, then, operates as a defensive means of justifying their own estrangement from the community of Sulaco.

As the novel unfolds, the motivations underlying Nostromo's heroism are questioned with increasing scrutiny. Decoud and Monygham see Nostromo's actions as a means of achieving the public esteem he craves: "He looks upon his prestige as a sort of investment" (220). In a letter to his sister, Decoud wonders what gives rise to Nostromo's inordinate yet all-too-human concern for reputation: "Is it sheer naiveness or the practical point of view, I wonder? Exceptional individualities always interest me, because they are true to the general formula expressing the moral state of humanity" (246). Decoud correctly discerns the colossal egoism that underlies Nostromo's heroic actions and fidelity. He sees the Capataz as the emblem of a general truth: egoism often appears in the form of virtuous action. "Decoud, incorrigible in his skepticism, reflected, not cynically, but with general satisfaction, that this man was made incorruptible by his enormous vanity, that finest form of egoism which can take on the aspect of every virtue" (300). However, Decoud believes that Nostromo's very egoism makes him absolutely dependable. When Nostromo is about to leave him stranded on the Great Isabel Island, Decoud reflects that, since the reputation of the Capataz rests on their success in saving the silver, Nostromo's tremendous pride paradoxically guarantees his integrity: Nostromo "would have preferred to die rather than deface the perfect form of his egoism. Such a man was safe" (301). Decoud does not suspect that Nostromo's deep egoism might simply take another

[13] Decoud's attitude is similar to the "declared pessimism" Conrad criticizes in his essay "Books" (1905), in *Conrad on Fiction*, p. 81: "The way of excellence is in the intellectual, as distinguished from emotional, humility. What one feels so hopelessly barren in declared pessimism is just its arrogance. It seems as if the discovery made by many men at various times that there is much evil in the world were a source of proud and unholy joy unto some of the modern writers."

form, one that does not ensure Decoud's safety.

Monygham, too, doubts Nostromo's integrity. Having been through his gruesome ordeal, Monygham thinks that if Nostromo has not yet been corrupted, it is because he has been lucky enough not to meet a supreme test that pits the demands of moral duty against the urgency of self-interest. He realizes that Nostromo's heroic actions result from his striving for prestige, and, in trying to persuade the "incorruptible Capataz" to undertake the perilous mission to Cayta, appeals candidly to Nostromo's concern for reputation: "the choice was between accepting the mission to Barrios, with all its dangers and difficulties, and leaving Sulaco by stealth, ingloriously, in poverty" (455). Monygham believes that, so long as his desire for recognition is satisfied, Nostromo is "capable of anything—even of the most absurd fidelity" (319). But he suspects to the very end that Nostromo has at some time betrayed his trust for personal gain, though he never obtains concrete evidence of corruption. When Mrs. Gould withholds the fact of Nostromo's deathbed confession from the doctor, Monygham is conclusively "defeated by the magnificent Capataz de Cargadores, the man who had lived his own life on the assumption of unbroken fidelity, rectitude, and courage" (561). The reader, of course, knows that Dr. Monygham's intuition was correct, for Nostromo has stolen the treasure. Nostromo's integrity was corrupted when the demands of moral duty and his own personal self-interest no longer conveniently coincided, but sharply conflicted.

In sum, the early and middle portions of *Nostromo* involve a gradual disclosure of the forms of self-interest that underlie the virtues of the main characters. In the later sections of the novel, Conrad explores the ways that self-interest can conflict with and undermine moral purpose.

The process of Nostromo's corruption shows the second aspect of Conrad's exploration of moral virtue in *Nostromo*: virtue's dependency on a public role and virtue's disintegration when deprived of supportive social conventions. This theme is prefigured early in the novel, when Nostromo is baffled by Teresa Viola's disparagement of his popular reputation. Teresa tells Nostromo that his great reputation provides inadequate compensation for his services: "They have turned your head with their praises. They have been paying you with words" (257). When Teresa mocks him, Nostromo feels "out of character," not himself, deprived of his rightful identity. He is particularly distressed when she ridicules the name the Europeans call him—"our man"—instead of his real name: Gian Battista Fidanza.

The crisis that brings about Nostromo's moral corruption and Decoud's suicide arises when the Europeans try to save some of the mine's silver from the Monterist mob by sending it out of Sulaco on a lighter with the two men. In one of Conrad's most memorable scenes, he portrays the sensations and thoughts of these two contrasted individuals when, after the tumultuous events in Sulaco, they suddenly find themselves utterly alone in the eerie blackness of the Golfo Placido. The first chapter of the novel had described the Golfo on certain cloudy, windless nights as a "black cavern" where "the eye of God Himself could not find out what work a man's hand is doing in there; and you would be free to call the devil to your aid with impunity if even his malice were not defeated by such a blind darkness" (7). Now Decoud is stunned, mentally annihilated by the silent, measureless black space in which their boat drifts: "Intellectually self-confident, he suffered from being deprived of the only weapon he could use with effect. No intelligence could penetrate the darkness of the Placid Gulf" (275). Meanwhile a new element comes to the surface of Nostromo's character: deprived of public adulation, he begins to feel "exasperated by the deadly nature of the trust placed, as a matter of course, into his hands" (263). When the lighter is struck by Colonel Sotillo's troopship as it stealthily approaches the harbor, the two men realize that, cut off from Sulaco's structure of social relationships, all that unites them is the immediate danger: "This common danger brought their difference in aim, in view, in character and in position, into absolute prominence in the private vision of each. There was no bond of conviction, of common idea; they were merely two adventurers pursuing each his own adventure, involved in the same imminence of deadly peril" (295).

When the silver has been buried on the Great Isabel and Nostromo has returned secretly to the mainland, he experiences a solitude he has never known. The necessity of his hiding from the Monterist mob roaming Sulaco makes "everything that had gone before for years appear vain and foolish, like a flattering dream come suddenly to an end" (414). For the first time Nostromo realizes that the Europeans have used his services with scarcely a thought for his safety. "He was as if sobered after a long bout of intoxication. His fidelity had been taken advantage of" (417). He fears that his heroic actions for the mine have displayed an unwitting servility to the rich. Giorgio Viola had compared the poor to dogs kept by the wealthy, "to fight and hunt for their service," and now Nostromo broods over this notion. To explain his new feelings of anger and estrangement, Nostromo fixes on the idea that he has been betrayed: "His imagination had seized upon the clear and simple notion of betrayal to account for the dazed feeling of enlightenment as to being done for, of having inadvertently gone out of his existence on an issue in which his personality had not been taken into account" (419–20). When he encounters Monygham he feels "an inexplicable repugnance to pronounce the name by which he was known" (425). The doctor's failure to understand the resentment felt by Nostromo confirms his sense of alienation from his former public role, and furthers the process of disillusionment that ultimately leads Nostromo to appropriate the silver secretly as the reward for his services and the revenge for his having been exploited.

A striking pattern of cross-references in *Nostromo* is the series of incidents in which one character exploits another's knowledge of his public reputation. The details of the scene depicting the confrontation between Nostromo and Monygham near the Custom-House show Conrad's fascination with the ways that a person's public reputation can blind others to his real moral character. Nostromo had reflected earlier that "men's qualities are made use of, without any fundamental knowledge of their nature" (265). When the doctor meets Nostromo lurking about the wharf he unquestioningly assents to the popular view of the Capataz de Cargadores:

> The doctor's misanthropic mistrust of mankind (the bitterer because based on personal failure) did not lift him sufficiently above common weaknesses. He was under the spell of an established reputation. Trumpeted by Captain Mitchell, grown in reputation, and fixed in general assent, Nostromo's faithfulness had never been questioned by Dr. Monygham as a fact. It was not likely to be questioned now he stood in desperate need of it himself. Dr. Monygham was human; he accepted the popular conception of the Capataz's incorruptibility simply because no word or fact had ever contradicted a mere affirmation. It seemed to be a part of the man, like his whiskers or his teeth. It was impossible to conceive him otherwise. (432)

The irony of the doctor's credulity here is that he has just completely deceived Colonel Sotillo by exploiting his own evil reputation in Sulaco. Monygham's "usefulness" in this situation is his "character" (409) because Sotillo fully believes that the doctor will betray the Europeans and reveal the location of the silver. Monygham offers to Mrs. Gould an ingenious plan "to serve you to the whole extent of my evil reputation" (410) by keeping Sotillo occupied in the harbor looking for the treasure. In this perilous undertaking Monygham is contrasted with Nostromo, who bitterly resents the danger his social role has incurred for him, and is about to betray his reputation by stealing the silver for himself. Monygham is also contrasted with Don Pepe, the foreman of the workers in the San Tomé Mine. Left in charge of the mine with enough dynamite to destroy it, this faithful steward's value depends on his reputation as a man who cannot be bribed by the Monterist party. "The incorruptibility of Don Pepe was the essential and restraining fact" (409) that guarantees the safety of the Goulds while they are held hostage in the town of Sulaco. Nostromo, Monygham, and Don Pepe all exploit the beliefs that others hold about their characters, whether for acts of deception or acts of integrity, for self-serving or self-sacrificing ends.

Like Nostromo, Decoud perishes when deprived of his social environment. After eleven days of total isolation on the Great Isabel, he kills himself. Critics have usually misinterpreted the meaning of Decoud's suicide as Conrad's attempt to repudiate skepticism as an attitude to life. It is true that the account of Decoud's ordeal on the island is accompanied by a great deal of explicit authorial condemnation of his inability to deal with adversity:

> The brilliant Costaguanero of the boulevards had died from solitude and want of faith in himself and others. . . . [Decoud] was not fit to grapple with himself singlehanded. Solitude from mere outward condition of existence becomes very swiftly a state of soul in which the affectations of irony and skepticism have no place. . . . The vague consciousness of a misdirected life given up to impulses whose memory left a bitter taste in his mouth was the first moral sentiment of his manhood. But at the same time he felt no remorse. What should he regret? He had recognized no other virtue than intelligence, and had erected passions into duties. Both his intelligence and his passion were swallowed up easily in this great unbroken solitude of waiting without faith. . . . His sadness was the sadness of a skeptical mind. (496–98)

His treatment of Decoud reveals Conrad's unresolved struggle with a deep tendency of his own imagination. Warren does well to call attention to the fact that "the act of creation is not simply a projection of temperament, but a criticism and a purging of temperament." But the metaphor of purging implies that Conrad's attitude to skepticism was entirely negative; Warren states this explicitly when he claims that "Conrad repudiates the Decouds of the world."[14] Conrad does not "repudiate" Decoud; he dramatizes the compounding of difficult circumstances that drive a certain kind of character to self-destruction. We can best see the total imaginative effort required to depict this character as a self-critical attempt to envision the dangers to a crucially important outlook on the world. Conrad's depiction of Decoud entails not moral condemnation of skepticism, but an attempt to anticipate and forestall the potential weaknesses of this crucial virtue. Conrad is even *more*, rather than less, skeptical than the skeptical Decoud.

Conrad points out that few persons are ever forced to meet a test of protracted solitude: Decoud "died from solitude, the enemy known but to a few on this earth, and whom only the simplest of us are fit to withstand" (496). Simplicity is immune to the dangers threatening Decoud's "virtue" of "intelligence" (498). Sharing Decoud's skepticism, Dr. Monygham well understands the terror and the enervating inertia that can attack an imaginative person cut off from the encouragement and example of others. "Having had to encounter single-handed many physical dangers, he was well aware of the most dangerous element common to them all: the crushing, paralyzing sense of human littleness, which is what really defeats a man struggling with natural forces, alone, far from the eyes of his fellows" (433). Though skepticism is an essential virtue rather than a fault in Conrad's moral world, it is vulnerable to certain dangers, especially when the skeptic is isolated from other persons. For

---

14 Warren, "The Great Mirage," p. 48.

skepticism demands its polar opposite, belief, to sustain itself; in this sense it is a secondary though indispensable virtue. Lacking a social context, the skeptic's critical intelligence becomes introverted and self-destructive.

But that belief alone cannot cope with life's complexity, and that skepticism is indispensable, are asserted explicitly by the narrator: "The popular mind is incapable of skepticism; and that incapacity delivers their helpless strength to the wiles of swindlers and to the pitiless enthusiasms of leaders inspired by visions of a high destiny" (420). Decoud's skeptical intelligence and realistic appraisal of human motivation provide a crucial antidote to the innate human tendency towards self-deception. The other perceptive and discerning characters in *Nostromo*, Emily Gould and Dr. Monygham, also develop a strong sense of skepticism through their experiences in Costaguana. Many critics have seen Mrs. Gould as an idealized figure, a sort of fairy-godmother; they forget her bitter remarks on her own marriage when she tells Giselle, grieving over Nostromo's death: "Console yourself, child. Very soon he would have forgotten you for his treasure. I have been loved too" (561).

In sum, then, Conrad presents skepticism as a crucial moral virtue, essential if one's pursuit of an ideal is not to result in self-deception. Yet he shows that a skeptic like Decoud, as well as the warrior-hero Nostromo, can be destroyed in a test that deprives him of the social context necessary to sustain virtue. Decoud and Nostromo, like Lord Jim on the night he abandoned the Patna or Kurtz on the upper reaches of the Congo River, are vulnerable to self-doubt and moral corruption when they are cut off from the "eye of others." And because of their courage and their heroic roles in their societies, these men are more likely than most to find themselves in situations of enforced solitude and isolation. Despite its rich political themes, *Nostromo*'s climactic scenes are the moments when characters recognize their utter apartness from their fellows. Engaged in political and military ventures of desperate urgency, Conrad's protagonists are placed in positions where they must keep secrets and refrain from open communication with others. As Nostromo warns Decoud, "Honesty alone is not enough for security. You must look to discretion and prudence in a man" (299). But secrecy and concealment easily lead to estrangement from the community one serves. Tragic heroes must keep secrets, but secrets destroy their solidarity with others. The moral virtuoso who acts on behalf of his community must expose himself to unusual risks and temptations. These perils overcome Nostromo's moral integrity and Decoud's self-confidence when they are deprived of the support and encouragement provided by the community of Sulaco.

The third aspect of Conrad's critique of virtue in *Nostromo* is his depiction of its blindness. Edward Said links the blindness common to every character to the many disjunctions between "action" and "record": each character is myopic about discrepancies between what really happened and the flattering accounts by which they "author" an acceptable history.[15] This blindness has a moral significance: both idealistic and skeptical characters inadvertently bring about their own suffering and danger or doom to others. The theme of moral blindness is worked out most extensively in the fate of the Goulds' marriage and their idea, and in the indirect effects of Dr. Monygham's fidelity. Charles Gould's all-consuming dedication to the mine has the practical effect of isolating him from his wife. While he is largely insensitive to their growing estrangement, Emily feels it keenly: "It was as if the inspiration of their early years had left her heart to turn into a wall of silver bricks, erected by the silent work of evil spirits, between her and her husband" (221–22). At several points Charles Gould is portrayed gazing abstractedly into space, past the head of his wife, who with dread sees his growing preoccupation. The narrator comments on the danger of mental obsession with even an "idea of justice": "Charles Gould's fits of abstraction depicted the energetic concentration of a will haunted by a fixed idea. A man haunted by a fixed idea is insane. He is dangerous even if that idea is an idea of justice; for may he not bring the heaven down pitilessly upon a loved head?" (379). Emily sees her husband as "incorrigible" (521) in his pursuit of his idea; this adjective expresses both his moral determination and his inflexible refusal to consider any good but that of the mine. Gould's project entails a "sentimental unfaithfulness which surrenders her happiness, her life, to the seduction of an idea" (245).

It is not only to his wife's unhappiness that Gould is oblivious. His blindness extends to the obvious danger to his own ideals when silver is used as a weapon: "Dangerous to the wielder, too, this weapon of wealth, double-edged with the cupidity and misery of mankind, steeped in all the voices of self-indulgence as in a concoction of poisonous roots, tainting the very cause for which it is drawn, always ready to turn awkwardly in the hand" (365). Gould refuses to recognize either his own moral guilt or the dangers his project entails for others. In the following passage, which accounts for the commingling of several elements in Gould's readiness to destroy the San Tomé Mine, his moral culpability is tied to his reckoning his own personal risk as a justification for imposing danger on others:

> For all the uprightness of his character, he had something of an adventurer's easy morality which takes count of personal risk in the ethical

---

[15] Edward Said, *Beginnings: Intention and Method* (New York: Basic Books, 1975), pp. 100–137. This tendency in every character reflects the split Said detects in Conrad between the agonized voice of the private letters and the serene, jocular, and publicly acceptable author of the Prefaces and Notes.

appraising of his action. He was prepared, if need be, to blow up the whole San Tomé mountain sky high out of the territory of the Republic. This resolution expressed the tenacity of his character, the remorse of the subtle conjugal infidelity through which his wife was no longer the sole mistress of his thoughts, something of his father's imaginative weakness, and something, too, of the spirit of a buccaneer throwing a lighted match into the magazine rather than surrender his ship. (365–66)

Uprightness and a tendency to rationalize, tenacity and remorse, imaginative weakness and grim desperation: Conrad was a master at showing how different elements of a person's character intertwine and blind him to all that lies outside his conscious purposes.

In one enigmatic passage, the narrator of *Nostromo* claims that it is Gould's "corrupt judgment" that induces him to try to establish justice in the land by backing Decoud's scheme for an independent Sulaco: "The mine had corrupted his judgment by making him sick of bribing and intriguing merely to have his work left alone from day to day. Like his father, he did not like to be robbed" (365). In Gould's "corrupt judgment" we see the subtle mixture of intellectual mistake and moral guilt that characterizes a tragic error. Gould's deepest wish is simply to go about his work. This justifiable ambition produces the ideal of a Sulaco where one could do business without constantly having to barter favors and bribe rapacious officials. But to try to achieve this goal by means of revolution is pragmatically naive, given the political history of Costaguana. Monygham claims that "a frank return to the old methods" (370) of ransom and bribery would quickly satisfy the Monteros' greed, and Gould could then get on with his work. Gould's judgment may be "corrupt" in the sense of erroneous, then. It is also implied that he is corrupt morally when he initiates a political revolution for the sake of his own business interests. Gould is the perfect example of what Decoud calls "the picturesque extreme of wrong-headedness into which an honest, almost sacred conviction may drive a man. . . . It seemed to him that every conviction, as soon as it became effective, turned into that form of dementia the gods send upon those they wish to destroy" (200). Decoud's reflections suggest the ancient Greek notion of *atē*, which joined the phenomena of human virtue, blindness, and god-sent madness. Even skeptical Decoud has a tendency to lose sight of what is essential to his own happiness: "He had pushed the habit of universal raillery to a point where it blinded him to the genuine impulses of his own nature" (153). Decoud's conviction that all action is ultimately futile undermines his faith in the reality of his love for Antonia when he is isolated on the Great Isabel. As much as Gould and Nostromo, Decoud blindly destroys his own peace of mind as well as the happiness of the woman who loves him.

Dr. Monygham, too, becomes "extremely dangerous to himself and to others" (431) as he risks all to avert the threat to Mrs. Gould. Monygham might have perceived and soothed Nostromo's feelings of resentment when the two men met by the Custom House, but "the doctor, engrossed by a desperate adventure of his own, was terrible in the pursuit of his idea" (434). He is quite indifferent to Decoud's fate, and sends Nostromo on another life or death mission with hardly a second thought. Most significant of all, the doctor is completely oblivious to the fatal repercussions for Señor Hirsch of Monygham's deception of Sotillo, until Nostromo directly accuses him: "If you had not confirmed Sotillo in his madness, he would have been in no haste to give the estrapade to that miserable Hirsch" (438). Even then, the doctor evades recognizing his guilt in this matter:

> The necessity, the magnitude, the importance of the task he had taken upon himself dwarfed all merely humane considerations. He had undertaken it in a fanatical spirit. . . . Though he had no sort of heroic idea of seeking death, the risk, deadly enough, to which he exposed himself, had a sustaining and comforting effect. To that spiritual state the fate of Hirsch presented itself as part of the general atrocity of things. (439)

Monygham is a truly courageous man, ready to sacrifice his life to protect the woman he loves. But his myopia about the side-effects of his activities is typical of the moral striving of all the main characters in *Nostromo*. Conrad uses metaphors of vision and blindness to probe the fallibility of idealist and skeptic alike.

The last aspect of Conrad's treatment of virtue in the novel is his exploration of "the degradation of the idea" when it is realized in action. The theme of moral corruption is worked out primarily in the depiction of the "terrible success" of the Goulds' idealism and in Nostromo's downfall. The price of the outward triumph of the San Tomé mine is the defeat of the Gould's ideals. Charles and Emily each face this recognition in a crucial scene that indicates their final fate. Charles Gould's most penetrating insight in the novel is his perception that he and the bandit leader Hernandez, with whom he allies against the Monterists, are in the same moral position. The two men are "equals before the lawlessness of the land. It was impossible to disentangle one's activity from its debasing contacts. A closemeshed net of crime and corruption lay upon the whole country" (360–61). Though his ideal has been fatally compromised in Costaguana's web of political corruption, Gould has no alternative but to go on in the desperate hope that somehow the mine will survive the conflict and produce a better justice in the long run. Like Macbeth, he determines to persist to the end in what he knows to be a morally doomed cause, hoping that success will justify his moral compromises. "He was like a man who had ventured on a precipitous path with no room to turn, where the only chance of safety is to press forward" (361). This is the climax of Gould's development as a character. Hence the irony that after Gould recognizes his similarity to Hernandez, he beholds the exhausted reformer Don José Avellanos, "vanquished in a lifelong struggle with the powers of moral darkness, whose stagnant depths breed monstrous crimes and monstrous illusions" (362). Gould suspects but never admits to himself that, despite the eventual triumph of "material interests" in Sulaco, his own moral aspirations are also defeated in action, betrayed in order to achieve outward success.

Though the Gould Concession survives the revolution and becomes the most powerful force in the new Republic of Sulaco, the peace and justice it was intended to usher in remain unrealized "illusions." This fact is brought home rudely to Mrs. Gould in the crucial scene from which comes the title for this chapter. Several years after the revolution she sits talking with Dr. Monÿgham in her garden after returning from a trip to Europe. Receiving Antonia Avellanos and Corbellán, now Cardinal-Archbishop of Sulaco, she finds that the two are conspiring to start yet another war, in order to invade Costaguana and free their former countrymen. Then the doctor informs her that Sulaco has developed "labor problems," secret societies, and Marxist revolutionaries. He declares forcefully that moral justice cannot be firmly based on "material interests," whose law "is founded on expediency, and is inhuman; it is without rectitude, without the continuity and the force that can be found only in a moral principle. Mrs. Gould, the time approaches when all that the Gould Concession stands for shall weigh as heavily upon the people as the barbarism, cruelty, and misrule of a few years back" (511). When the doctor leaves, Mrs. Gould suffers a profound loneliness and has a despairing insight into the corruption of the youthful ideal she and her husband had sought to realize in Costaguana:

> There was something inherent in the necessities of successful action which carried with it the moral degradation of the idea. She saw the San Tomé mountain hanging over the Campo, over the whole land, feared, hated, wealthy, more soulless than any tyrant, more pitiless and autocratic than the worst Government; ready to crush innumerable lives in the expansion of its greatness. He did not see it. . . . She saw clearly the San Tomé mine possessing, consuming, burning up the life of the last of the Costaguana Goulds, mastering the energetic spirit of the son as it had mastered the lamentable weakness of the father. A terrible success for the last of the Goulds. (521–22)

Charles is indeed the last of the Goulds, Emily having finally given up her hope of having children. She dreads the future, for, "with a prophetic vision she saw herself surviving alone the degradation of her young ideal of life, of love, of work—all alone in the Treasure House of the World" (522). Emily's bitter fate is moving, and Conrad does not stress her guilt for the effects of the mine's success. But it should be noted that the degradation of the Gould's ideal is not the fault only of Charles. Emily supported him at every stage in establishing the mine as the supreme power in the land; she, too, bears some of the responsibility for the consequences of the mine's terrible success. However, in her final reflections, which sum up many of the narrator's general claims about history, what is emphasized is not the naiveté of the Goulds' illusions or the unfortunate errors and miscalculations that fatally undermined the goal of "a better justice," but "something inherent in the necessities of successful action" itself. Given the anarchic conditions of Costaguana's political life, the idea of a moral reformation became inextricably linked to the stabilizing influence of the San Tomé mine, "a great power for good and evil" (486). Because Costaguana lacks a tradition of political liberalism and reform, when the Goulds try to alter the shape of the country's political life they find themselves forced to "stoop for their weapons." But the actions required to keep the mine functioning mean the betrayal of the original moral inspiration for their venture in Sulaco. Though Charles seems wilfully blind to his moral failure, the more discerning vision of Mrs. Gould fully appreciates the hidden costs of the mine's "terrible success."

Nostromo's fate reveals another kind of "degradation of the idea": the corruption of the ideal of personal heroism and fidelity into a mere pose, a social role. Critics have neglected Nostromo. Guerard, for example, calls him the novel's "lost subject" and does not discuss the development of his character at all.[16] We can justly criticize as sentimental and melodramatic the novel's last two chapters, which center on Nostromo's bondage to his stolen treasure and his romantic entanglement with the Viola sisters.[17] The ending comes as a disappointing anticlimax after Conrad's earlier political insights and his subtle characterizations of more complex individuals like Decoud and Monygham. But Nostromo is not as simple a character as has usually been thought, and Conrad's skillful rendering of the process of his corruption has not been appreciated. The end of the novel involves a compelling portrayal of the erring hero's temptation, moral fall, and remorseful agony. And the recapitulation in Nostromo's fate of the various dangers to virtue ties together the several elements of Conrad's exploration of moral conduct in the novel.

Usually critics locate Nostromo's fall in the moment of his "awakening" from a deep sleep which follows his rescue of the lighter and his swim back to an abandoned fort: "He threw back his head, flung his arms open, and stretched himself with a slow twist of the waist and a

---

[16] Guerard, p. 204.

[17] Frederick R. Karl, *Joseph Conrad: The Three Lives* (New York: Farrar, Straus and Giroux, 1979), p. 557: "Conrad appears to have been caught in the middle, trapped between his dilatory methods of working and his artistic intentions. An abrupt ending to the serial would have provided a certain ironic commentary on Nostromo's earlier success; whereas a fleshed-out ending could have tried to supply a rationale for Nostromo's transformation, that is, given greater credibility to his shift from Tarzan to businessman. In fact, Conrad did neither."

leisurely growling yawn of white teeth, as natural and free from evil in the moment of waking as a magnificent and unconscious wild beast. Then, in the suddenly steadied glance fixed upon nothing from under a thoughtful frown, appeared the man" (411–12). In fact this is only the first sign of Nostromo's moral dissolution. The last six chapters of the novel explore a process of increasing remorse and self-torture as Nostromo desperately tries to escape from his false role before others and his secret guilt about the treasure. Conrad presents an accumulation of improbable coincidences and circumstances that conspire to tempt Nostromo to steal the treasure. At the time of temptation Nostromo is in a highly unsettled state of mind. Earlier he had been placed in a painful moral dilemma that forced him to deny Teresa Viola's dying request so that he could undertake the mission to save the silver. His refusal to fetch a priest for her weighs heavily on his conscience when he awakens; he feels "the burden of sacreligious guilt descend upon his shoulders" (420). He puzzles over her final warning to him that the Europeans are "paying you with words" and that he should "get something for yourself" for once (256). Nostromo is forced to live in hiding, apart from "the eyes of others." He experiences a sense of bewilderment and loss of identity: "And at the end of it all—Nostromo here and Nostromo there—where is Nostromo?" (417). His obsession with the notion of betrayal reveals both his sense of disillusionment and alienation from his fellows, and his dim awareness of the threat the treasure poses for him. Nostromo sees Monygham as the devil's tempter when the two men discuss ways to lure Colonel Sotillo into a futile search for the treasure. Nostromo's vivid imagination of how Sotillo's avarice will drive him insane with rage and thwarted desire prefigures his own enslavement: "There is something in a treasure that fastens upon a man's mind. He will pray and blaspheme and still persevere, and will curse the day he ever heard of it, and will let his last hour come upon him unawares, still believing that he missed it only by a foot. He will see it every time he closes his eyes" (460).

The motives for Nostromo's heroic ride to Cayta are quite complex. Most immediately, the return of Barrios's troops is his only hope for avoiding the revenge of the Monterist mob. Furthermore, the ride provides a chance to keep out of sight and thus preserve the secret of the silver. Faced with the choice of whether or not to disclose the location of the treasure, he imaginatively projects all his own temptations to steal it onto others: no one, he tells himself, is trustworthy enough to confide in. Nostromo therefore doesn't inform Mitchell or Monygham or Viola of the presence of the silver and of Decoud on the Great Isabel; he allows everyone to believe that both the man and the treasure sank with the lighter. Leaving Sulaco allows Nostromo to temporize and avoid making a decision about what to do about the silver. In addition, he wants to save the Viola family, to avenge Sotillo's hideous murder of that "man of fear," Señor Hirsch, and to salvage his somewhat damaged reputation for heroism.

Still Nostromo has not actually decided to steal the silver. When he returns with Barrios's troops after eleven days, he has not told anyone of its location: "the idea of secrecy had come to be connected with the treasure" (493). He finds that Decoud has committed suicide in his absence. Conrad now develops the similarity between Nostromo's fate and Decoud's. As analyzed above, both men are destroyed by experiences of isolation from their social community. A significant parallel construction in the text contrasts their fates in terms of how the strength of each man's character is defeated in action. Decoud is "a victim of the disillusioned weariness which is the retribution meted out to intellectual audacity"; Nostromo is "victim of the disenchanted vanity which is the reward of audacious action" (501). At this point, realizing that he alone knows the location of the silver, Nostromo decides to "grow rich slowly." His defiant pride in being able to pay the price in guilt for Decoud's death and for Teresa's "lost soul" binds him to the treasure:

> He knew the part he had played himself. First a woman, then a man, aban-
> doned each in their last extremity, for the sake of this accursed treasure. It
> was paid for by a soul lost and by a vanished life. The blank stillness of awe
> was succeeded by a gust of immense pride. There was no one in the world
> but Gian' Battista Fidanza, Capataz de Cargadores, the incorruptible and
> faithful Nostromo, to pay such a price. (502)

As if to seal his fate, Nostromo finds four silver ingots inexplicably missing, not knowing that Decoud had used them to weight his body. Nostromo believes, or rationalizes, that he could not explain their loss to his employers. Finally, the theft of the silver expresses his revenge against the rich who had so casually exploited his heroism, and against the San Tomé Mine, "which appeared to him hateful and immense, lording it by its vast wealth over the valour, the toil, the fidelity of the poor, over war and peace, over the labor of the town, the sea, and the Campo" (503).

Conrad takes great care that his readers will not simply condemn Nostromo for wanting some reward for his services. All along we have witnessed his faithful and selfless service. Decoud testifies that Nostromo is "more generous with his personality than the people who make use of him are with their money" (248). Monygham points out that "he's not grown rich by his fidelity to you good people of the railway and the harbor" (321). And even after the revolution has succeeded, we see a rich merchant whose very life has been saved by Nostromo complain when the Capataz requests a cigar. These incidents establish Nostromo's desire for compensation as not merely mercenary greed, but in part an entirely justified wish for recognition of his inestimable services for the entire community. The reader's sympathy for the criminal is essential if his fate is to be apprehended as tragic.

The last three chapters show Nostromo's outward prosperity and inner ruin some six or eight years later. "A transgression, a crime, entering a man's existence, eats it up like a malignant growth, consumes it like fever. Nostromo had lost his peace; the genuineness of all his qualities was destroyed" (523). But if Nostromo's virtues have been corrupted, they are not completely eradicated. His suffering is tragic because he finds his hypocrisy a source of torment. Nostromo is not simply anxious about having his secret discovered; he agonizes about deceiving others and struggles futilely to escape his false position. His suffering is immeasurably increased by the fact that he must carry his treasure off the island piece by piece to avoid detection, thus re-enacting his crime over and over again. He makes a partial confession to Giselle Viola, and believes he is about to be released from the curse of the silver just as he is accidentally killed by Giorgio Viola. Nostromo's tragic error in not revealing his love for Giselle to Giorgio is significantly linked to the source of his moral guilt. Afraid of being denied access to the Great Isabel, on which Viola is now the keeper of a lighthouse, Nostromo allows the Garibaldino to believe that he will marry Linda when in fact he loves Giselle. Thinking Nostromo is Ramirez, a despised suitor, Viola shoots him one night as the Capataz approaches the treasure. The final coda of the novel thus recapitulates all the ethical themes explored in this section. The reader sees the deep underlying vanity that continues to motivate Nostromo's actions. The fatal split between public role and personal identity continues in the discrepancy between Nostromo's public engagement to Linda and his private romance with Giselle. The blindness of the tragic hero appears as, intent on his treasure, "the resourceful Capataz" is "caught unawares by old Giorgio while stealing across the open towards the ravine to get some more silver" (554). And we see Nostromo's idea of heroism degraded in action, as Nostromo acts like a petty thief in order to preserve his public reputation.

On his deathbed, Nostromo desperately tries to locate the source of his sense of betrayal, to find some external object he can reproach for his ruin. He casts about wildly, blaming Decoud, the four missing ingots, Monygham, the Goulds, and "you fine people" of Sulaco. But all explanations fail: "'I die betrayed—betrayed by—' But he did not say by whom or by what he was dying betrayed" (559). In fact, Nostromo himself has betrayed the trust of his employers, Linda for Giselle, Giselle for the treasure, and his own self-respect for the undiminished adulation of Sulaco. His "idea"— his purpose of winning the trust and admiration a community bestows on its heroes—has been degraded in action to the deception and concealment of a coward. It is not his fear of the law but his commitment to the "idea" of himself as a hero that leaves him powerless to throw away popular esteem by confessing his secret. As with Lord Jim, his primary motivation remains a deep fear of shame when, according to Marlow, what is really significant is the question of moral guilt: Jim "made so much of his disgrace while it is the guilt alone that matters" (*Lord Jim*, chapter 16).

A final irony of the novel is that Nostromo dies without fully clearing his conscience, because Mrs. Gould refuses to let him reveal the location of the silver to her: "No one misses it now. Let it be lost for ever" (560). When realized in action, Emily's intended charity has the practical effect of denying the Catholic Nostromo the spiritual release he craves through confession. Mrs. Gould's ideal of compassion and charity, like the "ideas" of all the principal characters in *Nostromo*, brings a "terrible success" when actualized. Human fallibility and weakness, accidental circumstances, and the pressure of vast historical forces all seem to conspire to bring about the degradation of worthy ideals and the thwarting of moral purpose.

III. *The Failure of the Moral Idea in History*

Though the protagonists of *Nostromo* help to bring about their own dooms, their choices and actions are shaped, even forced, by uncontrollable political forces. Fredric Jameson speaks of a "disjunction between the movement of history and its enactment by individual subjects" as "*Nostromo's* ultimate narrative message." The acts of Decoud and Nostromo are alienated and stolen from them by the necessities of institutional history: "History uses their individual passions and values as its unwitting instruments for the construction of a new institutional space."[18] Conrad located his tale in a specific socio-political context: a Latin American republic dominated by European and American entrepreneurs. However, while Conrad's critique of capitalist imperialism's "religion of silver and iron" (71) is an important aspect of *Nostromo*, I think it constricts the fullest significance of the novel to interpret Nostromo, the "man of the people," primarily as the symbol of the tragedy of a social class.[19] Conrad's deepest design in *Nostromo* lies less in depicting the vicissitudes of any particular political movement than in showing the common tragic aspects of all of human history.

[18] Fredric Jameson, *The Political Unconscious: Narrative as a Socially Symbolic Act* (Ithaca: Cornell University Press, 1981), pp. 278–79.

[19] See Avrom Fleischman, *Conrad's Politics: Community and Anarchy in the Fiction of Joseph Conrad* (Baltimore: Johns Hopkins University Press, 1967), pp. 163–64: "Nostromo's career represents the history of an entire class, the proletariat—its enlistment and exploitation in the industrialization of the country, its entry into the separatist revolution (fighting for class interests not directly its own), its growth of self-consciousness and discovery of an independent political role, its temptation by the materialistic drives of capitalism, and its purgation by traditional idealists in its own camp."

One of the most deeply-rooted and pervasive beliefs of nineteenth-century thought, and especially of Victorian England, was that history showed "progress": that the development of civilization was leading to both material and moral improvement in the conditions of human life. In the last half of the nineteenth century this confidence about history was increasingly threatened by such diverse intellectual developments as the philosophical pessimism of Schopenhauer and Nietzsche, Darwin's theory of natural selection and evolution, and the growing recognition that industrial and technological changes led to greater rather than lesser social strains and conflicts on both the class and international levels. While a thorough study of these intellectual influences on Conrad is beyond the scope of this study, it is clear that *Nostromo* reveals the author's fundamental skepticism about the Victorian belief in "progress" in history.[20]

Conrad expresses his deep pessimism about the possibility of progress by setting the Sulaco Revolution in a broad historical context that demonstrates the futility and senselessness of political action. The structure of the novel—the confusing order in which events are presented, denying any sense of consecutive development or even rational connection—reflects a grotesque or absurd view of history's essential "causes." The bizarre origin of the novel's central conflict, the Monterist insurrection, lies in Pedrito Montero's light reading of romantic Napoleonic novels. "This was one of the immediate causes of the Monterist Revolution. This will appear less incredible by the reflection that the fundamental causes were the same as ever, rooted in the political immaturity of the people, in the indolence of the upper classes and the mental darkness of the lower" (387). Revolution succeeds revolution, one leader replaces another, in a pattern of perpetual but meaningless political upheaval. To Mrs. Gould, "the constant 'saving of the country'" resembles "a puerile and bloodthirsty game of murder and rapine played with terrible earnestness by depraved children" (49). The political outrages perpetrated by each new government make Costaguana's history seem "a struggle of lust between bands of devils let loose upon the land with sabres and uniforms and grandiloquent phrases" (88). The reader's overall sense of the meaning of events is best summarized by what Father Roman learns through "long experience of political atrocities": "The working of the usual public institutions presented itself to him most distinctly as a series of calamaties overtaking private individuals and flowing logically from

---

[20] See Ian Watt, *Conrad in the Nineteenth Century* (Berkeley: University of California Press, 1979), pp. 147–68 ("Kurtz and the Fate of Victorian Progress") and p. ix: In analyzing the intellectual influences on Conrad, "the difficulties arise not because Conrad was anomalously immune to the historical process, but because his inheritances from the past were so rich and diverse."

each other through hate, revenge, folly, and rapacity, as though they had been part of a divine dispensation" (399).

If the Sulaco revolution is only the latest in a long series of political convulsions, the future does not promise stability. When she hears that Antonia and Corbelán are plotting the invasion of Costaguana, Mrs. Gould can only wonder how persons who had taken part in the Sulaco Revolution can "forget its memory and its lesson" (507). Her words suggest the answer to the question of whether the new government brings progress to the land or not.[21] Material prosperity has been brought to Sulaco, but to protect "material interests" the new government resorts to measures just as coercive and corrupt, if somewhat subtler, than those used in the past. The situation is basically the same as it had been in the days of the Ribierist regime, when one could look back on the days when politics was comparatively "more vile, more base, more contemptible, and infinitely more manageable in the very outspoken cynicism of motives. It was more clearly a brazen-faced scramble for a constantly diminishing quantity of booty" (115–16). The essentially vicious and mercenary nature of politics remains unchanged in the new Sulaco; indeed, the recent cosmetic alterations in its appearance make its hazards all the more insidious. As Decoud puts it, in old times "the persistent barbarism of our native continent did not wear the black coats of politicians, but went about yelling, half-naked, with bows and arrows in its hands" (231).

The effect of *Nostromo*'s epic historical scope is to make the corruption and defeat of the individual protagonists seem more inevitable and less blameworthy. This helps the reader to pity the main characters rather than simply condemning them for compromising their moral ideals. In setting the tragedy of individual heroes within an epic scale, *Nostromo* recalls the *Iliad*.[22] In both works, the sense of the past and the

---

[21] Warren, "Great Mirage," p. 50, claims that the new Occidental Republic of Sulaco represents a moral improvement over the ghastly injustices of the old order: "There has been a civil war but the forces of 'progress'—i.e., the San Tomé mine and the capitalistic order—have won. And we must admit that the society at the end of the book is preferable to that at the beginning." Guerard, *Conrad the Novelist*, p. 177, disagrees: "The novel's own view of history is skeptical and disillusioned, which for us today must mean true." Guerard suggests (p. 197) that the new government is at best a lesser evil: "There would thus be a choice of evils. But surely one evil is replaced by another evil." Irving Howe, *Politics and the Novel* (New York: Avon Books, 1957), p. 108, tries to mediate this dispute by pointing out that the new order contains the seeds of future strife: "Both critics seem to me right: the civil war brings capitalism and capitalism will bring civil war, progress *has* come out of chaos but it is the kind of progress that is likely to end in chaos. Perhaps the central political point in *Nostromo* is that imperialism does indeed bring order, but a false order."

[22] E. M..Tillyard, *The Epic Strain in the English Novel* (London: Chatto & Windus, 1958), p. 167, mentions his "experience of constantly thinking of Homer when reading *Nostromo*," and discusses the novel's mixture of tragic and epic elements.

future, and of an entire society at war, enable the reader to see heroic action in its historical and social context, and to understand how admirable characters can fail partly because of impersonal forces beyond their control. The epic depiction of a whole society in conflict also shows how different virtues become irreconcilably opposed in certain circumstances. Just as the *Iliad* presents the mutual dependence and the tensions between the civic virtues of the ordered domestic life and the warrior's ferocious valor, so in *Nostromo* Conrad depicts the antagonism between idealism and skepticism, and the incompatibility of these equally essential moral qualities in certain extreme situations. And both *Nostromo* and the *Iliad* show the ways a society's encouragement of its heroes' sense of pride easily leads to vanity and self-esteem that can have disastrous repercussions for the entire community. Finally, the vast scope of the epic places the downfall of the tragic protagonists in the context of various other human fates. But in the case of Conrad's novel, the fate of every character is seen in the light of the general doom of human idealism and aspiration on both the personal and collective levels.

Conrad's essay "Autocracy and War" (1905), written just after *Nostromo*'s publication, articulates his view that the "idea" is inevitably degraded not only in the lives of individuals, but in the fates of political ideals. Referring to the distortion of the French Revolution's ideas of freedom and justice in Napoleon's reign, Conrad wrote: "It is the bitter fate of any idea to lose its royal form and power, to lose its 'virtue' the moment it descends from its solitary throne to work its will among the people. It is a king whose destiny is never to know the obedience of his subjects except at the cost of degradation." [23] This essay interprets the implications of Japan's defeat of Russia in terms of the development of nineteenth century European history. Conrad argues, much like *Nostromo*'s Dr. Monygham, that the peace of the world will only "be built on less perishable foundations than those of material interests."[24] With prophetic insight, Conrad expressed deep skepticism about whether the European nations would refrain from a great war. Quite as much as the protagonists of *Nostromo*, states crave the illusion of mastering destiny by decisive aggressive action:

> States, like most individuals, having but a feeble and imperfect consciousness of the worth and force of the inner life, the need of making their existence manifest to themselves is determined in the direction of physical activity. Action, in which is to be found the illusion of a mastered destiny, can alone satisfy our uneasy vanity and lay to rest the haunting fear of the

---

[23] Joseph Conrad, "Autocracy and War," in Conrad's *Notes on Life and Letters* (New York: Doubleday, 1924), p. 86. Tillyard, *Epic Strain*, pp. 160–63 and Baines, *Critical Biography*, pp. 312–13 and 318–20, point out connections between this essay and *Nostromo*.

[24] Conrad, "Autocracy and War," p. 107.

future. . . . Let us act lest we perish—is the cry. And the only form of action open to a State can be of no other than agressive nature.[25]

Conrad despised the use of moral slogans to justify every political maneuver, however scandalous. In *Nostromo*, Decoud refuses to call himself a "patriot," for "in connexion with the everlasting troubles of this unhappy country it was hopelessly besmirched; it had been the cry of dark barbarism, the cloak of lawlessness, of crimes, of rapacity, of simple thieving" (187). Later Gould declares: "The words one knows so well have a nightmarish meaning in this country. Liberty, democracy, patriotism, government—all of them have a flavor of folly and murder" (408). Like Razumov of *Under Western Eyes* and Winnie and Stevie Verloc in *The Secret Agent*, the characters in *Nostromo* find their fates settled by absurd but deadly struggles for political power. As his biographers have pointed out, Conrad's complex attitudes to politics have deep roots in his knowledge and experience of Polish history and his bitter memories of his father's futile efforts for Polish independence. The painful struggle to work through his feelings about these matters, as well as the confrontation with the implications of his own skepticism in his portrayal of Decoud, probably account for Conrad's sense of utter exhaustion on finishing *Nostromo*.[26]

If the exertions of individuals prove ineffectual and self-defeating in the context of Costaguana's capricious political contentions, human history itself seems condemned to meaninglessness when viewed against the indifference of nature. The "snowy dome of Higuerota" is mentioned dozens of times, always silently dominating the petty conflicts of humankind. Conrad often presents an event from the point of view of a distant and detached observer, thereby emphasizing the puny scale of human affairs. For example, one battle is seen from afar by old Giorgio Viola, who is inevitably associated with Higuerota:

> His eyes examined the plain curiously. Tall trails of dust subsided here and there. In a speckless sky the sun hung clear and blinding. Knots of men ran

[25] Ibid., pp. 108–9. Similarly, in his essay on "Anatole France," Conrad claimed that this author perceived the truth that "political institutions, whether contrived by the wisdom of the few or the ignorance of the many, are incapable of securing the happiness of mankind" (*Notes on Life and Letters*, p. 33).

[26] See the chapter on *Nostromo* in Karl's *Three Lives*, especially pp. 566–67: "The lot of the Costaguanera was based on Conrad's knowledge of Poland's fortunes. . . . Decoud was grappling with profound issues: the nature of political commitment, the measurement of ideals against personal gain, the kind of reward one expects from the investment of time and energy. For Conrad, it was a testing out of Apollo Korzeniowski's very being and of his own reaction to his father's career. . . . The effort required to investigate two points of view for which there could be no apparent resolution was bound to bring him down; he had, for the sake of his imagination, to follow through the very concepts he wished, as a man, to evade."

headlong; others made a stand; and the irregular rattle of firearms came rippling to his ears in the fiery, still air. Single figures on foot raced desperately. Horsemen galloped towards each other, wheeled round together, separated at speed. Giorgio saw one fall, rider and horse disappearing as if they had galloped into a chasm, and the movements of the animated scene were like the passages of a violent game played upon the plain by dwarfs mounted and on foot, yelling with tiny throats, under the mountain that seemed a colossal embodiment of silence. Never before had Giorgio seen this bit of plain so full of active life. (26–27)

Conrad's distinctive narrative style and vision of life can be seen in these vivid contrasts between the agitated, desperate struggles of humans and the vast, indifferent world of nature; between the maneuvers of a skilled horseman and his sudden disappearance as if into a chasm; between a scene bursting with the most "active life" and its setting in what is only a "bit of plain."

Conrad brilliantly depicts the psychological effects of the impenetrable and inhospitable Golfo Placido as it isolates Decoud and Nostromo from their fellows and helps bring about their doom. While these characters become alienated from the human community partly through their own actions, the silent, indifferent world of nature impresses on the human psyche a sense of its aloneness and lostness in the universe. Alienation results as much from a person's being placed in such a natural setting as from his acts. Decoud's despairing suicide is prompted not only by his own weakness, but by a harrowing experience of eleven days in a "glory of merciless solitude" (500). When he kills himself, his body "disappeared without a trace, swallowed up in the immense indifference of things" (501). The efforts and purposes of individual humans—and even history itself— seem but an ephemeral appearance in this implacable natural world. If a God created such a world, He must be, in Gould's words, "very far away, . . . as they say in this country, God is very high above" (206). Human agents are quite alone in the cosmos, and awareness of this fact destroys confidence in the meaningfulness of the self's actions and in the value of life itself. Those characters who have the strength of mind to recognize their alienated position in the world are threatened by what Monygham calls "the crushing, paralyzing sense of human littleness" (433). And when individuals become conscious of the tragic defeat of their hopes, they are rarely able to overcome a sense of utter futility.

In this regard, *Nostromo* is quite unlike James's *The Princess Casamassima*. I argued earlier that Hyacinth's rich consciousness enables him to affirm the goodness and beauty of life even after he decides to kill himself, and referred to some of James's non-fictional writings which express the conviction that increases in human consciousness may enable individuals to survive and transcend experiences of defeat and despair. The contrast with Conrad's view of consciousness could not be more striking. For Conrad, it is human consciousness that makes life tragic:

What makes mankind tragic is not that they are the victims of nature, it is that they are conscious of it. To be part of the animal kingdom under the conditions of this earth is very well,—but as soon as you know of your slavery, the pain, the anger, the strife,—the tragedy begins. We can't return to nature, since we can't change our place in it. . . . There is no morality, no knowledge and no hope: there is only the consciousness of ourselves which drives us about a world that, whether seen in a convex or a concave mirror, is always but a vain and floating appearance.[27]

Conrad wrote to Cunninghame Graham of the probable effect of greater consciousness on Singleton, the simple heroic sailor of *The Nigger of the "Narcissus"*: "Would you seriously wish to tell such a man 'Know thyself! Understand that you are nothing, less than a shadow, more insignificant than a drop of water in the ocean, more fleeting than the illusion of a dream?' Would you?"[28]

In *Nostromo*, the birth of self-consciousness coincides with the beginning of Nostromo's corruption; before his awakening the Capataz was "simple and great" much like Singleton. Decoud's penetrating powers of mind lead to his mental anguish and suicide. Charles and Emily Gould and Monygham all experience paralyzing feelings of futility and absurdity. The contrast between their fates and Hyacinth's reveals a radical difference between James's and Conrad's attitudes towards human consciousness. Generalizing from other novels as well as *Princess* and *Nostromo*, Elsa Nettels has finely put the contrast this way:

The life of the imagination sustains James's characters and gives value to their lives; in Conrad's novels thought often robs characters of the grounds on which they can justify action and vitiates the will to live. At best, awareness is intelligence which enables characters like Monygham and Mrs. Gould and Marlow to understand the forces against which men struggle and to save themselves from self-deceiving optimism. . . . Whereas the source of greatest anguish for James's characters is the sense of deprivation, the fear that they have failed or will fail to live fully, the deepest anguish suffered by Conrad's characters is the blighting conviction that effort is futile, the goals of action illusory. James's characters are enlightened and strengthened by tragic recognition; in contrast Conrad's characters, like Monygham and Gould, merely see more clearly the futility of struggle, the certainty of pain, and the inevitability of failure.[29]

[27] Conrad to Cunninghame Graham, January 31, 1898, in *Joseph Conrad on Fiction*, p. 14.

[28] Conrad to Graham, December 14, 1897, in *Conrad on Fiction*, pp. 13–14. One must be cautious in quoting Conrad's letters; he can be deeply pessimistic or, more rarely, rather cheerfully confident about life depending on his moods and the character of his correspondent. Critics have often quoted Conrad's letters to Graham as the key to Conrad's basic view of life. Graham, to whom Conrad wrote his bleakest letters, was an optimistic reforming socialist; Conrad thought Graham did not sufficiently recognize the intractability and brutality of human nature.

[29] Elsa Nettels, *James and Conrad* (Athens, GA: University of Georgia Press, 1977), pp. 234–35.

While for James the mind's imaginative powers often help characters to triumph over outward defeat, Conrad emphasizes the corrosive and destructive effects of human consciousness and reflection, even when characters succeed in their projects. Whereas in *The Princess Casamassima* James presents Hyacinth's tragic situation without stressing its broader implications, Conrad's narrative generalizations emphasize the universal defeat of human consciousness in history. Conrad is what Warren calls a "philosophical novelist": "one for whom the documentation of the world is constantly striving to rise to the level of generalization about values, for whom the image strives to rise to symbol, for whom images always fall into a dialectical configuration, for whom the urgency of experience, no matter how vividly and strongly experience may enchant, is the urgency to know the meaning of experience."[30] In *Nostromo*, Conrad continually emphasizes the general frustration in history of the moral projects of both idealistic and skeptical characters. Furthermore, the recognition that this fate is universal brings not a sense of release from the loneliness of one's personal ordeal, but rather increased despair and mental anguish. Despite the bleakness of this vision, Conrad thought that moral realism depended on frank recognition of the tremendous dangers to human virtue posed by an incomprehensible history and an indifferent universe. Both the form of Conrad's *Nostromo* and his letters and essays, then, reveal a deep ambivalence about what a more complex consciousness does for human existence, and a radical skepticism about the possibility of human happiness in the world.

Critics have long puzzled over how to reconcile Conrad's expressions of extreme skepticism with other statements that assert the need for acceptance of "a few simple ideas": "Those who read me know my conviction that the world, the temporal world, rests on a few very simple ideas; so simple that they must be as old as the hills. It rests notably, among others, on the idea of Fidelity."[31] Too often critics have simplified Conrad's moral vision in trying to resolve elements which are, in fact, in essential discord. Critics have most frequently misrepresented Conrad's greatest works by finding in them only unrelieved skepticism and a vision of despair at the futility of all human effort.[32] The less common view of Conrad as

---

[30] Warren, "Great Mirage," p. 58.

[31] Joseph Conrad, "A Familiar Preface" (1912), in *Joseph Conrad on Fiction*, p. 124.

[32] This view of Conrad has been characteristic of the "achievement and decline" group of critics, who see the poor quality of Conrad's later work as attributable to the displacement of his pessimistic outlook by naive moralization. Douglas Hewitt, *Conrad: A Reassessment* (Cambridge: Bowes & Bowes, 1952), pp. 130–31, first argued this influential view: in his best works, Conrad "is intensely and continuously aware of the existence of moral and spiritual values, yet every quality, every virtue, every position in which he might hope to rest in security, is at once undermined; the 'impenetrable darkness' covers the world."

endorsing traditional ideals or the "work-ethic" or "job-sense" of the unreflective sailor is just as misleading.[33] In effect, these two interpretations
make *either* skepticism or idealism into a self-sufficient virtue at the heart
of Conrad's moral vision. However, *Nostromo* shows the indispensability
of both of these kinds of virtue. It dramatizes what Warren calls "the cost of
awareness and the difficulty of virtue."[34] The "cost of awareness" is the
corrosive power of skepticism, which sees the truth about man's fragile
position in the cosmos and vitiates a person's ability to act confidently in
the world. The "difficulty of virtue" involves all the hazards to idealism
analyzed above. I have argued that Conrad shows the need for two virtues,
skepticism and commitment to an "idea," a moral purpose or principle that
brings the individual into community with others. Tragedy arises because
these two virtues seem inimical in moral experience. For individuals can
only act under the "illusion" that action will effectively express their idealistic intentions, but skepticism undermines moral self-confidence, trust
in others, and single-minded commitment to action. Furthermore, the
pragmatic contingencies of successful public action seem inevitably to
lead to compromise and the moral degradation of the idea that motivated the action in the first place. The novel can hardly be said simply
to endorse one virtue, or even two virtues, as an answer to the human
predicament. The central imaginative thrust of *Nostromo*'s tragic vision
lies in the depiction of all the dangers to skepticism and idealism, both of
which are indispensable for meaningful action and yet are extremely
difficult to reconcile both with each other and with the conditions
required for action to be successful.

Given all the dangers to virtue analyzed in the previous section, and
the corrosive effects on human initiative of an individual's consciousness
of history's absurdity, it might seem that *Nostromo* would fail to be

[33] Because he interprets the novel as an epic, Tillyard, *Epic Strain*, p. 166, claims *Nostromo* reflects "the serene security of Conrad's beliefs in his ideals. He can talk of Justice
and Concord without affectation and sentimentality and with great conviction."

[34] Warren, "Great Mirage," p. 48. An equally penetrating and concise interpretation of
Conrad's central moral vision is Ian Watt's "Joseph Conrad: Alienation and Commitment,"
in *The English Mind: Studies in the English Moralists*, ed. by Hugh Sykes Davies and
George Watson (Cambridge: Cambridge University Press, 1964). Watt sees in Conrad's
work an early exploration of the condition of alienation that has fascinated such classic
modern writers as Joyce, Pound, Lawrence, and Eliot. But unlike these later writers, Conrad also tried to resist the temptation to simply withdraw from society, and to equate
alienation with mature individuality. Conrad dramatized the struggle to acknowledge
alienation but move beyond it to meaningful commitment: "The dominating question in
Conrad: alienation, yes, but how do we get out of it?" (p. 272). Watt's *Conrad in the
Nineteenth Century*, p. 167, compares critical responses to Conrad and to Freud: "The
general modern tendency has been to overlook this [ethical] aspect of Conrad and Freud
in favor of the more unsettling and nihilistic side of their vision; in effect, both of them
have been attacked or praised more for what they saw than for how they judged it; their
warnings against the truths they revealed have been overlooked."

tragic. Where every human action is inevitably defeated, a character's fate can hardly arouse our hope or fear or compassion. Yet this is not my own sense of the novel. The central characters are not simply struck down mechanically. The fates of the protagonists are various, and their own contributions to their destinies intricately meshed with the workings of coincidence. The novel portrays a broad scope of degrees of self-deception and self-interest in the pursuit of an idea, ranging from the "perfect egoism" of Nostromo's heroism to Monygham's "imaginative exaggeration of a correct feeling" (375). And the characters do not disappear into the same black abyss. Dr. Monygham, in fact, undergoes a striking rehabilitation, as "marked inwardly by the almost complete disappearance from his dreams of Father Beron" (508). Though all the other protagonists undergo a moral defeat, their sufferings are caused by and convincingly "fit" the strengths and weaknesses of their own characters.

Furthermore, the novel shows that idealism and skepticism do not absolutely preclude each other; they may be joined in an uneasy union. Though this possibility is seen to be extremely difficult to achieve, it is nonetheless the only adequate "way to be" in the Conradian world. Conrad has intellectual sympathy for a skeptic like Decoud, but the fate of this cynical observer of others' follies reveals the necessity for enduring moral purpose and commitment to others. Conrad plainly admires simple warriors and seasoned men of action like Barrios, Roman, or Mitchell, but he shows that it is luck and their lack of intelligence or imagination that save these men from doubt or despair. Their unswerving commitment to the immediate job at hand is praiseworthy, but it hardly represents the mature moral wisdom Conrad sought. It is in the characters of Monygham and Emily Gould that Conrad presents the possibility of a tentative alliance of the virtues of idealism and skepticism. Emily Gould has a far broader and deeper vision of human solidarity than does the doctor, or indeed anyone else in the novel. And though one hesitates to call her a skeptic, she is the one with the insight and courage to recognize the dark truth that "there was something inherent in the necessities of successful action which carried with it the moral degradation of the idea" (521). In Monygham's character, by contrast, skepticism is the dominant virtue, while his idealism is quite limited in scope. Though his "idea" is so narrowly focused on a single human life as to make him egregiously indifferent to Hirsch's death, Monygham overcomes his deep skepticism about human illusions enough to risk his life for Mrs. Gould and finally to achieve a partial and hesitant reintegration into the ongoing community life of Sulaco.

The moral center of the novel, indeed of Conrad's most enduring and significant work, lies in his depiction of the difficult struggle to combine skeptical intelligence with commitment to an idea—and the further attempt to realize the idea in concrete actions. His profundity as a tragic novelist in *Nostromo* lies in his probing analysis of the terrible dangers to this conception of human virtue as individuals commit themselves to the certain compromises and the uncertain consequences of action in history.

5

"Making Good Out of Bad"
In *All The King's Men*

Two styles of moral virtue conflict in Robert Penn Warren's *All the King's Men*: the ideal of "being good," or personal integrity, and Willie Stark's goal of "making good out of bad" at the cost of "dirty hands." The first part of this essay analyzes Warren's presentation of the tragic conflict between these two styles of virtue, or moral goodness. The second section explores the political and religious roots and the cultural preconditions of Willie's ideal of "making good out of bad." Finally, Jack Burden's regeneration is interpreted in terms of his understanding of the tragic limitations of the two styles of moral virtue.

I. *Cousin Willie and the Boss*

The structure of *All the King's Men* follows the parallel development of two primary characters: Willie Stark, the governor of a Southern state during the 1930s, and Jack Burden, Willie's friend and assistant, who narrates their stories. The novel involves frequent time shifts, as Jack's wandering memories and reflections focus on different stages of his own life and Willie's political career. In the first chapter, two central images of Willie Stark are strikingly contrasted: the "Cousin Willie" that Jack first meets in 1922 and "the Boss" at the height of his power as governor in 1936.

The moral status of Willie's conduct and character as "the Boss" is highly problematic. Often the reader experiences a sharp conflict between sympathy for and repulsion from the figure of the Boss. Most readers will approve of Willie's progressive social programs: building schools, roads, and hospitals, redistributing the wealth more equitably, and throwing out corrupt bureaucrats who dominated the state government for decades. But we find abhorrent Willie's complete lack of scruple or inhibition in devising political tactics, especially his resorting to blackmail, bribery, and intimidation to bully his projects through the state legislature. Many of Willie's personal qualities recall the protagonists of Elizabethan revenge tragedy: his tremendous reserves of energy and feverish determination, the sardonic wit often employed in humiliating friends and enemies alike, and the commanding, somewhat melodramatic presence that inspires and awes his supporters. Willie resembles Macbeth and Lear in his cynical view of the basic needs of human nature, his frequent analogizing of man to various animals, and his obsession with the absolute loyalty of his followers.

Willie's chief moral aspiration is his yearning to "make good out of bad." The central dramatic conflict of *All the King's Men* arises when Willie's attempt to make good out of bad in politics clashes with a radically differing ethical perspective. Willie believes that his ideal of creating good justifies the use of any means. Adam Stanton, Judge Irwin, and several other characters believe that certain acts are intrinsically right or wrong, and that, as a matter of conscience, such acts should not be used as means to a supposedly good end. The conflict between these two contrasting moral styles is introduced in the first chapter in an encounter between Willie and Judge Irwin. When Willie learns that Irwin has endorsed another man for the Senate instead of Willie's candidate, Jack and Willie make a midnight call on the Judge to try to persuade to change his mind. Irwin refused to endorse Willie's candidate, Masters, because Irwin had learned of some unspecified crime or misconduct in Masters' past; as Willie surmises, "somebody dug up some dirt" on Masters. This is the first appearance of the primary symbol of "dirt," which is associated with moral evil and with the truth about the past. Willie defends Masters by claiming that dirt is not inherently good or bad, but becomes so by the use to which it is put: "There ain't a thing but dirt on this green God's globe except what's under water and that's dirt too. . . . It all depends on what you do with the dirt" (50).[1] Willie claims that he can "deliver" or control Masters, and that he could easily dig up some dirt on the other candidate, Callahan. But the issue has become a matter of conscience for Irwin, who refuses to switch his endorsement. On the drive back to the capitol, Willie orders Jack to "find something" from the past with which to put pressure on Irwin. Jack wonders whether in fact there may not be any "dirt" in Irwin's past to dig up. But Willie claims with finality that "there is always something" and asserts a fundamental belief about human nature in phrases that Jack remembers several times during the novel: "Man is conceived in sin and born in corruption and he passeth from the stink of the didie to the stench of the shroud. There is always something" (54). Willie avows that there is evil in any person's history, and that he is justified in using this dirt politically to create good, even if to do so dirties his own hands. This understanding of political ethics is rejected by Irwin, and later by Hugh Miller and Adam Stanton, all of whom refuse to compromise their personal integrity for the sake of some proposed good end.

As the novel develops, Willie's political and moral style of "making

---

[1] *All the King's Men* (New York: Harcourt, Brace & World, 1946). All references are to this edition and are cited parenthetically in the text.

good out of bad" is contrasted with Dr. Adam Stanton's ethical idealism and incorruptible integrity. Willie wants Adam to be the director of a new hospital. Jack is assigned the task of persuading Adam that his integrity and personal purity will not be contaminated by association with Stark. Jack sees Adam as "a romantic, and he has a picture of the world in his head, and when the world doesn't conform in any respect to the picture, he wants to throw the world away" (262). As Jack tells Anne Stanton, Adam's view of morality is at once too romantic and too scientifically precise to allow for the ironies and ambiguities of good and evil in history. But Adam agrees to work with Willie when a "history lesson" changes his picture of the world. The history lesson is a discovery Jack made in the course of his research on Judge Irwin. Adam's father, a former governor of the state, had protected his friend Irwin when the latter had broken the law. Adam is shocked when he learns of his father's secret crime, and angrily agrees to take the hospital job.

When Adam and Willie first meet, a deep-rooted antagonism between them surfaces immediately. Each man feels the need to defend his basic response to evil and his own ideal of virtue. Willie's reasoning receives far more articulation in the text than Adam's. The rationale behind his moral style emerges when he claims that former Attorney General Hugh Miller resigned because he was afraid to "get his hands dirty" in order to make goodness:

> He resigned because he wanted to keep his little hands clean. He wanted the bricks but he just didn't know somebody had to paddle in the mud to make 'em. He was like somebody that just loves beefsteak but just can't bear to go to a slaughter pen because there are some bad, rough men down there who aren't animal lovers and who ought to be reported to the S.P.C.A. Well, he resigned . . . just because he inherited a little money and the name Miller he thought you could have everything. Yeah, and he wanted the one last damned thing you can't inherit. And you know what it is? . . . Goodness. Yeah, just plain simple goodness. Well you can't inherit that from anybody. You got to make it, Doc. If you want it. And you got to make it out of badness. Badness. And you know why, Doc? . . . Because there isn't anything else to make it out of. (272)

Willie insists he has to use badness to make good, even at the price of his moral integrity. In contrast, Adam's deepest impulse when confronted with "dirt" is to protect his integrity and purity: he doesn't want to get his hands soiled. But Adam is not just concerned with his own integrity. He sees, as he tells Jack, that something cannot be "made good" apart from its context: "A thing does not grow except in its proper climate, and you know what kind of climate that man creates" (252).

Adam and Willie each tend to exaggerate the self-sufficiency of their own approach to "making good" and to caricature the other's position. To Adam, Willie's assertion that "you have to get your hands dirty" only rationalizes his political crimes. To Willie, Adam's preoccupation with the morality of his personal actions is selfishly narrow and ignores the ambiguity of politics. He sarcastically assures Stanton, "I'll keep your little mitts clean. I'll keep you clean all over, Doc. I'll put you in that beautiful, antiseptic, sterile, six-million-dollar hospital, and wrap you in cellophane, untouched by human hands" (275). Hegel's theory of tragedy fits well the "conflict of ethical claims" between Willie and Adam: their confrontation has a moral structure similar to the collision between Creon and Antigone. Both Adam and Willie express crucial moral insights, but their ethical stances become stubbornly one-sided and inflexible when asserted against each other.

The conflict between these two antagonistic moral positions produces not only the external clash between Willie and other characters; it is the primary cause of Willie's internal self-division, the split between Cousin Willie and the Boss. Even after Willie stoops to the basest means of maintaining his power, he retains an idealistic desire to "make good" according to a standard much like Adam Stanton's. This desire prompts Willie's decision, immediately after Hugh Miller's resignation, to build a huge hospital solely out of "good." It reveals his need to placate a guilty conscience, and to appease nagging doubts and regrets about his political misconduct. The hospital project functions as Willie's atonement for his corruption.

It is Willie's ideal of keeping the hospital free of corruption and graft that eventually leads to his tragic error and downfall. His yearning to create one purely good action draws him to seek Adam Stanton as the director of the hospital. And this ideal drives him to oppose letting his dissolute and venal Lieutenant Governor, Tiny Duffy, sell the contract to build the hospital to Tiny's old crony Gummy Larson. Jack notices the inconsistency between Willie's theory that the good can only be made from the bad and Willie's obsession with keeping Tiny from becoming involved in the hospital deal: "Now if Willie Stark believed that you always had to make the good out of the bad, why did he get so excited when Tiny just wanted to make a logical little deal with the hospital contract? Why did he get so heated up just because Tiny's brand of Bad might get mixed up in the raw material from which he was going to make some Good?" (276). The explanation for this puzzling and inconsistent behavior lies in the nature of Willie's relationship to Tiny. The Boss employs an obvious crook because he needs to abuse the part of himself which he despises for having been corrupted. With part of his being, Willie desperately wants to be as morally innocent as Adam Stanton. Willie's desire to keep the hospital "pure" and his contempt for the corrupted part of himself, then, reveal the continuing conflict between Cousin Willie and the Boss.

Despite his intention to keep the hospital "clean," Willie is forced to make a deal with Gummy Larson to protect the reputation of Willie's son Tom. In the complicated chain of events in the ninth chapter of *All the King's Men*, Tom suffers a crippling accident in a football game because Willie allowed him to break training and "have some fun," as Willie never did. This shattering event triggers an abrupt change in Willie, who determines to reform. His first act is to cancel the hospital contract with Larson, telling Jack, "you got to start somewhere" (387). This decision is the tragic error that precipitates Willie's death. There is a deep irony in the fact that it is Willie's only attempt to do good in something like Adam Stanton's terms—that is, without permitting any admixture of evil—that brings about his destruction. According to his own view of the nature of humankind, Willie should have known such an effort to be futile. It is too late for the Boss to reform, to purge himself and his projects of evil. Willie cannot escape the web of corruption he has created. Tiny Duffy, bitter that Willie canceled the deal from which Tiny would have received a fat kickback, secretly informs Adam Stanton that Willie is having an affair with Adam's sister Anne, and that this is the reason Willie hired Adam. Adam is outraged at the insinuation that he profited from playing "pimp to his sister's whore" (413). In a hallway of the state capitol, Adam assassinates Willie Stark and is himself shot down by Willie's bodyguard.

Willie and Adam thus switch roles at the climax of the novel, each adopting for a moment the moral position of the other. Willie refuses any moral compromise in choosing the means to build the hospital, wanting to keep out any "dirt" that would contaminate it. Adam resorts to the means of murder in order to uphold his ideal of family and personal honor. A radical inconsistency in each man wrecks their ill-fated attempt to work together for good. In the denouement of the novel, Jack Burden tries to understand the limitations of each man's virtue, and of Judge Irwin's, and to assert the need for a balance or synthesis of their inimical kinds of moral goodness. But before we turn to Jack's reflections on the tragedy of Willie and Adam, and to Warren's presentation of Jack's growth as a character, let us interpret some of the cultural sources of Willie's moral perspective and political vision. Thus we inquire into the cultural preconditions that make possible his ideal of virtue as "making good out of bad."

II. *The Cultural Roots of Willie's Moral Perspective*

All the King's Men was originally inspired partly by the career of Governor Huey Long of Louisiana. The ascendency of a figure like Long or Willie Stark is made possible by certain features of mass *democratic politics*, and by the nature of Willie's appeal to his constituency, "the tongue-tied population of honest men" (68). Willie fulfills the common man's longing for a hero who embodies his aspirations for a better life, rising above the fears and inarticulateness of the average citizen. Willie's campaign slogan—"My study is the heart of the people" (8)—stresses his humble background and his knowledge of the needs of the common man. Throughout his political career, Willie genuinely desires to serve the impoverished folk of his state. He wants one thing above all: social justice. Initially, Willie's speeches are full of tax formulas and figures, and he puts his audience to sleep. But he soon learns how to manipulate a crowd's emotions as a demogogue. He arouses their passions with inflammatory rhetoric, directing their anger against his chief political opponents, the wealthy families and businesses that have long controlled the state. Willie's charismatic power, oratorical skills, and knowledge of human emotions are dramatized in a number of striking crowd scenes. He appeals at once to several basic passions, catering at once to the multitude's latent religious fervor and to its basest, most bloodthirsty instincts of revenge.

Willie appeals to the crowd's sense of justice at the same time that he flatters its smug self-righteousness. His political style depends on an attitude that Warren has called "Common Man-ism." This perversion of democracy expresses the defensiveness and resentment felt by the average, the common, the normal person for superiority or excellence of achievement. The voice of Common Man-ism was "a doctrine of complacency" that "by implication at least, denied that democracy should mean the opportunity—and the responsibility—for the development of excellence, and uttered a doctrine carrying at its core the appalling convictions that the undeveloped, the unaspiring, the frustrated, the un-responsible, is somehow mystically superior to the excellent, and that a refusal of effort toward excellence is a gesture of moral worth."[2] Besides the element of honest candor, there is a strong element of "Common Man-ism" in Willie's appeal to "'friends, red-necks, suckers, and fellow hicks. . . . In the quiet the crowd would be restless and resentful under these words, the words they knew people called them but the words nobody ever got up and called them to their face" (101). Willie arouses for the first time the belief of the common folk in their own worth. But his power also depends on his exciting and enlisting their animosity and desire for revenge against the state's established powers. The "king's men" who work for Willie function as "double" figures to show the psychological process by which a charismatic leader holds sway over his followers. According to Warren, Willie's "power was based on the fact that somehow he could vicariously fulfill some secret needs of the people about him."[3] Willie's supporters all see in him

---

[2] Warren, "Knowledge and the Image of Man," in *The Merrill Studies in "All the King's Men,"* ed. James Light (Columbus: Charles Merrill Publishing Co., 1971), p. 22.

[3] Warren, "Introduction to the Modern Library Edition of *All the King's Men,"* in *Twentieth Century Interpretations of "All the King's Men,"* ed. Robert H. Chambers (Englewood Cliffs: Prentice-Hall, Inc., 1977), p. 93.

something that they lack, and identify themselves vicariously with his successes.

Yet as Willie fulfills the needs of those around him, he discovers, "more and more, his own emptiness and his own alienation."[4] The "king," as much as his men, suffers from a sense of self-division and incompleteness. Though he appears to others as a fully integrated and self-sufficient individual, Willie is internally split by the struggle between Cousin Willie and the Boss. And he is tormented by an inability to understand or express what it is that he hopes to achieve. For all his energy and skill at improvising, Willie is often depicted as uncertain or inarticulate about his basic goals. Adam Stanton and Judge Irwin attract him because their integrity provides a moral substance and structure he lacks; their firm adherence to a moral code compensates for his own hollowness. Willie's moral confusion produces the inconsistencies, the abrupt changes, and the desperate attempt to create pure goodness that brings about his downfall. In sum, Warren explores the psychological processes in both a political leader and his followers that lead to the demagogic perversion of democracy. Such an interpretation of the novel explains Warren's reference to the name Willie Stark bore in the original verse play from which the novel grew: "Talos." Talos is the "name of the brutal, blankeyed, 'iron groom' of Spenser's *Faerie Queene*, the pitiless servant of the knight of justice. . . . In other words, Talos is the kind of doom that democracy may invite upon itself."[5] Willie Stark's rise and fall dramatize an inherent danger in the democratic political process.

"Long was but one of the figures that stood in the shadows of imagination behind Willie Stark. Another one of that company was the scholarly and benign figure of William James."[6] Warren's brief allusion to James points to one of the main elements shaping Willie's moral outlook: the philosophy of *pragmatism*. Pragmatism tends to focus on the best means of achieving some end rather than on first principles or fixed assumptions. The pragmatist judges the truth of a belief by its practical consequences. One advantage of Willie's pragmatic orientation is his flexibility and ingenuity in responding to problems. Willie cannot

[4] Ibid., p. 94.

[5] Ibid., p. 97. Warren's continuing interest in how internal self-division threatens democracy can be seen in his *Democracy and Poetry* (Cambridge: Harvard University Press, 1975). There he argues that democracy is only possible in a society of fully individuated selves, and that one reason we should value poetry is its diagnostic and therapeutic role in providing images of the self in disintegration and in "significant unity."

[6] Warren, "Introduction," in *Twentieth Century Interpretations*, ed. Chambers, p. 97. Cushing Strout, in *"All the King's Men* and the Shadow of William James," *Southern Review*, n. s. 6 (1970), 920–34, discusses some of the general influences of James's philosophy on Warren's novel, but focuses not on Willie, but on Jack Burden's suffering as a "sick soul" and his moral rebirth.

explain facts, but he can see things for what they are. "There ain't any explanations," he claims, "all you can do is point at the nature of things" (204). However, Willie's readiness to improvise and act without precedent brings conflict with traditional legal and moral codes. In his argument with Hugh Miller, Willie claims that, because the law always lags behind the needs of the times, it sometimes has to be disregarded in order to meet the demands of developing human societies.

Willie's first meeting with Adam Stanton elicits a lengthy articulation of his pragmatic justification for political and moral compromises. He claims that the good is something "you just make up as you go along":

> What the hell else you think folks been doing for a million years, Doc? When your great-great grandpappy climbed down out of the tree, he didn't have any more notion of good or bad, or right and wrong, than the hoot owl that stayed up in the tree. Well, he climbed down and he began to make Good up as he went along. He made up what he needed to do business, Doc. And what he made up and got everybody to mirate on as good and right was always just a couple of jumps behind what he needed to do business on. That's why things change, Doc. Because what folks claim is right is always just a couple of jumps short of what they need to do business. (273)

Willie asserts that notions of right have to be adjusted to changing values, giving the example of society's gradual acceptance of divorce. His argument is partly convincing: law is created to serve human needs rather than vice-versa. But Willie's pragmatic method leads by an irresistable logic to the justification of terrible evils. He identifies "human need" with his administration's policies, and forsakes all moral continuity and consistency in a short-sighted focus on the most expedient means to these political goals. It is not surprising that while writing *All the King's Men*, Warren was "deep in Machiavelli."[7] Many of Willie's techniques might have been suggested by the author of *The Prince*. Willie would rather "bust a man than buy him," for he thinks he can depend more surely on a man's fear of him than on his continued gratitude: "Bust 'em and they'll stay busted, but buy 'em and you can't tell how long they'll stay bought" (246).

Willie's denial of any enduring standards leads inevitably to moral guilt. He treats persons as animals or mere objects, and their actions as only means to an end. Politics becomes "just a question of who has got his front feet in the trough when slopping time comes" (417). Half facetiously, but revealing his underlying attitude to moral issues, Willie doubts whether "the category of guilt and innocence can be said to have any relevance to something like Byram B. White": "My God, you talk like Byram was human! He's a thing! You don't prosecute an adding machine if the spring goes bust and makes a mistake. You fix it. Well, I fixed Byram"

---

[7] Warren, "Introduction," in *Twentieth Century Interpretations*, ed. Chambers, p. 94.

(144). Individuals are only cogs to be used in Willie Stark's political machine. Willie's guilt should be seen in the light of Warren's interpretation of the guilt of the Ancient Mariner and his companions, who make man's "convenience the measure of an act. . . . They judge the moral content of an act by its consequence."[8]

In comparison with Adam and Irwin, Willie appears as an unbridled violator of tradition and law, an immoral practitioner of the most unscrupulous politics. The strengths of Willie's version of pragmatism need to be reasserted before we leave this issue. Warren places Willie in a mediating position between unbending idealists like Adam or Hugh Miller, who seem ineffectual or irrelevant to the realities of politics, and corrupt figures like Tiny Duffy, Byram White, or Macmurfee. Willie's pragmatism has its moral perils, but it is realistic about the material necessities of human life, and it recognizes the place of negotiation and flexibility in politics. Like the pragmatist, the skillful politician must be a mediator, one who enables conflicting parties to come to a working compromise. Here lies the deeper significance of the motifs linking Willie's career to Abraham Lincoln's. In his interpretation of the American Civil War, Warren interprets pragmatism as an outgrowth of the conflict between two absolutistic ways of thinking: the "legalism" of the South's defense of states' rights and the "higher law" of the Abolitionists of the North. He sees Lincoln as the mediator between a party insisting on strict legality and a party wanting to act according to an uncompromising moral position.[9] Willie's ability to mediate between different positions, as well as his vision of social justice, resemble Lincoln's wisdom about human nature and his creative political imagination. In its promise, though not in its fulfillment, Willie's pragmatic outlook recalls that of Abraham Lincoln.

Certain peculiarly American, and specifically *Southern*, conflicts of value shape Willie Stark's life and death. While Warren's experiences in the Agrarian and Fugitive movements of the 1920s and 1930s developed his skepticism about modern science and material progress, he has not

[8] Warren, "A Poem of Pure Imagination: An Experiment in Reading," in *Selected Essays by Robert Penn Warren* (New York: Random House, 1966), p. 232. This long essay on Coleridge's "Rime of the Ancient Mariner" was composed in 1945–46, while Warren was working on *All the King's Men*. There are a number of parallels between the novel and the essay: the theme of a "crime against nature" (p. 229); Warren's ideas about guilt and *hamartia* (pp. 227–28); and his view of the spiritual problem of modern man as "divided purpose and lack of conviction" (p. 252). For studies of other connections between these two works, see James Justus, "The Mariner and Robert Penn Warren," *Texas Studies in Literature and Language* 8 (1966), 117–28; and Christopher Katope, "Robert Penn Warren's *All the King's Men*: A Novel of 'Pure Imagination,'" *Texas Studies in Literature and Language* 12 (1970), 493–510.

[9] Warren, *The Legacy of the Civil War: Meditations on the Centennial* (New York: Random House, 1961), pp. 17–18.

simply called for a return to traditional Southern values.[10] He has been concerned to examine critically the South's moral heritage, and to expose the hollowness of self-congratulatory clichés. Warren sees a recurring moral conflict in Southern history in the struggle between normless ambition and the decaying values of the status quo. Willie is driven by ambition, the tragic crime that Warren associates with a young society seeking escape from the constraints of traditional morality. An essay on Faulkner aptly describes Willie's conflict with established Southern values: "Ambition is the most constant tragic crime, and ambition is the attitude special to an open society; all villains are rationalists and appeal to 'nature' beyond traditional morality for justification, and rationalism is, in the sense implied here, the attitude special to the rise of a secular and scientific order before a new morality can be formulated."[11]

In *All the King's Men*, an ambitious young politician faces hostility from established power. The weakening authority of past standards of morality is represented in the novel by the decadent aristocratic community at Burden's Landing. Willie's rise to power threatens the Stanton, Irwin, and Burden families, who see Willie as an unscrupulous despoiler of inherited values. In particular, Willie violates the ideal of the chivalrous Southern gentleman bound by a code of honor and a sense of *noblesse oblige*. Jack has very mixed feelings about Willie's conflict with the Southern aristocrats. He admires the genuine representative of the ideal of the Southern gentleman, Judge Irwin. Yet Jack helps Willie challenge the established powers and he supports Willie's efforts to introduce basic reforms. For standards of decorum and gentility have led to an unresponsive, static government. Special pleading, the weight of inertia, and class bias all underlie the objections wealthy conservatives offer against Willie's populist reforms. Jack throws back the charge made against Willie by one of his mother's friends: "Graft is what he calls it when the fellows do it who don't know which fork to use" (134). The Southern gentlemen who ruled the state in the past resent Willie because of his social background and his undignified "impatience" to make changes. Willie is hardly concerned with such standards of propriety, telling Irwin: "There's lots of things you never get, Judge, if you wait till you are asked. And I am an impatient man. I am a very impatient man, Judge. That is why I am not a gentleman" (48). Warren suggests that the myth of the Southern gentleman's chivalrous nobility sometimes confuses manners and morality. At the same time, let us note Jack's, and Warren's, clear admiration for Judge Irwin as

[10] For studies of Warren's involvement in the Fugitive and Agrarian groups, see Leonard Casper, *Robert Penn Warren: The Dark and Bloody Ground* (Seattle: University of Washington Press, 1960) and Louis D. Rubin, Jr., *The Faraway Country: Writers of the Modern South* (Seattle: University of Washington Press, 1963).

[11] Warren, "Cowley's Faulkner, Part I," *New Republic* 140 (1946), p. 177; cited in Casper, *Dark and Bloody Ground*, p. 51.

the authentic realization of the Southern ideal of the gentleman.

Willie's ideal of social justice pits him against the inherited traditions of the past. His attitude towards the past exemplifies a persistent American habit of mind: the assumption that *history* is a burden that must be sloughed off in order to realize an ideal of freedom or human fulfillment. Warren has long reflected on how pursuit of abstract ideals can threaten a community with violence. His first book, *John Brown: The Making of a Martyr* (1929), interpreted the abolitionist as a fanatic possessed by the ideal of freedom. As in the character Jeremiah Beaumont in *World Enough and Time*, Warren's novels have often depicted an idealist destroying himself when frustrated by a society's resistance to his moral convictions. The fates of both Adam and Willie, too, show the self-defeating recklessness of a person believing his moral acts can break with the weight of the past.

All the King's Men opens with a description of Jack's car ride to Mason City on Highway 58. Highway 58, one of Willie's main achievements, is hacked out of dense jungles and intractable swamps. Many passages in the novel portray a symbolic struggle between human effort and *nature*: "We bored on into the dark for another twenty miles and eighteen minutes. The ectoplasmic fingers of the mist reached out of the swamp, threading out from the blackness of the cypresses, to snag us, but didn't have any luck. A possum came out of the swamp and started across the road and might have made it, too, if Sugar-Boy hadn't been too quick for him" (54). Sugar-Boy's deliberate extermination of snakes and possums acts out one of the Boss's primary traits: his urge to conquer nature. Willie's desire to build roads and schools and bridges expresses the idealistic aspirations for which we admire him. But, like the vindictive quest of *Moby-Dick*'s Captain Ahab, Willie's projects also show sinister aspects of the American view of nature as something to be eradicated or consumed.[12] This defiance of the natural order is expressed, too, in Willie's tragic error. Though usually highly aware of the role of the "natural" element in human life and activity, Willie "violates nature" when he tries to build the new hospital without the cooperation of Tiny Duffy, who symbolizes the gross and brutish part of man. His insistence that only the idealistic part of human nature, the part he sees in Adam, can take part in the hospital construction ironically brings about the cooperation of Adam and Tiny Duffy in destroying the Boss. Thus Warren shows the interdependence of the animal and the idealistic elements in human nature by dramatizing how self-division, conflict, and violence

---

[12] Further evidence for this view of the novel is Warren's account of the origin of *All the King's Men* in "a continuation of writing *At Heaven's Gate*." In that novel, all the main characters are, like the members of Dante's Seventh Circle, "violators of nature" (Warren, "Introduction," in *Twentieth Century Interpretations*, ed. Chambers, p. 95).

follow when Willie attempts to operate only with the aid of the "goodness" in humankind.

This tragic error blatantly violates the major tenet of Willie's view of human nature: his belief in its *sinfulness*. The central symbol of "dirt" links the theme of nature and the theme of sin. Man is literally dirty by nature: he is "conceived in sin and born in corruption and he passeth from the stink of the didie to the stench of the shroud" (54). And human nature is "dirty" in that it is sinful. Each individual is essentially self-interested, though he knows this to be wrong. He is more concerned with his own welfare than God's moral law. Willie explains to Jack that his Presbyterian upbringing is a primary influence on his belief that there is "always something"—always some secret evil in a person's history: "I went to a Presbyterian Sunday school back in the days when they still had some theology, and that much of it stuck" (358). Willie is accurate when he claims that he never has to frame anyone, because the truth is always sufficient to incriminate them. Sooner or later, to a greater or lesser degree, everyone commits evil and creates a dirty past. The truth of Willie's view of human nature is conclusively established for Jack when, after an exhaustive search into the past, his work on "The Case of the Upright Judge" turns up the evidence proving Irwin's past misconduct as Attorney General.

Warren also shows the inherent potential for abuse in the doctrine of original sin. Willie's "use" of what he knows about the moral guilt of others often means blackmailing them into complicity with his political operations. And his belief that all men are sinners, along with the view that the good can be judged only in terms of consequences, leads quickly to justification of his own corrupt actions. The notion of original sin provides the perfect rationalization for using "dirty tricks" against opponents. But despite this perverse application of the doctrine of original sin to defend his crimes, the truth of Willie's view of the sinfulness of human nature is shown by his own fate when he tries to operate using only the good in human nature, hoping to reform his life by canceling the contract with Gummy Larson. His impulsive wish to dissociate himself from dirt, which denies all that he knows about the origin of goodness, represents a symbolic regression to his initial political innocence. Willie's first and last blunder involve repressing the knowledge that brings him to power, the knowledge of human sinfulness. *All the King's Men* shows the twisted and perverse use to which Willie puts his belief in original sin, but the novel also affirms the validity and truth of the idea of original sin as an understanding of human nature.

In addition to examining the many strands forming Willie's moral perspective, *All the King's Men* explores the virtue Warren contrasts with Willie's readiness to "get his hands dirty" to create goodness. Willie is opposed by several individuals deeply committed to the ideal of personal moral integrity: *"being good."* Warren shows that an individual can refuse to compromise his ethical beliefs because of either admirable, dubious, or blameworthy motives. We respect Irwin's refusal to back Willie's candidate for the Senate, even when the Judge is threatened with blackmail. Irwin acknowledges the partial validity of Willie's position, admitting the principle that "you don't make omelettes without breaking eggs" (132). Irwin sees, however, that Willie has gone too far in applying this notion, telling Jack: "I was almost for him at one time. He was breaking the windowpanes out and letting in a little fresh air. But . . . I began to worry about him knocking down the house, too. And some of his methods" (364). Having committed the crime that saved his house from foreclosure but led to Littlepaugh's suicide, Irwin has no naive illusions about his own moral innocence. But though he recognizes his own capacity for evil, he refuses to compromise his integrity; he will not be cajoled or coerced into helping Stark to do what he knows is wrong. He sticks to his principles and will not be "flexible." Similarly, the reader judges favorably Cass Mastern's emancipation of his slaves and his conscientious objection during the Civil War. These actions, based on deep conviction, involve considerable risk but neither a fear of contamination by evil nor a presumption of personal sanctity.

By contrast, strong elements in Adam Stanton's commitment to maintaining his own personal purity are a fear of life's ambiguity and a fanatical assurance about his own righteousness. Anne Stanton tells Jack that she sometimes thinks Adam's "work—even the doing good—is just a way to cut himself off" (261). Adam's dedication to doing good is praiseworthy in itself, but his singleminded obsession with this goal makes his character narrow, incomplete, and unattractive. His ideal of purity is cold and abstract, revealing an alienation from the messiness of life and the imperfection of other persons. Adam's rigid moral position indicates an underlying wish to withhold and insulate himself from the world. This explains his violent reaction when Coffee tries to bribe him. Adam "must have been in the grip of an instinctive withdrawal, which took the form of moral indignation and moral revulsion, but which, no doubt, was different from either, and more deep seated than either, and finally irrational" (341). In like manner, the value of Ellis Burden's turning to tasks of religious charity is diminished because his primary impulse is simply to flee from the painful discovery of his wife's adultery with Irwin.

Jack recognizes in his own life a phenomenon he calls "virtue by defect" (393). Catching himself sneering at the so-called "good times" of the office secretaries, he realizes that, if he does not indulge in their tame pleasures anymore, he hardly qualifies as a saint. He merely endures "abstinence by nausea": "I didn't have to be proud because a good time wouldn't stay on my stomach" (393). The process of rationalization by which a person assures himself of his moral goodness is well

illlustrated in the progression of Jack's thoughts after his involuntary
hesitation in sleeping with Anne Stanton. His fear of violating his boy-
hood image of Anne's purity results in the "luck" that Jack's mother does
not discover them in bed together:

> As that thought scared me into a cold sweat, I suddenly had the feeling of
> great wisdom: I had acted rightly and wisely. Therefore we had been
> saved. And so my luck became my wisdom (as the luck of the damned
> human race becomes its wisdom and gets into the books and is taught in
> schools), and then later my wisdom became my nobility. (315)

Jack realizes that, just as one person's active virtue may lead to crime,
the apparent virtue of another sometimes results simply from passivity
and lack of desire or temptation. If Judge Irwin had committed a crime
to save the house he dearly loved, Jack cannot take pride in his relative innocence: "Perhaps my unwillingness to commit a crime to save the
house (assuming that I should have the opportunity—which is doubtful)
is simply a way of saying that I do not love the house as much as Judge
Irwin loved it and a man's virtue may be but the defect of his desire, as
his crime may be but a function of his virtue" (463). So luck, passivity,
and indifference, as well as self-righteousness and fear of life's moral
complexity, may explain a person's decision not to perform some wrongful deed. By showing the ways these motives and attitudes can assume
the shape of an act of conscience, Warren clarifies the authentic basis for
such acts in the cases of Irwin and Cass Mastern. At the same time, Warren shows the partial validity of Willie's claim that sometimes concern
for one's own moral innocence should be subordinated to the needs of a
wider community.

III. *Tragedy's Affirmative Dimensions:*
Jack Burden's Moral Regeneration

Just as "the story of Judge Irwin, which seemed so complete in itself,
was only a chapter in the longer story of the Boss," so Willie's story is
"itself merely a chapter in another bigger story" (377). That longer story
describes how Jack Burden comes to a new understanding of himself and
the world. His relationship to Willie is not the only factor involved in
Jack's moral regeneration, but it is certainly the most important one:
"I must believe that Willie Stark was a great man. What happened to his
greatness is not the question. . . . Believing that Willie Stark was a great
man, I could think better of all other people, and of myself. At the same
time that I could more surely condemn myself" (452).

Jack speaks in the present tense in the last few pages of the novel
about what Willie Stark's life now means to him. Analyzing the conflict
that destroyed his two friends, Jack sees their downfall growing out of a
conflict between two kinds of moral virtue, each of which is inadequate

by itself. Both the "man of fact" and the "man of idea" suffer from an incompleteness which leads both Willie and Adam to pervert their own ideals of virtue: "Adam Stanton, whom he came to call the man of idea, and Willie Stark, whom he came to call the man of fact, were doomed to destroy each other, just as each was doomed to try to use the other and to yearn toward and try to become the other, because each was incomplete with the terrible division of their age" (462). Willie, whose greatest desire was to do good, and Adam, whose chief wish was to be good, were both good men, in different ways. But they both violate their own deepest values. Adam's self-righteous zeal in defending his honor prompts an act of assassination that utterly defeats his quest for personal purity. Willie, certain that his own efforts establish something as good, that right and wrong are something that "you just make up as you go along," breaks altogether with the standards of law and justice that originally inspired him. His refusal to allow Tiny Duffy a role in the hospital construction is the culmination of Willie's moral self-righteousness; at the same time it contradicts his guiding principle that the good must be made from the bad.

Many of the other narrative strands of Warren's novel show a character's virtue producing evil. Irwin's last words to Jack assert that when Governor Stanton impaired his honor to protect Irwin, "his failing was a defect of his virtue. The virtue of affection for a friend" (369). Cass Mastern's attempt to operate a farm in ante-bellum Mississippi with freed slaves leads only to suffering; according to his worldly brother Gilbert, "all you have managed to do is to get one nigger killed and one nigger whipped" (194). Surveying the pitiful results of human efforts to work for the good, Cass can only conclude that "the world is full of good men . . . and yet the world drives hard into darkness and the blindness of blood . . . and I am moved to ask the meaning of our virtue" (198).

But though his virtue leads to evil, the example of the strong but erring sinner discloses more of life's moral possibilities than that of the weak saint. This phenomenon is shown in Warren's handling of Jack's search for a father figure. Jack is tremendously relieved by the discovery that Irwin rather than Ellis Burden is his true father. Though Ellis Burden was a good man, Jack says, "his goodness had told me nothing except that I could not live by it" (375). Jack sees the religious and charitable activities of the "Scholarly Attorney" as a sign of weakness rather than strength: "He had a beautiful and eager young wife and another man had taken her away from him and had fathered his child, and all he had done was to walk away, leaving her in possession of everything he owned, and crawl into a hole in the slums and lie there like a wounded animal and let his intellect bleed away into pious drivel and his strength bleed away into weakness" (375). Jack's "new father," by contrast, had not "been good," but he had "done good": "He had cuckolded a friend, betrayed a wife, taken a bribe, driven a man, though unwittingly, to death. But he had done good. He had been a just judge. And he had carried his head high. That last afternoon of his life he had done that" (375). It is the "impurity" of Willie and Adam and Irwin—the intertwining of their virtues and vices, of their highest aspirations with their secret temptations—that makes their characters fertile soil for tragic literature.[13] Even in defeat, and in the perversion of his own virtues, the tragic hero's fate reveals an image of what Jack simply calls "greatness." Ultimately "what happened to his greatness is not the question"; what most matters is simply that "he had it" (452).

Jack's affirmation of Willie's greatness in defeat is closely connected with his reassertion of the reality of moral responsibility despite the universality of guilt. "Believing that Willie Stark was a great man, I could think better of all other people, and of myself. At the same time that I could more surely condemn myself" (452). At the end of the novel, Warren suggests that the idea of moral responsibility is a more balanced and comprehensive conception of virtue than Willie's goal of "making good" or Adam's ideal of integrity. The virtue of responsibility is supposed to synthesize the two incomplete ideals of doing good and being good, which become locked in a mutually destructive conflict. Jack affirms that, though his two friends were doomed in the "terrible division of their age," their lives show the inescapable reality of human moral responsibility for one's actions: "They were doomed, but they lived in the agony of will" (462). Recognizing these individuals' responsibility for their deeds, Jack ceases to believe the theory of the Great Twitch: "He did not believe in it because he had seen too many people live and die." The Great Twitch cannot account for Willie's last words: "It might have been all different, Jack. You got to believe that" (461).

This new understanding of the meaning of moral responsibility enables Jack to comprehend the "truth" of Cass Mastern's story. What had most puzzled Jack was Cass's claim that "the world is all of one piece." Cass's journal begins to make sense as Jack traces the web of responsibility for Willie's death. He learns that *all* the "king's men"— Sadie, Tiny, Sugar-Boy, and Jack himself—are implicated in the chain of events leading to the twin deaths of Adam and Willie. A web of guilt makes them all accomplices with blood on their hands. Jack now perceives the relevance to his own experiences of the central image in the Cass Mastern story, an enormous spider web. The image of the spider's web symbolizes the interconnectedness of all persons in good and evil,

---

13 Warren said in an interview, "Once you start illustrating virtue as such you had better stop writing fiction. Your business as a writer is not to illustrate virtue but to show how a fellow may move toward it—or away from it" (Ralph Ellison and Walter Eugene, "The Art of Fiction XVIII: Robert Penn Warren," in *Robert Penn Warren: A Collection of Critical Essays*, ed. with an introduction by John L. Longley, Jr. [New York: New York University Press, 1965], p. 44).

and the reverberations of each individual's actions through the years of history. The ideal of responsibility therefore requires historical knowledge and self-knowledge. The consequences of one's actions must be discovered, acknowledged as one's responsibility, and appropriated into the self's identity. Cass has to admit to himself that: "All of these things—the death of my friend, the betrayal of Phebe, the suffering and rage and great change of the woman I had loved—all had come from my single act of sin and perfidy, as the boughs from the bole and the leaves from the bough" (189). Irwin and Jack, too, inadvertently discover how their deeds have affected others. They all learn that moral responsibility is not simply "given" to them; they must actively *take* responsibility for the fruits of their actions. Jack does this when he admits—first to himself and then to Anne—his share of responsibility for the deaths of Irwin and Adam and Willie. Discovering one's responsibility brings dread and fear because it always means acknowledging that one has caused evil or suffering.

"It does not matter whether or not you meant to brush the web of things" (200): one's careless actions may release a spider's venom. Warren suggests that there is an element of *tragic guilt* involved in every individual's coming to understand the meaning of moral responsibility. A person's actions usually need to be intentional if he or she is to be held morally guilty. Tragic guilt, however, may require a person to take responsibility for the unintentional results of action. Jack did not foresee or intend the disastrous results of his research for Willie, but he feels he must take responsibility for them. He speculates that "all knowledge that is worth anything is maybe paid for by blood. Maybe that is the only way you can tell that a certain piece of knowledge is worth anything; it has cost some blood" (455). Despite a person's good intentions, the consequences of action are bound to be mixed in moral quality; sooner or later one will have to acknowledge responsibility for something not directly willed. Willie's fate helps Jack to understand the tragic dimensions of his own more limited guilt.

Because the reader sees Willie Stark's tragedy through the perspective of Jack Burden, the ending of *All the King's Men* is optimistic and hopeful. Yet it seems necessary to point out the numerous ambiguities and qualifications that critics have overlooked. Though Jack claims that individuals are morally responsible for history, he never repudiates "the theory of the moral neutrality of history." According to this view, Willie Stark was a Promethean hero who justified in doing evil to create good for humankind (417–18). Willie's approach is partially vindicated by events, for he does "create good." His achievements—the roads, hospitals, etc.—are presented as genuine boons to the state, and his personal example inspires many of the other characters. Willie's view of the moral ambiguity of politics and history receives a good deal of support from Irwin, who defends his loyalty to the questionable figure of Mac-murfee in terms much like Willie's own: "Politics is always a matter of choices, and a man doesn't set up the choices himself. And there is always a price to make a choice" (364). Yet if "history is blind," individuals are not. Results are not all that matter in judging the rightness and wrongness of actions, and all is not permitted to a hero. Even Willie seems to know that his actions have been wrong, and that his character has been corrupted. In the end, Jack can neither affirm nor deny "the theory of historical costs"; he is "willing to let those speculations rest" (418).

History is a web of connected events, but the connections are usually morally ambiguous, and often ironic. The good agent may perform the evil deed; a man's "virtue" may result from the lack of temptation or desire; and a person's failing or crime is often a defect of his virtue. Warren shows a number of ironies and ambiguities that defy the schemes and theories by which humankind tries to make moral sense of history. The evil for which one may be responsible does not always result from clear moral choices—one may have accidentally brushed the "spider's web" of being that connects events and persons. Furthermore, Jack's notion of responsibility remains only a proposal; we are not shown how it would fare in history. Two figures who are supposed to embody Jack's ideal of morally responsible politics remain mere shadow-figures: Hugh Miller, for whom Jack intends to work in the future, and Gilbert Mastern, whom Cass suggested "can in the midst of evil retain enough of innocence and strength . . . to do a little justice in the terms of the great injustice" (195–96). There is hardly a simple or universal solution to the dilemma of moral choice, for "there is always a price to make a choice." Judge Irwin, who has some of the best qualities of Willie and Adam, is the most morally admirable of the fully-developed characters in the novel. But Irwin committed a crime that, discovered by Jack thirty years later, led him to kill himself rather than publicly acknowledge his guilt; this way of taking responsibility for the past hardly seems the best one.

Even acknowledging all these ambiguities and qualifications, however, *All the King's Men* is an extremely affirmative work that stresses the positive results of the tragic protagonist's career. Jack emphasizes Willie's greatness, not his corruption—or rather Willie's greatness *despite* corruption. Willie's last words—"It might have been all different, Jack. You got to believe that" (461)—suggest a recovery of his integrity and a promise of hope for the future. He does not despair over his coming death, but seems to accept it as an atonement for his crimes. He even manages to forgive his assassin: "He was all right. The Doc" (424). Willie's example inspires Jack to commit himself to working with Hugh Miller when the latter returns to politics. Jack marries Anne and goes back to work on Cass Mastern's story, which he now understands. The ending of the novel strains a little awkwardly to bring good out of evil. By killing his father, Jack is said to have "saved his mother's soul," because at last she admits her love for Irwin. The obstacles that had prevented Jack and Anne from having a good relationship drop away too suddenly, leaving us dissatisfied with this aspect of the novel. And Jack is rather abruptly reconciled with all of his "fathers"; Willie, Irwin, and even Ellis Burden, whom he no longer despises for fleeing from the discovery of his wife's adultery. Finally, however, Jack's regeneration is not sentimental or idyllic, but convincing and compelling. It seems "earned" by all he has been through.[14]

All the admirable men Jack has known committed some evil deed. In their own ways, Adam and Irwin and Willie, like Cass Mastern, have gotten tangled and trapped in their own strategies to be good or to do good. But Jack's recognition of the universality of humankind's "fall," its loss of innocence in moral experience, does not make him pessimistic about history's possibilities or cynical about individual moral responsibility. Rather, his historical research and his experiences with Willie release him from his previous sense of alienation and callousness. He sees in Willie's career suggestions of the creative possibilities of political life, and he affirms that Willie's corruption does not diminish the essential fact of his greatness. The novel's ending gives the impression that the good qualities of Irwin and Adam and Willie have decisively influenced the lives of the characters who survive them and go on with the work of reordering the political community. *All the King's Men*, then, reveals the affirmations of which tragedy is capable.

Warren's nonfictional writings articulate his belief in the affirmative dimensions of tragedy. In his key essay, "Knowledge and the Image of Man," he says that once a person "realizes that the tragic experience is universal and a corollary of man's place in nature, he may return to a communion with man and nature. . . . The return to nature and man is the discovery of love, and law. But love through separateness, and law through rebellion. . . . His unity with mankind will not now be the unity of a member of the tribal horde with that pullulating mass; his unity will be that of a member of sweet society."[15] It is by offering "a vision of

---

[14] Even Murray Krieger, who usually expresses boundless enthusiasm for undiminished Manichean conflict in tragic literature, finds the end of *All the King's Men* completely convincing: "I know of no other work in which so sophisticated, so self-conscious a life-scarred creature—especially a narrator-creator of a monumentally tragic figure—wills himself into such a simplicity of final commitments and comes close to getting away with it. . . . It is a daring stroke, this walking off into the sunset (sunrise?); but, in view of what we know of Jack Burden, what we know he knows, it is—I believe—more daring than sentimental" (*The Classic Vision* [Baltimore: Johns Hopkins University Press, 1971], p. 308).

[15] Warren, "Knowledge and the Image of Man," in *Merrill Studies*, ed. Light, p. 24.

experience . . . fulfilled and redeemed in knowledge, the ugly with the beautiful" that literature provides man with "an image of experience being brought to order and harmony . . . a myth of order, or fulfillment, an affirmation that our being may move in its totality towards meaning."[16] This statement succinctly describes the rendering of Jack's experiences in *All the King's Men*, a work that provides "an image of order" by showing how Jack's discovery of the universality of tragic experience leads to his renewed "communion with man and nature."

In showing how Willie's tragic fate affects Jack, Warren convinces us that, though his virtues were perverted by success, Willie was indeed a great man, one who discloses to men and women something of their own capabilities and possibilities. Warren's depiction of Jack's effort to understand the conflict between two kinds of virtue provides an invaluable "image of order" with which to understand the strengths and liabilities of a peculiarly American vision and strategy for "making good out of bad."

[16] Ibid., p. 28.

6

The Moral Structure of Tragic Literature

Though tragedy arises in different ways in *The Princess Casamassima*, *Billy Budd*, *Nostromo*, and *All the King's Men*, these novels share certain features which make it possible to speak of a common moral structure of tragic literature. We may summarize in advance our understanding of tragedy's basic moral structure. (1) Tragedy depicts the suffering or downfall of a character with a particular kind of virtue. (2) In tragedy, the hero's moral obligations conflict with his self-interest or with something essential to his well-being. (3) The protagonist also faces an irreconcilable conflict between different moral duties or obligations. (4) The hero's tragic error is an irrevocable decision which leads to extreme suffering or death for himself or another character. (5) The tragic situation is exacerbated because of the hero's virtue. (6) Tragedy makes a critique of a form of virtue: an assessment of its strengths and potential liabilities. (7) Tragedy discloses broader conflicts among the social and cultural values within which context a virtue finds its purpose and justification. (8) Literary tragedies often suggest that a tragic situation has broader implications: tragedy may be presented as a common or rare aspect of human moral experience, and it may suggest grounds either for despair, for renewed confidence, or for a muted and enigmatic sense of irony about the downfall of virtue.

(1) The four narrative tragedies all focus on a striking moral situation: the phenomenon of a basically good character performing actions which lead to evil and self-destruction. That is, the novels follow the downward career of one or more characters who represent particular conceptions of *moral virtue*. In Henry James's *The Princess Casamassima*, Hyacinth Robinson's discerning consciousness, personal impressionability, and aesthetic sensibility are the attributes of a young man "on whom nothing was lost." Melville's Captain Vere has all the virtues of the ideal sea commander, especially the indispensable quality of prudence for the safety of his crew and his ship. In the fates of Nostromo, Charles and Emily Gould, Decoud, and Monygham, *Nostromo* explores dangers to two essential Conradian virtues: idealism and skepticism. All the characters in the novel meet disillusionment or death when they try to translate their personal moral "idea" into the sphere of public action. In *All the King's Men*,

Robert Penn Warren depicts the political career of a charismatic leader whose actions are guided by the belief that he can "make good out of bad." Warren shows the real fruitfulness of this notion of moral goodness along with its inherent susceptibility to corruption.

(2) The protagonists of these tragedies all find themselves in a situation in which their moral obligations conflict sharply with some essential aspect of their well-being, or with life itself. In tragedy, *virtue conflicts with self-interest*, and the protagonist must make a difficult sacrifice in order to live according to his ideals. Hyacinth Robinson's sense of the pressing need for social justice impels him to take an oath to be prepared to sacrifice his life. The young bookbinder again disregards his personal security when, ignoring repeated warnings, he becomes deeply involved with the Princess. Though Hyacinth derives much pleasure from her company and from his new aesthetic experiences, the growth of his sense of moral obligation to his culture's artistic heritage brings him great suffering, and he finally realizes that he must give up his own life rather than take another's. James's use of metaphors of sacrifice and payment, and his pointed comparisons of Hyacinth with other characters, show that it is the young man's capacity to "give up," his readiness to renounce his own interests, that indicates the full measure of his moral goodness.

"Self-interest" is a somewhat misleading term for what conflicts with Captain Vere's military duties. It is his deep concern and love for Billy that must be suppressed if Vere is to carry out his responsibilities in the youth's trial. What Vere most deeply desires—to spare Billy's life—cannot be reconciled with what he must do as the commanding officer of a ship at war. As Melville's use of the Abraham and Isaac metaphor makes clear, Vere loves Billy as a son but believes he must sacrifice him. For Vere, as for the other tragic protagonists, moral obligations demand that he renounce something essential to his happiness.

The analysis of *Nostromo* showed how Conrad gradually discloses that egoism and forms of self-interest underlie all the main characters' attempts to realize some "idea" in action. Decoud reflects that the heroic Nostromo "was made incorruptible by his enormous vanity, that finest form of egoism which can take on the aspect of every virtue." Conrad's treatment of the character Nostromo culminates in the temptation and moral fall that occur when the Capataz is confronted with a situation in which public duty and private self-interest no longer conveniently coincide, but require diametrically opposed actions. Isolated from the supportive community of Sulaco and the watchful "eye of others," Nostromo steals the silver and ensures his own moral damnation. Conrad ensures that his readers will be sympathetic to his erring protagonist; because we are shown the partial legitimacy of Nostromo's self-interest and his genuine grievances, we see him as a tragic hero and not simply as a petty thief. The other central characters make moral compromises in order to make possible the success of an "idea" or the survival of a loved one. But concern for practical success in the public sphere always undermines altruistic goals or threatens another important value or person. Thus Gould's hope of establishing conditions of law and order in Sulaco requires him to instigate a political insurrection that breeds anarchy. At the same time, his single-minded commitment to the revolution ruins his marriage. Dr. Monygham carelessly risks any number of lives to protect Mrs. Gould. There is "something inherent in the necessities of successful action" which leads to "the moral degradation of the idea" that each character tries to realize. In the form of concern for practical success in society, self-interest undermines the moral projects of idealists and skeptics alike.

In *All the King's Men* Warren dramatizes the politician's perennial struggle to reconcile the public good with the temptation to use political power for personal gain. The corrupting influence of power is particularly insidious in Willie's career because his deepest desire is not for personal aggrandizement, but for the fulfillment of his project to "make good out of bad." Willie Stark, too, faces the necessity for a sacrifice of something essential to his being: his understanding of politics requires him to sacrifice his own integrity in order to "do good" on the larger scale of the state he governs. The temptation to misuse his power to further his own political interests proves irresistible and Willie is corrupted. Yet Willie never loses his idealistic desires both to be and to do good, and in the end is destroyed because he desperately and inconsistently wants to realize these two conceptions of good. He dies partly because, in his final attempt to reform, he cares little for his own safety or security in comparison to his scheme to "make good" on both a public and a personal level.

(3) In each of these tragedies, the protagonist's responsibilities and obligations diverge not only from his personal self-interest, but from *each other*. *Moral duties conflict* in tragedy so that the hero can not meet all his obligations. He faces what Hegel called a "conflict of ethical claims," though the hero is not always equally loyal to both claims. Hyacinth Robinson makes a political commitment to overthrow what he believes is an unjust social system. With the growth of his sense of loyalty to Europe's artistic and cultural achievements, Hyacinth realizes that he cannot consistently work to undermine society while enjoying its refinements and treasures. His "socialist" and "social" sympathies—his sense of obligation to both "the people" and to "civilization as we know it"—point to antithetical courses of action. He must either defend or attack the established alliance between art and political power. In addition to the conflict between his yearning for a more just society and his horror of destroying the precious achievements he has learned to love, Hyacinth is torn between loyalties to several persons. His relationships to

Paul Muniment, Hoffendahl, Milly, and the Princess place irreconcilable demands on him. Hyacinth's intense devotion to all his friends, even when they disappoint and abandon him, contributes greatly to the bewilderment that ends in his suicide.

Captain Vere faces a conflict between the need for prudence about the safety of his ship and a moral obligation to do all he can to preserve an individual's life. Under the conditions of military action Melville so carefully specifies, the demands of collective security clash with the "rights of man." Any middle course is excluded: Vere is forced to choose either "to condemn or let go."

In *Nostromo*, the two virtues of idealism and skepticism prove to be terribly difficult to reconcile in action. The five main characters, despite their varying degrees of idealism and skepticism, all become embroiled in a desperate political conflict in the course of trying to realize some "idea." Conrad shows the strange blindness that accompanies the idealistic illusion that one can successfully realize an idea in the public arena. Charles Gould seems oblivious to the dangers his political scheme poses for his wife: "A man haunted by a fixed idea is insane. He is dangerous even if that idea is an idea of justice; for may he not bring the heaven down pitilessly upon a loved head?" All the main characters fail to perceive that their dedication to one project threatens other essential values or other human lives. Decoud reflects that "every conviction, as soon as it became effective, turned into that form of dementia the gods send upon those they wish to destroy." Even the most skeptical characters, Decoud and Monygham, take action in the belief that they can master destiny, though the fates of others have shown them that this is an illusion. Taking action requires decisive commitment, which in Conrad's world usually involves both insensitivity to others and self-deception about one's actual control over events. In action, the main characters find it impossible to be skeptical of their own endeavors, and to see clearly the possibilities for disastrous side-effects or failure. But on the other hand, skepticism destroys those cut off from the continuous activity and supportive institutions of society. Without the routine and rewards attached to a public role, even the most energetic and unreflective actor, Nostromo, loses faith in his idea of himself as a hero, doubts his identity, and betrays the trust of his community. None of the central figures in *Nostromo* can maintain a clear-sighted commitment to an idea: they oscillate between dazzled fascination with their idea and disenchanted detachment from society. The two virtues of idealism and skepticism inevitably seem to conflict in any practical course of action, though either one alone leads readily to a fatal blindness.

All the King's Men presents a conflict between the imperative to "be good" and the goal of "doing good." Warren establishes a dramatic conflict between Willie Stark's political ambition to "make good out of bad" and several characters who refuse to cooperate with his plans at the cost of violating their deepest moral convictions. Willie not only meets resistance from Adam Stanton, Irwin, and Hugh Miller: he is also internally torn between the honest "Cousin Willie" who entered politics as a clean-cut reform candidate and the "Boss" who will use any corrupt means to attain his ends. Jack Burden's reflections return again and again to the contrast between these two moral styles as alternative responses to the "dirt" of moral evil. Willie feels keenly the dilemma of the politician who must choose dubious means to achieve some essential goal and yet somehow retain his own moral integrity. But in *All the King's Men* the dramatic conflict occurs primarily between individuals, rather than within the consciousness of the protagonist, as in *The Princess Casamassima*. Jack Burden interprets the basic conflict as one between a "man of fact" (Willie) and a "man of idea" (Adam). The "conflict of ethical claims" in tragedy is usually portrayed both within the soul of the tragic hero and in his struggles with other characters, but the emphasis can lie primarily on internal conflict, as in *Princess*, or on a dramatic struggle between individuals, as in *All the King's Men*. One might also contrast Warren's work with James's in that, while James devotes equal care to showing both sides of Hyacinth's dilemma, Warren assumes the general validity of the position of the individual who wants to "be good," and devotes most of his effort to showing the partial legitimacy of Willie's ideal of "making good" even at the cost of his personal integrity.

(4) In this situation of conflicting moral obligations, tragedy is realized when the hero is forced to make a *tragic error*: a decision that leads to irreversible and destructive consequences. In each tragic novel, the multiple obligations a character faces must be resolved in a single decision or series of decisions which cannot be revoked. Such a choice is made when Hyacinth makes his vow; when Vere decides to bring Claggart and Billy together, and later to press for Billy's execution; when each character in *Nostromo* aligns himself with the insurgents in the Sulaco revolution; and such a choice is made when Willie Stark decides to fire Gummy Larson from the hospital project. Of course, any completed action is irreversible in the sense that it cannot be undone. What is peculiarly characteristic of tragedy is the way in which disastrous circumstances follow from a decision that, at the time when it was made, seemed at least partially justified. Tragedy involves a great reversal of fortune: the hero is shocked when, contrary to expectation, his decision proves to have been a terrible mistake leading to great suffering.

The hero's tragic error involves the moral ambiguity of a conscientious choice that leads to evil. The protagonist must decide what to do in a confusing situation, under conditions of temporal urgency and limited knowledge. He cannot foresee the consequences of his actions, and he is often in ignorance of crucial information that would affect his deliberations. The reader can understand and even approve of the choice that proves to be a tragic error: for instance, Willie's attempt to reform by firing Larson. The analysis of *Billy Budd* showed how Melville's emphasis up to and through the trial scene consistently focuses upon the reasonableness of Vere's actions in extremely dangerous circumstances. For prudence is shown to be a necessary virtue in a man-of-war world, and it is prudence that determines Vere's proceedings in the trial of Billy Budd. It is only *after* the trial that prudence and Vere's decision are called in question. Hyacinth Robinson's vow to be ready to sacrifice his life seems a meaningful and courageous (if ill-considered) act in the context of the posturing and futile discussions in the "Sun and Moon." Yet in spite of his good intentions, the protagonist's choices create negative consequences that he cannot alter or correct. The moral decision which seemed justified at the moment of choice is suddenly seen as a catastrophic mistake.

The hero makes a tragic error partly because of factors beyond his control. Circumstances conspire to expose him to irresistible temptations, as in Nostromo's or Willie's cases, or to make his acts destructive in unexpected ways, as happens when Monygham inadvertently brings about Hirsch's death or Jack's blackmail of Irwin leads to the Judge's suicide. Captain Vere's actions are set within the context of the contingencies of naval war, the threat of mutiny, and Vere's limited knowledge of the characters of his crew. An advantage of the narrative mode of tragic literature is the opportunity it offers for showing in detail over a lengthy period of time the massing of conditions, the compounding of contingent factors, which together may corrupt a person or cause his best efforts to miscarry.

The temporal span of these tragic novels shows how not only the external environment, but the hero's own history exerts a determining power on his fate. His previous deeds engender an inexorable momentum; when the hero tries to avoid a looming disaster, he is hemmed in by the consequences of his past acts. History becomes a "burden" for all the protagonists; this theme is especially prominent in *All the King's Men*, where Willie Stark fails to break out of the web of corruption he has created. He cannot violate with impunity the network of dependencies and expectations established when he employed crooks like Tiny Duffy and Gummy Larson. In tragedy, commitments can not be retracted, actions can't be undone, and the terrible consequences of past decisions can't be avoided, but destroy the hero or something essential to his happiness.

Sometimes when moral values or duties conflict, one can act in accordance with one of them and merely neglect the other one. But in tragedy, the hero's tragic error leads to consequences that not only neglect, but destroy other essential values. When Hyacinth's "call" to assassinate a duke comes, he cannot honor it without directly attacking part of the social fabric he has come to cherish. If he does not act, he

will break his sacred vow to Hoffendahl, which represents his commitment to social justice. Whatever he does will destroy some value fundamental to his being. Similarly, Vere must violate either of two of his
essential concerns. He will flaunt one of the basic forms of naval life if
he lets Billy escape the established legal penalty for murdering an officer. Or, if he follows the letter of the law, he will have to execute a person whom he knows is essentially "innocent," in the sense that Billy was
falsely accused of mutiny by Claggart and did not intend to kill him
when he impulsively struck him. After the trial scene, Vere's decision is
presented as a tragic error, as its evil consequences and broader social
implications are seen more clearly.

In *Nostromo*, Gould cannot overthrow the corrupt Costaguana regime
without allying himself with the bandit Hernandez, though this pact subverts his commitment to the rule of law. Gould's all-consuming political
quest also brings great suffering to Emily; his successful revolution only
imprisons her "all alone in the Treasure House of the World." All the characters in the Conrad novel seem as blind to the suffering they cause others
as Dr. Monygham, who is prepared to sacrifice any number of lives for the
one woman he loves. Commitment to one person or ideal inevitably leads
to the destruction of another one.

In *All the King's Men*, too, two kinds of moral value become locked
in a mutually destructive conflict. The characters who insist on strict
standards of personal morality in politics, like Adam Stanton and Hugh
Miller, seem naive, ineffectual, and unconcerned about the public welfare. Willie, on the other hand, comes to believe—in more and more
instances—that he can only "make good out of bad" by defying accepted
standards of personal integrity. In blackmailing Judge Irwin and others,
he violates even his own beliefs about individual morality. When Willie
reverses himself and belatedly tries to reform his hospital project, he
contradicts everything he has asserted about original sin in politics and
about the fertility of "dirt." Like the other tragic protagonists, Willie's
attempt to realize one fundamental moral value leads to the tragic error
that destroys another value.

(5) The tragic nature of this kind of moral dilemma is *exacerbated*
because of the *virtue of the hero*. A difficult moral conflict might be
evaded by a person who was inconsistent in meeting responsibilities, or
who avoided having to perform painful duties, or who rationalized about
his motives and behavior so that he never became aware of his moral guilt.
But even though he may be morally corrupted and commit evil actions, the
tragic hero is basically a virtuous person: someone who desires to carry out
his moral obligations, feels keenly the dilemma of conflicting duties, and
persists in the struggle to act rightly when a less conscientious person would
compromise his ideals or shirk some of his responsibilities. As readers, we
admire and respect the tragic hero because he does not shrink from, but

courageously faces an agonizing moral dilemma. Moral courage is an indispensable virtue of the tragic hero if his ethical situation is to be fully explored.

Thus it is Hyacinth's "power to be richly aware and finely responsible" that enables him to recognize fully all the considerations that produce his perplexing dilemma. Hyacinth discerns the moral culpability both of revolutionary political movements and of the established social powers that support artistic culture. To feel keenly both the urgency of the problem of social injustice and the intrinsic values of culture, James's protagonist must have intelligence, aesthetic sensitivity, and a strong sense of fair play. He must have a highly developed conscience that probes his own motives and reckons how his deeds will affect others. Hyacinth must be a man of his word, someone who does not simply disregard a former vow when it no longer suits his interests. And the young man's dilemma will be further exacerbated if he persists in his unwavering loyalty to all the persons who try to enlist his support for one or another political position, even though these individuals abandon him just when he most needs their counsel. By means of pointed comparisons with Hyacinth's friends, James makes clear that Hyacinth alone reaches a bewildering moral impasse because he is the only character on whom "nothing is lost."

Melville emphasizes that Captain Vere is "an exceptional man," the only one on his ship who fully understands the complexity of Billy's case. Vere's scrupulous effort to do the right thing and his love for Billy make his ordeal all the more agonizing. He feels bitterly the weight of his responsibility for Billy's death because he must stifle his compassion for Billy as he carries out the forms of military justice. The narrator of *Billy Budd* informs us that Vere's mental suffering is far greater than that of the man he condemns to execution. Vere's moral situation would not be so painfully tragic if he did not both love and want to save Billy and also have the practical wisdom to accurately reckon all the pressing military and legal considerations calling for a prompt execution.

The central section of the chapter on *Nostromo* explored the fallibility and vulnerability of the hero in the world of public action. Conrad shows that certain individuals are highly susceptible to internal moral corruption and to external perils because of their public roles in society. Conrad places in acutely dangerous situations heroes with different kinds of skepticism and idealism. These Conradian virtues expose them to hazards that would not threaten less discerning and less committed persons. When Conrad's protagonists become aware of their isolation and alienation from society, skepticism undermines self-confidence and trust in the worth of their own actions. Nostromo, Decoud, Monygham, and the Goulds all feel what R. P. Warren calls, "the cost of awareness": a paralyzing sense of futility that accompanies insight into how little control agents really have over the effects of their actions in the world. *Nostromo* also shows the difficulty of the virtue of idealism by probing how the attempt to realize an idea poses a number of attendant perils: the undermining of idealism by self-interest, the disintegration of the self's identity apart from society, the self-destructive blindness of commitment, and "the moral degradation of the idea" amid the compromises of public action. The suffering of the protagonists of *Nostromo* is immeasurably increased because their idealism persists even in defeat, so that the characters must live with the knowledge of their own moral failure. Nostromo's final days are so bitter because he cannot stand being a hypocrite; his idea of himself as a hero endures, making shameful his life of deception. Unable to rationalize his theft of the silver, he is tormented by guilt and remorse. Similarly, Emily Gould's compassion, generosity, and devotion to her husband and the entire community make her suffering all the more acute when in the end she is forced to recognize her estrangement from Charles Gould and the defeat of their youthful ideal for Sulaco.

Warren's Willie Stark is corrupted because he cannot resist certain temptations inherent in his project to make good come out of evil. Willie's passion for social justice leads him to enter politics in the first place, and motivates his progressive social programs. He believes that his ideal of creating good out of bad justifies the use of any means. Yet the fact that he constantly defends his tactics reveals his underlying awareness that other moral claims must also be considered. Willie feels both the moral imperative to be good as an individual and a desire to do or make good on the scale of state politics. A politician who did not feel the urgency of *both* moral imperatives would not have fallen into the kind of vacillation and inconsistency that lead to Willie's downfall when he makes a last desperate attempt at reforming his administration. Willie's dying words to Jack—"It might have all been different"—testify that his conscience continues to judge his actions until the very end. Willie Stark, then, is a good man corrupted by the necessary compromises and subtle temptations of political power.

Of course a still better man, morally speaking, would not have been corrupted at all. But it has not been my purpose to argue that tragedy simply illustrates examples of moral perfection. Tragedy deals with heroes, not saints. A tragic hero's character shows the intertwining of virtue with the other personal qualities that give him complexity and uniqueness as an individual. A tragic hero's fate shows that virtue is not enough to ensure success or happiness. In certain circumstances, a person's very moral goodness makes all the more agonizing a terrible dilemma, and all the more bitter the knowledge of guilt or defeat.

(6) The critique of virtue in each narrative tragedy has been the central focus of the argument of every chapter, and a summary statement of this theme here must be rather abstract. In each novel, the virtue of the

protagonist—Hyacinth's sensibility, Vere's prudence, Willie's strategy for making good out of bad, or the idealism and skepticism of Conrad's characters—is shown both to contain a dangerous potential for conflict with other values, and unexpectedly to bring about evil and suffering. Some critics might argue, in fact, that these personal qualities are not virtues at all, but vices, or "tragic flaws." It has been my thesis, however, that the authors of the four novels neither repudiate nor idealize the virtues of their protagonists, but offer a balanced assessment of both the virtue's value and its potential weaknesses. The novelists do this by exploring ambiguities in the meaning and value of a virtue within a social context and by dramatizing its operation in time. Tragedy displays a virtue's temporal functioning and its origin and effects in the protagonist's social environment.

(7) The interpretations of *The Princess Casamassima*, *Billy Budd*, *Nostromo*, and *All the King's Men* did not concentrate solely on the moral qualities of individual characters, but have shown that, in all of these works, tragedy arises because of contradictions and *conflicts among a society's values*. Analysis of the cultural roots of Willie's moral perspective in *All the King's Men* disclosed a number of specifically American influences on the notion of "making good out of bad." The meteoric career of Huey Long, Warren's view of the demagogic tendencies of democratic politics, the philosophy of pragmatism, the Southern conflict between tradition and ambition, the American view of nature as a wilderness to be subjugated, and a homespun version of the doctrine of original sin: all these influences shape Warren's depiction of Willie Stark. Besides being a uniquely individual character and a representative of tensions in the American experience, Willie Stark's story discloses recurring features of the basic process by which a human culture reimagines and revises its moral priorities. Willie's fate especially illustrates the continual friction between the criticism, development, and reform of a society's moral notions, and a society's need for enduring standards of personal goodness. The story of Stark's life and death shows Warren wrestling with the fundamental problem of how to achieve worthy social goals when the price of reform and progress is violation of an essential standard of personal ethics.

In *Nostromo*, society seems to require the heroes to take the courses of action that destroy them. The focus of our analysis of Conrad's novel was on how the protagonists' ideals are corrupted or defeated in the arena of public action. Disinterested motives and altruistic aspirations are first compromised and finally surrendered as the central characters adopt dubious tactics merely to survive the upheavals of a chaotic political revolution. The novel's central symbol, "the silver of the mine," unifies the fates of the five main characters, all of whom are forced to translate their personal desires and ideals into this one universal currency of human exchange. For Decoud and Monygham and Mrs. Gould, even personal love between man and woman becomes indissolubly linked to the fate of the San Tomé silver. In *Nostromo*, the individual's moral purpose becomes diluted and debased as it is absorbed into the medium of economic wealth, and thus intimately bound up with the public world of force and violence. Even when Charles Gould achieves outward success in the aftermath of the Sulaco Revolution, the reader sees that his original design of social justice has been lost in the inevitably corrupting fabric of political life.

In the last chapters of *Billy Budd*, Melville showed that the virtue of prudence is rooted partly in the necessity for a certain stability in a society's institutions. Melville shows that the need of the warmaking machine for "forms, measured forms" takes priority over the possibility of exceptions to the rule, and of a grace or mercy that might operate in favor of individuals who run afoul of the law. The forms of military life parody religious symbols and institutions, functioning as the basic loyalties that shape Vere's decisions. In some scenes, Vere is presented as but the agent of his society's commitment to the rule of rigid forms and violence. Melville's critique of the virtue of prudence, then, reveals not only possible deficiencies of character in the prudent individual: excessive cautiousness, self-concern, the withering of the heart and the feelings, or oversolicitude for correct social forms. Melville explores, too, the way that prudence is a virtue whose rationale and justification are generated by society's need for efficient mechanisms for disciplining and punishing individuals engaged in organized violence.

The fate of James's impressionable young bookbinder reveals not only the danger of a certain kind of personal sensibility, but a deep-rooted conflict within European culture. Examination of *The Princess Casamassima* supported Lionel Trilling's claim that, in the character of Hyacinth Robinson, James discloses implications of the tacit alliance between art and established power. Hyacinth may be a rather wide-eyed and passive young man, but he accurately discerns that "the general fabric of civilization as we know it" is based upon a history of violence and injustice, and that either to defend or to attack the legacy of this history involves a degree of moral guilt. In *The Princess Casamassima* James probed not only the possible complications arising for an unusually sensitive consciousness, but also the moral ambiguity of European civilization's support of the arts. All these tragedies, then, probe basic moral tensions in the structure of a particular society, and they explore the roots of these tensions in the very nature of human existence in society.

(8) Though the four narrative tragedies center on the phenomenon of a virtuous character bringing about his own destruction in a situation of conflicting moral demands, the novels vary considerably in their presentation of the *broader implications of a tragic situation*. In *Nostromo*, vast historical forces and the blindness of human agents conspire to make

the thwarting of individual moral purpose seem inevitable. The dispersed focus on five main characters, the epic scale of the novel, and Conrad's rendering of the indifferent natural setting present the protagonists' defeats as brief episodes within a long history of doomed ideals and aspirations. Conrad shows tragedy on a cosmic scale, probing the many ways a collective destiny and the apparent disorder of the universe can engulf the moral projects of individuals. And Conrad's relentless examination of the enormous and insidious power of self-interest in all human activity also shows how each character's own divided aims help defeat moral aspirations. The way each character becomes fatally committed to the Sulaco revolution and to the San Tomé silver illustrates again and again "the failure of the moral idea in history." The most perceptive and discerning characters feel what Monygham calls "the crushing, paralyzing sense of human littleness." Particular tragic situations in *Nostromo* are used as evidence for broader generalizations made by Decoud, Monygham, and the narrator: statements that assert that tragedy is a universal fact of human moral experience. Even Emily Gould finally must admit to herself that "there was something inherent in the necessities of successful action which carried with it the moral degradation of the idea."

In *The Princess Casamassima*, by contrast, James localizes the tragedy, portraying Hyacinth's self-destruction as specific to a particular kind of person in fairly unusual circumstances. James does show the alliance of art and power to be a disturbing problem rooted in the very nature of civilized life. But without belittling the stature of his protagonist, James shows that Hyacinth's suicide was not the only or the best way of reconciling the conflicting demands of social justice and the aesthetic life. As a narrator, James has much more distance from his protagonist than does Conrad, whose voice is often indistinguishable from Decoud's or Monygham's. James's presentation of comic and pathetic elements in Hyacinth's plight suggests that a more experienced person, someone with a greater toleration for ironic contrasts, might resolve the dilemma at less grievous cost. Furthermore, the dilemma which brings about Hyacinth's personal tragedy is presented not only as the cause of anguish and despair, but—even for the hero himself—as a source of positive insights into the beauty and meaning of life. Hyacinth learns to estimate the importance of social justice and of imaginative experience in direct relation to each other. That is, he realizes that the deprivation of "the people" lies not just in the material sphere of life, and at the same time he sees that the huge scale of suffering in Europe makes the possibility of aesthetic experience all the more precious a privilege. James uses Hyacinth's tragic situation not to suggest that a similar defeat must be the common fate of many individuals, but rather to affirm the essential values Hyacinth learns to revere. The reader's deepest feeling on putting down *The Princess* is not, as after Conrad's novel, a sense of the inevitable futility and defeat of admirable individuals; rather one finishes with an increased appreciation for the complexity and beauty of the world Hyacinth sacrifices, and with a sense of sadness at the waste of this youth's capacity for generous admiration and appreciation.

All the King's Men presents still other implications of a tragic situation. Unlike the other novels, Warren's work is narrated by a character who is also an actor in the main events. We understand Willie Stark's tragedy primarily in terms of its impact on Jack Burden, whose basic reorientation in the course of the novel gives him a renewed sense of meaning and purpose. The last section of the chapter on *All the King's Men* explained how Jack Burden's moral regeneration shows the affirmative dimensions of which tragedy is capable. Jack's final reflections emphasize not so much the disturbing deaths of his friends Adam and Willie and of his father, Judge Irwin, but rather their greatness even in defeat: "Believing that Willie Stark was a great man, I could think better of all other people, and of myself." Willie's tragedy allows Jack to understand for the first time the meaning of moral responsibility, and to take responsibility for his own life.

But if *All the King's Men* resembles *The Princess Casamassima* in stressing the affirmative significance of a central individual's tragedy, it is like *Nostromo* in that Warren, too, strives to show that tragedy is a common feature of human moral experience. Willie proves right in claiming that "there is always something," some evil in a person's past that may return to haunt or destroy him. The deaths of Willie and Adam and Irwin show history to be a "burden" in every case, because each person's deeds produce terrible consequences he has to pay for. The tragic guilt of Jack's friends helps him to understand and live with his own accountability for his actions, as he struggles to come to terms with his crucial role in causing the deaths of his friends and father. In *All the King's Men*, then, a great man's downfall discloses tragic dimensions in human moral experience generally, but the universality of tragic experience is presented not as a source of despair or lament, but rather as the basis for Jack's revived strength to take responsibility for his life and to commit himself anew to "the burden of history."

The nature of *Billy Budd*'s broader implications are the most difficult to formulate. Melville clearly presents the events on board the *Bellipotent* as evidence of a basic recurring pattern in human societies. Society often crucifies innocent goodness, and it is often well-meaning and conscientious administrators who preside over the execution. Melville's contrasts between imagery of the natural world and of civilized life, as in the scenes of Billy's execution and burial, show his vision of a permanent tension between the essential goodness and uncontrolled energy of unspoiled nature and the necessary but rigid forms of society, which prove life-denying to those who violate them. Melville portrays Billy's death and

Vere's agonized response to it as a pattern of events rooted in the nature of every society's institutional forms, which require prudent administrators, rules, and specified punishments for criminals.

Yet other implications of Vere's tragic situation remain very enigmatic. Does the reader find in Vere's suffering and death a picture of the ultimate futility and moral mediocrity of the prudently good man, the person who remains loyal to his society's forms? Or is Vere's serene death an indication that understanding the broader implications of a tragic situation enables one to go on trying to act morally with the assurance that Plinlimmon's prudent morality is not only the best one can do in this "horological" world, but what one indeed should do? Is the reader's sense of the ending of *Billy Budd* more like *Nostromo*'s portrayal of the inevitable moral defeat of the good man, or more like *All the King's Men*'s presentation of the possibility that tragedy can lead to renewed meaning and purpose? Melville's narrative voice in *Billy Budd* is systematically muted and enigmatic. Vere's dilemma is the choice between chronological and horological virtues; Melville shows both the limitations of each kind of virtue and also the necessity for choice by the individual in a position of authority. Even more than the other modern tragedians, Melville leaves us with an impression we get in reading Sophocles: matters of moral agency—the mysteries of the will and the enigmas that baffle ethical reasoning—can not be understood in terms of simple formulas or oppositions between optimism and pessimism. Melville's many ironic qualifications seem calculated to leave the reader in a state of doubt and uncertainty about the wisdom of Vere's choice, and about its broader implications. In Melville's final vision, tragic choice and action are presented as an enigma, a problem whose double meanings can be clarified but never reduced to simpler terms.

This, in summary, is my understanding of the moral structure of tragedy, which can help us conceptualize the tragic dimension of moral experience. Tragedy is threatened when a basically admirable character's multiple responsibilities conflict with his or her self-interest, and with each other. Tragedy is realized when the hero makes a decision whose irreversible consequences destroy him or that which is essential to his happiness. The hero's tragic error thus makes him guilty of some terrible moral evil that he would never have chosen willingly. The tragic nature of this situation is exacerbated by the very virtue of the protagonist, who courageously struggles to meet all his obligations and usually feels both guilt and bitter remorse for his moral failure. The four narrative tragedies show how the fate of the hero is determined partly by his own moral choices, and partly by inconsistencies and conflicts of value within his society. Finally, the authors of the works we have considered use various literary techniques to present broader implications of an individual's tragedy. Tragic experience may be seen as fairly unique or rare, or as a common and basic aspect of human moral experience. And tragedy may suggest despair or discouragement about the value of certain virtues, and about moral life generally, or else it may involve either a clear or a somewhat muted reaffirmation of the significance of a moral virtue in spite of its defeat or fallibility in particular circumstances.

7

Tragedy and Ethical Reflection

Tragedy depicts a striking moral situation: an admirable character performs actions which lead to evil and to self-destruction. One would think that tragedy would be an extremely interesting topic and a subject of intense concern for philosophers and that they would naturally turn to literature as a source of insight and illumination. However, surprisingly little has been written about the moral issues raised by tragedy. As we note instances in which the topic of tragedy is skirted, it appears that this subject is an uncomfortable one for many ethical thinkers. Indeed, tragedy has often been perceived as a "problem" to be either dissolved or entirely avoided.

One of the purposes of this study of modern tragedy is to raise the question of how literary tragedy can nourish ethical reflection. This culminating chapter will explain why tragedy has been seen as a problem for ethical thinking and will elaborate ways in which tragedy can serve as an incentive to further ethical reflection. Literary tragedies direct attention to certain aspects of moral experience for which particular understandings of ethics fail to account, for interestingly different reasons. Two aspects of tragic literature have particular moral significance: the depiction of a character's virtue leading to evil, and the representation of irreconcilable conflicts between different moral values and between different virtues.

I. *The Problem of Tragedy in Ethical Reflection*

Why have ethical thinkers often avoided recognizing tragic aspects of moral experience? The sources of this tendency are as old as Plato's account in *The Republic* of a "quarrel between the philosopher and the poet." Plato criticizes literary depictions of the gods' involvement in human suffering, contending that the gods are only responsible for the good things that befall humans. He argues, therefore, that the rulers of the ideal state, "must either forbid them [the poets] to say that these woes are the work of God, or they must devise some such interpretation as we now require, and must declare that what God did was righteous and good, and they were benefited by their chastisement."[1] In this way Plato tries to avoid one of the haunting problems that tragedy poses: the question of theodicy. Plato's second criticism of tragedy is based on the belief that this kind of literature will have a negative influence on human morality. Fear and the impulse to lament misfortune endanger self-control and moral fortitude. While Plato does not refer exclusively to tragedy in his attack on literature's emotional effects, censorship of the plays of Sophocles and Euripides would figure prominently in his proposal to "taboo in these matters the entire vocabulary of terror and fear."[2] Human morality is threatened also by the suggestion that acting justly may bring a person nothing but misery and that one could be happy by being secretly immoral. Because it shows that virtue may not lead to one's own advantage and that the wicked and unjust are often successful and happy, tragedy would have to be outlawed in Plato's Republic.

Walter Kaufmann suggests that one source of Plato's hostility to the tragic poets involves the first philosophers' reaction against traditional authority. "Refusing to read their ideas into ancient texts or to invoke either the poets of the past or philosophic predecessors as authorities, they let their dicta stand on their own merits and went out of their way to emphasize their disagreements with those who had come before them."[3] The birth of philosophy as a movement of independent thought necessitated rebellion against a historically revered literary tradition. For Socrates and Plato and Aristotle, belief that their own reasoning was superior to the tragic poets' insights was accompanied by a certain defensiveness and querulousness. Perhaps something like the ancient quarrel between the philosopher and the poet continues to lie at the root of the difficulty ethical thinkers often seem to have in taking seriously the genuine insights into moral experience that are embodied in literature. Ethical thinkers have not always seen that literature does not just mirror the moral beliefs of an age, but subjects them to critical pressure. They have therefore proceeded as if progress in ethical thought could be achieved only by breaking with their culture's artistic achievements, little suspecting the price this imaginative impoverishment exacts in their accounts of human moral experience.

A further reason for Plato's hostility to the tragic poets is his presentation of a new norm of moral virtue radically opposed to that of the usual hero of literature. Plato's dramatizations of Socrates' life portray "virtue as its own reward." That is, Plato shows that "no evil can befall a just man because his virtue is its own reward, creating in him a serene

---

[1] Plato, *The Republic*, 380a–b, trans. Paul Shorey, in *The Collected Dialogues of Plato*, ed. Edith Hamilton and Huntington Cairns (Princeton, NJ: Princeton University Press, 1961), p. 627.

[2] Ibid., 387b. p. 632.

[3] Walter Kaufmann, *Tragedy and Philosophy* (Princeton, NJ: Princeton University Press, 1968), p. 5.

self-confidence and calm, heroic happiness that triumphs over calumny, persecution, and death."[4] I would extend Kaufmann's insight to later thinkers who have insisted that the truly good man should face suffering with stoical equanimity, secure that no earthly fate can diminish the worth of his virtuous actions. As did Plato, many moralists have thought that the tragedians place too much emphasis on happiness in this life. For the tragic hero does not find it an easy matter to renounce his happiness in the world for the sake of moral duty. Ethical thinkers have sometimes seen in the depiction of the tragic hero a glorification of such dangerous human impulses as ambition and arrogance and sensuality. And they have seen in tragedy an insidious temptation for men to value success or happiness or even life itself too dearly in relation to the absolute and peremptory demand of moral claims.[5] Most tragic protagonists would fit neither the philosopher's prescription for the good man nor the religious ideal of the saint who humbly submits his will to God. I suspect that the wish of philosophers and theologians to propose alternative notions of the morally good person has been an important factor in their continuing reluctance to dwell upon tragedy, where the conflict between moral virtue and personal self-interest is not resolved by a character's simply adopting an attitude of stoical indifference to all that tempts him away from duty.

Before discussing certain distinctive modes of ethical assessment that have allowed thinkers to avoid considering moral tragedy, I want to suggest one reason why they all have some difficulty in accounting for tragedy. Tragedy calls into question the boundaries of ethical judgment that every moralist must define or assume. Any system of moral evaluation must distinguish between matters for which a person can be morally assessed and things for which he or she cannot be assessed. The requirement of control is a crucial presupposition of moral assessment. When we are not just evaluating a state of affairs as good or bad but judging a person's moral responsibility, we assume that he or she must have had the capacity to alter events. Except in cases of negligence, a person is not accountable for an act unless he had the power and the relevant knowledge to have chosen to do or not to do it. Thus the making of moral assessments depends on certain deep-rooted, and usually unarticulated, beliefs about the limits of the sphere of human moral accountability which define the boundaries of ethical judgment. Tragedy threatens to undermine our sense of moral accountability because it shows that agents can become culpable for things for which they are not, strictly speaking, at fault. In actuality

---

[4] Ibid., p. 27.

[5] An interesting example of a philosopher's alternative paradigm of virtue lies in Kant's "Methodology of Pure Practical Reason" in the *Critique of Practical Reason*, trans. Lewis White Beck (Indianapolis: Bobbs-Merrill, 1956), pp. 155–59. In discussing the value of biography in moral education, Kant argues that not heroic actions, but actions performed entirely out of regard for duty, form the best subject matter for moral instruction.

individuals are held (and hold themselves) responsible for a number of things that different moral theories tend to downplay in their stress on other elements involved in moral judgment. Hence the following analysis of how a number of factors—such as the consequences of action, intentions, the legitimacy of an agent's concern for his own happiness, and society's role in generating moral conflicts—all shape moral judgment of a person and his acts. Any of these factors may be seen as adventitious and basically external to the scope of moral assessment by certain thinkers and ethical systems. By showing the significance of one of these elements, tragedy challenges the way a particular theory of moral assessment characteristically defines an agent's responsibility.

Thomas Nagel has called attention to the phenomenon of "moral luck" and explained how it seems to call in question the legitimacy of moral assessment:

> Where a significant aspect of what someone does depends on factors beyond his control, yet we continue to treat him in that respect as an object of moral judgment, it can be called moral luck. Such luck can be good or bad. And the problem posed by this phenomenon, which led Kant to deny its possibility, is that the broad range of external influences here identified seems on close examination to undermine moral assessment as surely as does the narrower range of familiar excusing conditions. If the condition of control is consistently applied, it threatens to erode most of the moral assessments we find it natural to make. The things for which people are morally judged are determined in more ways than we at first realize by what is beyond their control.[6]

In tragedy, bad "moral luck" appears in the form of fate. The hero becomes guilty because of any of several things that are partly beyond the control of his will: the kind of person he is, with characteristic inclinations and aptitudes; improbable coincidences and circumstances; contingent external factors influencing the way his actions turn out; or the unfortunate juxtaposition of conflicting demands placed on him by his social roles. It is dismaying and disconcerting to see the tragic hero condemned by his society and usually condemning himself for things that he could in no way have prevented or altered. Such a problematic situation makes especially uncomfortable thinkers concerned to discriminate the lines separating the sphere of moral assessment from all that is supposed to be external or irrelevant to it. This is perhaps the underlying reason why tragedy is felt to be a problem for ethics, and, in a number of ways, to confound thinking about moral responsibility.

Ethical thinkers who judge the morality of an act primarily in terms of an agent's intentions often fail to account for the fact that consideration of consequences may disclose a tragic dimension of certain choices.

---

[6] Thomas Nagel, "Moral Luck," in *Mortal Questions* (Cambridge, England: Cambridge University Press, 1979), p. 26.

This tendency is characteristic of deontological moral theories. Despite many dissimilarities among deontological thinkers, they all tend to stress the intrinsic significance of the actions of moral agents. In its extreme form, deontological theories assert that moral agents must determine how to act solely from consideration of the intrinsic rightness or wrongness of an action, and must do their duty "whatever the consequences." Kant is the extreme example of a thoroughgoing deontologist, for, in his focus on the "good will" of the moral agent, he sometimes explicitly rules out considering the consequences of an action in assessing its rightness. This leads him to a kind of studied and stubborn near-sightedness in cases where performance of a moral duty seems to lead directly to evil. The most famous example of this is his controversial discussion of the duty of truthtelling and the absolute prohibition of lying. Kant held that one should always tell the truth, even in the bizarre case of a man's being asked by a murderer where his victim was hiding. Kant claimed that the questioned man would be morally guilty if he lied to the murderer. Furthermore, by lying he becomes responsible for any bad consequences resulting from his acts; while, if he tells the truth, he cannot be held responsible for another person's—the murderer's—acts.[7] Sissela Bok has pointed to the basic problem with Kant's position: "There is much truth in saying that one is responsible for what happens after one has done something wrong or questionable. But it is a very narrow view of responsibility which does not also take some blame for a disaster one could easily have averted, no matter how much others are to blame."[8] Kant's view of responsibility is unreasonably restricted. For we do in fact hold others, and ourselves, responsible for the consequences of actions (or abstentions from action) performed with the best of intentions.

Tragedy shows in the most striking way that the actual results of a person's acts cannot help but influence how they are morally assessed, even though the agent may not have been able to control how things turned out. This is so because what one's action *is* is defined in part by its consequences. For example, in Henry James's *The Princess Casamassima*, Hyacinth Robinson's vow to Hoffendahl is a disastrous tragic error rather than simply an impulsive youthful folly because in fact Hoffendahl commands him to fulfill the vow by murdering a duke. If Hyacinth's "call" had never come, his vow would still have been a rash

---

[7] The extent of our responsibility for unfortunate consequences that follow from virtuous action was an issue which preoccupied Samuel Johnson in *Rasselas*. But Johnson stresses not the fact that we are not responsible for bad consequences but the consolation for our conscience provided by the knowledge that we have acted rightly. See *Rasselas*, chap. 34, in *Samuel Johnson: Selected Poetry and Prose*, ed. with introduction and notes by Frank Brady and W. K. Wimsatt (Berkeley: University of California Press, 1977).

[8] Sissela Bok, *Lying: Moral Choice in Public and Private Life* (New York: Vintage Books, 1978), p. 44.

and foolish statement, and he might well have regretted it, but it would not have directly precipitated the dilemma of divided loyalties that drives him to suicide. In Conrad's *Nostromo*, Charles Gould's actions in the Sulaco revolution are judged adversely by the reader partly because in fact they lead to his wife's suffering, even though this result was neither part of his original intention nor even within the realm of anticipation. The reader's interpretive response to tragedy shows how the scope of moral assessment encompasses consequences that seem extraneous and irrelevant to the character's intentions and good will. The fact that extreme forms of deontological moral theory do not account for this kind of moral situation without distorting its complexity raises doubts about the adequacy of such theories.[9]

Just as Plato presented the moral man as indifferent to pleasure or happiness, many ethical thinkers have tried to dissociate morality from questions of self-interest. Kant thought that the attempt to show that morality coincides with rational self-interest threatens to corrupt morality by making it only a more efficient means of pursuing natural human interests. Without criticizing Kant's attempt to protect the autonomy and integrity of ethical thought, I submit that Kant's influence has sometimes led later thinkers to sever all connection between morality and human well-being in its broadest sense. H. A. Prichard, for example, claimed that for a philosopher to attempt to "justify" moral duty is a basic mistake. Prichard held that moral obligations are immediately, intuitively known, and should be carried out regardless of their contribution or detriment to our happiness.[10] Though an approach like Prichard's need not dispute the fact that the performance of moral duty may lead to great suffering for an individual in a particular case, it will refuse to consider as a serious issue the question of why a person should act morally when such action brings disaster. Tragic literature, which raises this question in the starkest terms, can present only a disturbing problem for the ethical position that morality must be dissociated from considerations of the general human search for happiness.

An ethical perspective that focuses primarily on whether the consequences of action are good or bad has difficulty accounting adequately for a tragic choice when the agent must actively will evil as part of his moral intention. Utilitarianism is the best-known school of thought which evaluates actions primarily in terms of their consequences. The utilitarian viewpoint often misinterprets the tragic situation in which a person is faced

---

[9] I do not wish to imply that all deontological theories are incapable of considering consequences. See Alan Donagan's *Theory of Morality* (Chicago: University of Chicago Press, 1977), chapter 6, especially pp. 172 and 206.

[10] H. A. Prichard, "Does Moral Philosophy Rest on a Mistake?" (1912) in Prichard's *Moral Obligation* (Oxford: Oxford University Press, 1949).

with a choice between two evils. The utilitarian tends to redescribe the outcome of such a choice so that its character as "the lesser evil" is entirely lost, and it becomes simply "the right thing to do."[11] Tragedy is impossible for the utilitarian because, in judging mainly the consequences of action, one need not "count" the guilt attached to having intentionally brought about some evil.[12] It seems an evasion, though, to ignore the tragic implications of a person's having to choose to do the lesser of two evils. By making this choice simply a matter of rational calculation, such a position denies the real costs of a decision actively to will some evil. In the sphere of public policy, this often means that insufficient attention is given to injustices done to individuals for the sake of some social gain. The utilitarian tends to devalue the individual person in the interest of social benefits, thus establishing a justification and a precedent for terrible abuses.[13] The utilitarian also neglects the difficult uncertainty and the real (not illusory) sense of guilt of the person who must choose between two evils. Such tragedies as *Antigone* and *Hamlet* and R. P. Warren's *All the King's Men* reveal blind spots in this sort of moral perspective as they explore the agony of decision and the burden of guilt borne by an individual who knows that even his most conscientious efforts to do the right thing cannot release him from moral culpability.

The moral ambiguity involved in "doing evil to achieve good" is a key issue at stake in discussions of the merits of the Roman Catholic theory of "double effect." The theory of double effect is a complex notion which specifies the conditions under which a person may perform an act likely to have evil consequences. Basically the theory requires that the evil effect be "indirect": not the agent's primary end or a means to

[11] See Bernard Williams, *Morality: An Introduction to Ethics* (New York: Harper and Row, 1972), pp. 92–93: "The various claims he may feel on him can be brought to the common measure of the Greatest Happiness Principle, and there can be no coherent idea of a right or wrong thing to do, other than what is, or is not *the best thing to do on the whole*. . . . For utilitarianism, tragedy is impossible."

[12] This approach to a choice between evils is illustrated in a recent forum on *War and Moral Responsibility*, ed. Marshall Cohen, Thomas Nagel, and Thomas Scanlon (Princeton, NJ: Princeton University Press, 1974). Nagel raises the issue of the possibility of a "moral blind alley": "The world can present us with situations in which there is no honorable or moral course for a man to take, no course free of guilt and responsibility for evil" (p. 23). R. B. Brandt and R. M. Hare argue that such a situation is impossible, for the person in such a situation can always resolve the apparent dilemma by going through calculations that show one or the other course of action to be preferable.

[13] Stuart Hampshire, *Morality and Pessimism* (Cambridge, England: Cambridge University Press, 1972), pp. 30–31: "The error of the optimistic utilitarian is that he carries the deritualisation of transactions between men to a point at which men not only can, but ought to, use and exploit each other as they use and exploit any other natural objects. . . . When the mere existence of an individual person by itself has no value, apart from the by-products and uses of the individual in producing and enjoying desirable states of mind, there is no theoretical barrier against social surgery of all kinds."

that end, but an unavoidable "side-effect" which, while it can be fore-seen, is not part of the agent's intention. That is, the agent's intention is defined as not encompassing the evil effect that he foresees and helps bring about. While the principle of double effect does illuminate certain moral situations, recent discussions have shown that the theory of double effect often justifies a kind of studied aversion to recognizing one's responsibility for some evil.[14] Whatever a person does intentionally is subject to moral assessment, however indirect causally it is from his main purpose. In certain tragic situations, a person may incur moral guilt no matter what he does, because whatever course of action he wills entails some evil.

Moral thinkers who wish to see all values as commensurable are dis-inclined to reflect on tragedy. The clearest form of this tendency arises out of the utilitarian's attempt to quantify all values. Bernard Williams argues that utilitarians are committed to the quantification of values because this is the only apparent way in which the "greatest happiness" can be computed where different values conflict.[15] Especially on issues of public policy, moral thought must compare dissimilar values, compute risks and costs and benefits, and search for methods and decision proce-dures to help adjudicate difficult choices. However, there is a real danger of false clarity and of simplifying the problems that arise when diverse values conflict. We need to be able to reflect on such conflicts without assuming that a sort of ethical calculus will always yield the right "solu-tion." The "problem-solving" approach can reduce to a mere matter of technique the complex and open-ended process of assessment that is involved in moral deliberation.

Literary tragedy shows the "messiness" of moral decision between incommensurable values, and for this reason many moralists find it only confusing. Tragedy reminds moral thinkers of the painful elements of ambiguity and uncertainty that are inescapable aspects of hard choices, and it shows how affective loyalties and intentional commitments are nec-essary to resolve an issue. How is *The Princess Casamassima's* Hyacinth Robinson to measure the value of his culture's artistic heritage against the need for social justice? Or how is Captain Vere of Melville's *Billy Budd* to calculate whether prudence for his ship's safety or concern to spare Billy's life should resolve his moral dilemma? When these protagonists commit

[14] For contrasting criticisms of the principle of double effect, see Donagan, *Theory of Morality*, pp. 157–64; Richard McCormick and Paul Ramsey, eds., *Doing Evil to Achieve Good* (Chicago: Loyola University Press, 1978); and Michael Walzer's critique of Paul Ramsey's position in *Just and Unjust Wars* (New York: Basic Books, 1977), pp. 278–83.

[15] Williams, *Morality*, p. 97: "Nor is it an accidental feature of the utilitarian outlook that the presumption is in favor of the monetarily quantifiable, because quantification in money is the only obvious form of what utilitarianism insists upon, the commensurability of value."

themselves to one value, they do not and cannot justify their turning against the other one. And yet, given their situations, they must choose one value or the other. Tragedy's depiction of agonizing conflicts between irreconcilable and incommensurable values raises grave doubts about any moral theory that does not at least acknowledge (if not explain the reasons for) the elements of ambiguity and indeterminacy in moral choice.

Tragedy depicts powerful forces in the world that are hostile to human virtue. Many philosophers and religious thinkers have found such a vision of the world deeply distressing, even repugnant. Recognizing the limited power and knowledge of any individual, they have felt that moral activity can be effective only if it is sustained by deeper and broader forces than the isolated human will. Virtue seems a futile effort if the universe does not ultimately support the good man's endeavors. Therefore, faced with the destruction of a virtuous person, one habitual tendency of ethical thinkers is to isolate the individual's will and blame the disaster on some fault of the individual, rather than seeing the sources of tragedy in the structure of society and the world itself. In this way, the basic human need to be reassured about the ultimate goodness of the universe produces an impulse to moralize and to lay blame. If a person's suffering can be attributed to his own fault, we feel that the suffering was avoidable, and our confidence in the world is not called radically into doubt. Moral thinkers find it immensely reassuring when they can locate the source of a moral conflict in the fault of the moral agent: in what Alan Donagan, following Aquinas, calls perplexity *secundum quid*—perplexity conditional upon some misdeed—rather than perplexity *simpliciter*: a case in which a person, through no fault of his own, is faced with a situation in which he can only escape or prevent one evil by doing another.[16]

This tendency begins, as we saw above, with Plato's claim in the *Republic* that it is men and not the gods who are responsible for human misfortunes. It can be detected, too, in Aristotle's account of tragedy in the *Poetics*, in his notion of *hamartia*: tragic error. The hero should be an "intermediate kind of personage, a man not pre-eminently virtuous and just, whose misfortune, however, is brought upon him not by vice and depravity but by some error of judgment."[17] Aristotle ruled out the quite conceivable possibility that a good man could be destroyed through no moral fault of his own because of an underlying ethical assumption about the world. Aristotle's moral theory depends on the universe being organized so that prosperity accompanies the virtuous man. He can only find ethically shocking the portrayal of a superlatively good man, for

---

[16] Donagan, *Theory of Morality*, p. 144.
[17] Aristotle, *Poetics*, chap. 13, trans. Ingram Bywater, in *Introduction to Aristotle*, ed. Richard McKeon (New York: Modern Library, 1947), pp. 639–40.

such a fall "shakes the foundations of Aristotelian ethics."[18] (Also, Aristotle asserts that the virtues form a unity in the good man: they do not conflict.)

Though Aristotle's theoretical conception of possible tragic heroes seems unduly restrictive, he was empirically correct that the protagonists of most tragedies are not morally faultless. Tragic characters make mistakes, compromise their integrity for dubious ends, and rashly make incompatible commitments. However, is the fact that the source of a painful conflict of duties lies partly in some past misdeed of the agent really much less disturbing than the possibility of a person's being faced with perplexity *simpliciter*? Tragedy shows how individuals can suddenly find themselves in a situation in which it is almost impossible for them not to do wrong. In tragedy, a good man is often called upon to make incompatible promises or commitments or to reconcile divided aims and contentious political factions. A tragedy such as Warren's *All the King's Men* explores why an idealistic and energetic figure like Willie Stark, in trying to reform his state's political institutions, believes he must compromise in choosing his means and finally becomes corrupted. Once we have realized the difficulty of a protagonist's meeting all the demands placed on him, we cannot feel that his misery is less great, or his fate less terrible, simply because his downfall is partly his own fault. Tragedy shows that the sources of catastrophe, while they take effect through the human will, lie ultimately in the structure of the world. The origins of tragedy are not in the isolated agent, but remote: in the family line, in the incessant strife between society's factions, in humankind's sense that the conditions of security must be wrested from nature. As Max Scheler put it, "In every genuine tragedy we see more than just the tragic event. . . . The remote subject of the tragic is always the world itself, the world taken as a whole which makes such a thing possible."[19] When philosophers try to locate the source of tragedy exclusively within the will of the individual, they turn away from an open invitation to reflect on how the structure of the world and of particular societies generates conflicts that a person cannot resolve without incurring moral guilt and suffering.

The phenomenon of a virtuous person acting wrongly is so paradoxical that sometimes philosophers will deny that it can happen. That is, they define the role of character in the moral life so that only vices, never virtues, can lead to evil. For Aristotle, virtue is a mean between extremes; when carried to excess, the qualities associated with a virtue become a vice. Augustine accounted for the way that virtues can lead to

[18] A. W. H. Adkins, "Aristotle and the Best Kind of Tragedy," *Classical Quarterly* 16 n. s. (1966), 100.
[19] Max Scheler, "On the Tragic," trans. Bernard Stambler, in *Tragedy: Vision and Form*, ed. Robert Corrigan (San Francisco: Chandler, 1965), pp. 7–8.

evil by interpreting such qualities as "splendid vices." Courage or charity in a pagan, or prudence in a thief, are not true virtues, but vices, because they are not directed to the highest good, God.[20] The Catholic tradition has pointed to the need for prudence to mediate possible conflicts between different virtues. Without prudence, acting according to one virtue can be wrong, as in the case of a person who is tempted to do an act of injustice out of loyalty or charity to a needy friend. Recently Phillipa Foot has tried to account for our puzzlement at the idea that virtues may be displayed in bad actions.[21] All of these insightful attempts to explain the puzzling connections between virtues and evil share a common problem. Certain human capacities are praised or recommended in themselves, in isolation from any concrete actions. At the same time, particular evil actions are by definition severed from any connection with virtue. Such a strategy glosses over a basic truth about human moral experience. Tragic literature shows that the attributes and qualities of individuals produce actions very mixed in moral value. Tragedy reveals that, while virtues and character are essential factors in the moral life, the qualities of agents cannot be neatly correlated with types of action. As Warren's character Jack Burden puts it in *All the King's Men*: "The morally bad agent may perform the deed which is good. The morally good agent may perform the deed which is bad." The connections between the characters of persons and the qualities of their acts are neither as systematic nor as fortunate as most theories of virtue claim. On the contrary, the very virtues of a person can dispose him to act in such a way that, given his circumstances and the values he holds, he brings disaster for himself and others. Tragedy discloses a radical gap or breakdown between human intentionality and the actual shape of action. It reveals the disharmony between a person's deepest needs and goals and his power to affect the course of the world. We close our eyes to this reality at the cost of our own moral understanding.

The Christian tradition, as well, has sometimes avoided acknowledging the reality of a tragic situation. The idea that the world could present a good man with a choice between two evils, either of which must lead him to commit evil, is intolerable to many religious believers. And tragedy's depiction of the radical disproportion between a person's virtues and his fate in history raises all the baffling questions of theodicy. One way that Christians have shunned the tragic poet's insights has been to

[20] Augustine, *City of God*, Bk. 19, ch. 25, trans. Henry Bettenson (Harmondsworth, England: Penguin Books, 1972), p. 891.

[21] In *Virtues and Vices and Other Essays in Moral Philosophy* (Berkeley: University of California Press, 1978), Foot says that virtue-words refer to powers of producing good actions, in a way similar to that in which the terms "poison" or "solvent" name properties of physical things. "Just as poisons, solvents, and corrosives do not always operate characteristically, so it could be with virtues. . . . Courage is not operating as a virtue when the murderer turns his courage, which is a virtue, to bad ends" (p. 16).

attribute evil to an individual's own sin. This is the theological version of the tendency to blame evil exclusively on the fault of the individual.[22] When Christian thinkers have recognized tragic situations, they have usually concentrated on fixing the blame for misfortune on the sin of the individual involved. "Pride must have a fall" expresses a profound insight into the human condition, but this summary statement is often lacking in compassion and even understanding of the sufferer of a moral fall. A less common tendency of Christian thought seeks to emphasize that disaster in this world is never final, and that the end of history will involve a divine act of reckoning and the granting of justice and mercy to suffering human-kind. Beliefs about God's eschatological actions have sometimes been invoked to argue that tragedy is but a moment in human experience which will ultimately be succeeded by God's setting right, and even justifying, radical disproportions between human virtue and earthly happiness. Eschatological beliefs are a vital and essential part of Christian faith. However, when theologians move too quickly beyond the conflicts of history to affirmations of final justice, the tragic aspects of experience are blurred, and religious faith becomes an escape from troubling facts rather than a source for truthful illumination of the human condition.

Sometimes philosophers do not avoid the tragic, but embrace it. Since Hegel and Nietzsche, various thinkers have interpreted life itself as tragic. While metaphysically and theologically suggestive, however, a work such as Unamuno's *Tragic Sense of Life* is so all-encompassing in its use of the term "tragic" as to be of little aid in understanding the moral aspects of life.[23] When tragedy is seen as co-extensive with human existence, such a perspective results in failure to perceive crucial differ-ences among tragic moral situations, and differences between tragic situations and ones that are not tragic. The danger of using the term "tragic" to apply to every moral choice can be avoided only by a moral theory that distinguishes between a tragic moral situation and the sweep-ing claim that life itself is somehow tragic. Furthermore, it seems rather curious for thinkers to recommend "the tragic sense" as a kind of philoso-phy of life. All too often such assertions involve a sort of perverse pleasure in defeat and despair, a melodramatic pessimism or professional gloomi-ness. Tragedy is only real when it is forced on us; it is not a philosophical

---

[22] Peter Geach, in *The Virtues* (Cambridge, England: Cambridge University Press, 1978), p. 155, indignantly rejects the possibility that God could allow an innocent person to face a dilemma requiring a choice of evil: "This can be envisaged as a possibility only by people who do not believe in God's Providence or do not think consequently about what such belief implies. . . . A man cannot get into such a dilemma innocently or by the fault of others. God does not require of a faithful servant the desperate choice between sin and sin."

[23] Miguel de Unamuno, *Tragic Sense of Life* (1912), trans. J. E. Crawford Flitch (New York: Dover Publications, 1954).

view that one can argue for.[24] My conclusion that literary tragedy can help us to understand certain aspects of moral experience is by no means the same thing as the claim of the validity of a "tragic sense of life," or a sweeping generalization about the tragic nature of existence.

In human experience, tragedy is surely not something to be sought or to be accepted when it can be avoided. Unfortunately, tragedy is sometimes inescapable. It is therefore objectionable when ethical thinkers ignore tragedy, and habitually direct attention away from certain intentions or conflicts of duty or consequences that show virtuous action bringing about suffering.[25] Our understanding of moral experience is vitiated when, in the ways discussed above, certain factors are conveniently declared outside the boundaries of moral reflection, irrelevant or inaccessible to ethical assessment. We need methods and systematic theories of ethics to offer illumination and practical guidance in conflict situations (that is their primary rationale), but we also need to recognize that in some situations our theories and decision procedures break down: they don't provide a solution to a difficult dilemma. However, tragedy need not be seen solely as a problem to be "solved" by thought if tragedy is recognized as a fact of life. And ethical reflection need not cease when faced with the tragic aspects of moral experience. Sometimes our understanding of particular situations extends beyond our capacity to explain them in terms of a single coherent theory of ethics. Then ethical thought may simply have to recognize certain features of moral experience and reflect on their deeper implications for human life. I submit that literary tragedy is an invaluable source of insight into the shapes of human moral experience and provides a fruitful starting point, and an incentive toward, deeper and more honest ethical reflection.

II. *Tragedy as an Incentive to Ethical Reflection*

The term "tragedy," originally an aesthetic concept referring to a genre of literary art, is now loosely applied to any misfortune or sudden loss. When what we call a tragedy takes place near us, we find it shocking

---

[24] See Lionel Abel, "Is There a Tragic Sense of Life?" in Lionel Abel, ed., *Moderns on Tragedy* (Greenwich, CT: Fawcett, 1967), p. 178: "We cannot urge the tragic sense on ourselves or on others. To try to attain it or to recommend it is comical and self-refuting, tragedy being real only when unavoidable. There would be no such things as tragedy if a tragic fate could be rationally chosen."

[25] Resistance to the idea that a person may be faced with an irreconcilable conflict of moral obligations extends from the theoretical positions discussed above to specific practical issues. See Stephen Toulmin's analysis of the aversion to acknowledging possible conflicts of duty within legal and medical professionals' codes of ethics, "The Meaning of Professionalism: Doctors' Ethics and Biomedical Science," in *Knowledge, Value and Belief*, ed. H. Tristram Engelhardt, Jr. and Daniel Callahan (Hastings-on-Hudson, NY: Institute of Society, Ethics and the Life Sciences, 1977).

and repugnant. A puzzling feature of the aesthetic experience of tragedy is that we find moving, beautiful, and thought-provoking the depiction of events that would utterly appall us if they happened to someone close to us. The psychology of tragic pleasure depends on the fact that the reader or spectator is aesthetically detached and "distant" from suffering that would be overwhelmingly horrible in his or her own life. Yet the phenomenon of aesthetic distance, far from leading to a complete hiatus between literature and life, is the reason literature gives rise to ethical reflection. We do not simply dismiss the events depicted in tragedy; we take them seriously as a representation of possible human experiences. Our aesthetic detachment from the sufferings described in tragedy is intellectually productive, for we are forced to recognize and invited to ponder the harsher realities of human existence that we can only try to avoid in our own lives. Literary tragedy appeals to us to acknowledge painful truths about human experience that ethical theories and systems sometimes finesse, distort, or ignore. Simply by forcing us to confront "inconvenient facts" and potential conflicts between certain values and ideals, tragedy performs a crucial moral function. But tragedy also calls out for interpretation in terms of an account of the factors in the human moral condition that make tragedy possible.

Tragedy shows in vivid detail the significance of circumstances in moral experience. A tragic situation comes about because of particular circumstances that seem highly fortuitous, even irrelevant to our usual sense of that for which a person is morally accountable. That Billy Budd's stutter leaves him unable to defend himself verbally against Claggart's accusation, or that Lear finds Cordelia just minutes too late to save her from murder: how striking it is that these characters' moral accountability, and their very life or death, should hang on such apparently minor, trivial circumstances. Though there are common factors involved in any moral assessment (intentions, consequences, motives), it is impossible to set out in advance exactly what needs to be considered as significant in order to understand and evaluate each work's central events. While to some this particularity seems to show the process of ethical assessment as frustratingly fluid and open-ended, it is part of a tragedy's value for the moralist that it is not simply a "case study" that can be subsumed under a generalized pattern. It is not just that what "counts" as morally significant in each tragic work is unique and unpredictable, for this is true as well of nontragic literature. What makes tragedy such a rich source of insight is its traditional theme of the determining power of circumstances: as, for instance, in the significance of Desdemona's handkerchief to a jealous Othello. Tragedy shows a kingdom lost for want of a nail.

Because of this richness and specificity of circumstantial detail, one major value of literary tragedy for ethics is its role in developing the mind's powers of discernment. James Gustafson suggests that a "discerning" person "has an unusual capacity to isolate significant detail, to perceive subtleties, to be penetrating and accurate in his observations. While in one sense, to discern something is simply to notice it, to see it, in another sense we reserve the word for a quality of perception, of discrimination, of observation and judgment."[26] Gustafson's comparison of the act of moral discernment to "the combination of elements that go into good literary criticism and good literary creativity" points to a significant aspect of our interpretive response to tragedy. Tragedy provides the ethical thinker with a body of experience which shows in particular cases how we actually make complex moral judgments. By depicting in concrete instances the crucial role of certain circumstances in shaping human actions, tragic literature serves as an invaluable aid and resource for ethical reflection, which should be understood to encompass not only generalizations about the common elements of all human actions and choices, but the development of interpretive skills of discernment in relation to human action.

The moral dilemmas at the heart of tragedy give rise to thought about the incommensurability of moral values. When values have no common measure, choice between them becomes extremely uncertain and difficult. In *All the King's Men*, Willie Stark faces a choice between two values equally crucial to him: maintaining his own personal integrity or bringing about what he believes is a great good. In *The Princess Casamassima*, Hyacinth must finally give his allegiance either to the anarchist movement for social justice or to the established society that conserves aesthetic values. Tragic characters experience a wracking uncertainty, stemming from the necessity for a single irrevocable decision between courses of action that not only conflict, but seem independently justifiable, because supported by fundamentally different kinds of value. The protagonists' dilemmas reveal a basic fact about human moral experience: the sources of value are diverse and can conflict so that a person may be forced to choose one at the expense of the other.

Thomas Nagel has described how "the fragmentation of value" gives rise to this kind of dilemma: "The strongest cases of conflict are genuine dilemmas, where there is decisive support for two or more incompatible courses of action or inaction. In that case a decision will still be necessary, but it will seem necessarily arbitrary. . . . Either choice will mean acting against some reasons without being able to claim they are outweighed."[27] Nagel describes five types of value that can conflict: (1) "specific obligations to other people or institutions" that an individual

---

[26] James M. Gustafson, "Moral Discernment in the Christian Life," in *Norm and Context in Christian Ethics*, ed. Gene H. Outka and Paul Ramsey (New York: Scribner's Sons, 1968), p. 18.

[27] Nagel, "The Fragmentation of Value," in *Mortal Questions*, pp. 128–29.

incurs; (2) "constraints on action deriving from general rights that everyone has, either to do certain things or not to be treated in certain ways"; (3) utility: consideration of the effects of one's actions on everyone's welfare; (4) "perfectionist ends or values . . . the intrinsic value of certain achievements or creations"; (5) "commitment to one's own projects or undertakings."[28] Any of these values can conflict with another one; any value could also conflict with a person's self-interest. Nagel argues that it would be absurd to try to order these values in a system of fixed priorities: for example, to hold that specific obligations could never outweigh general rights, or that utility could never override obligations. The sources of value are multiple, reflecting the fact that persons as moral agents are "complex creatures who can view the world from many perspectives—individual, relational, impersonal, ideal, etc.—and each perspective presents a different set of claims."[29]

It would be possible and germane to analyze tragic literature in terms of these values, but such a complex exercise can only be suggested here. In the James novel, for example, Hyacinth's quandary pits (Nagel's) values 1 and 3 against 2 and 4: he faces a conflict between, on the one hand, a specific obligation he has incurred (by his vow) and his concern with "utility" (the welfare of everyone, but especially "the greatest number", the poor), and, on the other hand, a general constraint on action (the prohibition of murder) and a "perfectionist value" (the intrinsic worth of artistic achievements). He also confronts conflicts between his loyalties to various friends as well as, whatever he does, certain dangers to his self-interest. Ethical reflection on the problem of conflicts of value would be complicated greatly by turning to tragic literature, but insight might be gained into the major factor that produces ambiguity in moral choice: the incommensurability of moral values.

One aspect of the moral structure of tragedy is a sharp discrepancy between the good intentions of a person and the disastrous consequences of his acts. The tragic hero's ambiguous responsibility for misfortune shows interesting features of the process whereby an agent defines a field of moral responsibility. The area of an agent's moral responsibility is a "field," usually bounded by the limits of human foresight and the limits of the will's power. Yet the boundaries of moral responsibility are far from unalterably fixed, and individuals are interestingly different in their understandings of their accountability. Tragedy often presents a case of problematic responsibility: a character holds himself (or is held by others) accountable for events that are not obviously his fault. It is as if the hero must adhere to a kind of "strict liability" in the moral life. Thus, for instance, Conrad's Nostromo feels he is accountable for Decoud's suicide

[28] Ibid., pp. 129–30.
[29] Ibid., p. 134.

even though his connection with that death was fairly indirect. The paradox of tragic guilt is that the hero becomes guilty because of a minor error, or in spite of the lack of a significant moral failing. In this regard, Kaufmann has suggested that tragic responsibility (which is something one actively "takes") is a better term than tragic guilt for describing the hero's relation to his deeds.[30]

The tragic hero, then, holds himself accountable for certain events or consequences of his actions, even though they were not only unintended but unanticipated and unforeseeable when he acted. Usually the tragic hero feels morally responsible when a less scrupulous person would not. His nobility consists partly in this intense sense of moral accountability, often haltingly achieved through painful struggles of conscience. The hero's act of defining a field of responsibility raises questions that deserve further reflection. What factors influence an agent in defining the boundaries of his or her moral responsibility? Is it the nature of the consequences of his acts—the amount of suffering that his acts bring others? Is it his commitments or relationships to the particular individuals involved? (Tragedy has traditionally depicted the violence that disrupts bonds of family and friendship.) Is the establishment of some connection with suffering and evil an essential component of the self's ongoing quest for moral identity (as in *All the King's Men*)? What distinguishes a genuine moral hero who is imaginatively sensitive to his implication in other persons' suffering from the neurotic who wallows in his guilt feelings? Tragedy suggests a need for further reflection on the process by which a moral agent defines his field of responsibility.

In such political novels as *The Princess Casamassima*, *Nostromo*, and *All the King's Men*, the protagonists are tempted to commit an act they know is wrong in order to bring about some good. This moral dilemma is clearest in Willie Stark's case, but it applies as well to Hyacinth's vow to be ready to use violence to bring about a juster society and to the moral compromises all the main characters in *Nostromo* make in order to realize their "idea" amid the tumultuous Sulaco uprising. These tragic novels all raise a central issue in political ethics: the problem of "dirty hands." Tragedy poses the question of whether and when a good cause ever justifies the use of wrongful means. Many moralists deny that the problem of ends and means is a genuine dilemma. Kant argued that we cannot determine our moral conduct by means of an uncertain prediction of future consequences; Johnson contended that "man cannot so far know the connection of causes and events as that he may venture to do wrong in order to do right."[31] But the problem of "dirty hands"

---

[30] Kaufmann, *Tragedy and Philosophy*, p. 246: "Responsibility can be free of guilt feelings and can mean that we define our field of action."
[31] Johnson (note 7 above), p. 126.

has been a recurring issue in political ethics since Machiavelli's *The Prince*.[32] Raising the question of the legitimacy of dirty hands opens one to the charge of justifying various infamous historical crimes. However, there may be cases in which "doing evil for the sake of good" is not only a tremendous temptation but really justified, especially for political leaders entrusted with the fates of many lives. It may be that in some situations a genuine social good can only come about, or a terrible misfortune be averted, when an individual deliberately violates some basic moral prohibition or injunction. This, in fact, is how many tragic protagonists understand their moral positions. From *Agamemnon* through *Julius Caesar*'s Brutus to *All the King's Men*, the tradition of tragedy has depicted the ambitions, temptations, and moral risks inextricably bound up with the exercise of political power. Though often self-deceived about some of their motivations for choosing morally compromised actions, tragic protagonists usually wish to achieve some admirable goal and attempt to justify their decisions. It distorts our understanding of these characters to treat their conscientious struggles about the means to their ends as only a camouflage for self-deception and rationalization.

Tragedy raises at least three questions about "dirty hands." First, are there, and should there be, significant differences between what is morally expected of political leaders in their public roles and what is expected of a private individual? While recognizing that politicians have long rationalized abuses of power by promising future social benefits, several philosophers have claimed that there are instances when a political leader is morally justified in doing some wrong. According to Stuart Hampshire, this is because of three factors involved in assuming a public role: "first, accountability to one's followers, secondly, policies that are to be justified principally by their eventual consequences, and, thirdly, a withholding of some of the scruples that in private life would prohibit one from using people as a means to an end and also from using force and deceit."[33] Public and private moralities are not unrelated spheres of activity, but they have significant differences. Ethical reflection on the effect of public roles on morality might well turn to tragic literature for insight into the peculiar difficulties faced by political leaders.

A central tragic theme, as in *Nostromo* and *All the King's Men*, is

---

[32] A classic exposition of the dilemma is Max Weber's "Politics as a Vocation," in *From Max Weber*, trans., ed. with an introduction by H. H. Gerth and C. Wright Mills (New York: Oxford University Press, 1946), pp. 77–128, which presents the politician as a tragic hero who must sacrifice his own integrity to use the distinctive means of political power: violence. Michael Walzer, in "Political Action: The Problem of Dirty Hands," *War and Moral Responsibility*, ed. Cohen, Nagel, and Scanlon, pp. 62–82, argues that this dilemma is a central feature of political life.

[33] Stuart Hampshire, "Public and Private Morality," in *Public and Private Morality*, ed. Stuart Hampshire (Cambridge: Cambridge University Press, 1978), pp. 51–52.

the gradual corruption of public figures who come to believe that their hands are so stained that they must renounce—at least until their goals are achieved—all effort to act rightly. If tragedy shows the pressing considerations that seem to justify dirty hands, it raises a further question. How can a politician avoid the "slippery slope" of relativism, the process whereby the precedent set by some unusual case becomes generalized, so that it is applied indiscriminately to justify other violations of established moral rules?[34] Tragic literature offers significant insights not only into the conditions under which dirty hands might be justified, but also into the subtle temptations, the rationalizations, and the hypocrisy that can so insidiously corrupt well-meaning public leaders like Willie Stark or the Goulds in *Nostromo*. And tragedy shows the difficulty or impossibility of atoning for wrongs or reestablishing values that are violated or temporarily overridden, given the animosity and bitterness of actual political disputes.

A final question about dirty hands: to what extent can the good or bad consequences of a politician's choices justify him or make him more culpable? In many tragedies the protagonist gambles that history will justify his actions. Tragedy irresistably gives rise to speculation about the connection between "might" and "right." That is, it shows that, to a significant degree, political acts are judged as wrong or right because of their consequences. While it is necessary to assess actions from the point of view of the decision-maker who does not know the outcome of events, the way things turn out in fact has an enormous influence on the way we finally judge a course of action.[35] Faced with the necessity of decision

[34] A historical example shows the difficulty of reaffirming norms once they have been violated or "overridden." In his discussion of British terror-bombing of Germany during World War II, Walzer, *Just and Unjust Wars*, pp. 251–63, argues that the practice of deliberately bombing civilians, an action prohibited by the rules of war, was justified under the conditions of "necessity" in 1941: it was a case of dirty hands for a good end. After the terrifying threat of Hitler's totally overrunning all Europe had passed, such bombing became morally indefensible, but the Allies continued nonetheless.

[35] Nagel, in "Moral Luck," in *Mortal Questions*, p. 30, gives thought-provoking historical examples of how the way things actually turn out affects moral assessment: "If the Decembrists had succeeded in overthrowing Nicholas I in 1825 and establishing a constitutional regime, they would be heroes. As it is, not only did they fail and pay for it, but they bore some responsibility for the terrible punishments meted out to the troops who had been persuaded to follow them. If the American Revolution had been a bloody failure resulting in greater repression, then Jefferson, Franklin and Washington would still have made a noble attempt, and might not even have regretted it on their way to the scaffold, but they would also have had to blame themselves for what they had helped to bring on their contemporaries. (Perhaps peaceful efforts at reform would have eventually succeeded.) If Hitler had not overrun Europe and exterminated millions, but instead had died of a heart attack after occupying the Sudetenland, Chamberlain's action at Munich would still have utterly betrayed the Czechs, but it would not be the great moral disaster that has made his name a household word."

between conflicting imperatives, the tragic hero gambles—unsuccessfully—that a favorable outcome of events will diminish his moral culpability or even justify actions that he suspects or knows to be wrong. To a certain degree, such calculations have a place in political morality. Yet there seem to be limits to the kinds of practices that could be justified by even the happiest consequences. Further work needs to be done on how public leaders can be vindicated or blamed according to their success or failure. Such work could surely profit from consideration of the tradition of tragic literature.

Tragedy offers insights into the role of character in the moral life. Scholars of philosophical and religious ethics have recently turned to concepts of character and virtue as ways of approaching moral issues.[36] These thinkers seek a better understanding of the person as a moral agent as a corrective to theories that focus exclusively on discrete decisions or actions. While this approach has demonstrated how aspects of a person's moral character positively enhance his or her desire or capacity to lead a good life, relatively little attention has been given to character as a source of moral failure. Tragedy depicts the way a character has the "virtues of his vices" and the "vices of his virtues." In tragedy, the protagonist is destroyed or brings catastrophe to others because he is the kind of person he is, with characteristic dispositions and inclinations. In *Nostromo*, Decoud's skeptical lucidity leads to his disillusionment and suicide, while Monygham's fidelity and the courage and idealism of the Goulds all help bring about moral compromises, corruption, and suffering. The temperament and interests of "a youth on whom nothing was lost" enable Henry James's Hyacinth Robinson to perceive a dilemma that less scrupulous characters deny or ignore. And, in Warren's *All the King's Men*, Willie's predicament of whether to get his hands dirty to "make good out of bad" comes about because of his creative political vision, his boundless energy, and his determination to be good as well as to do good.

The tragedy of the failure of a good man suggests a number of questions that should concern moralists. What are the limits to which character can be assessed morally, given the large effect on character of earlier choices, good or bad fortune, and influences beyond the control of the individual? Can we explain conceptually how a person's character may lead to failure? To what extent is the virtuous person's failure attributable to human finitude—to the limitations of anyone's ability to foresee

---

36 See Foot, *Virtues and Vices*; James M. Gustafson, *Can Ethics Be Christian?* (Chicago: University of Chicago Press, 1975); and three works by Stanley Hauerwas: *Character and the Christian Life: A Study in Theological Ethics* (San Antonio, TX: Trinity University Press, 1975); *Vision and Virtue* (Notre Dame, IN: Fides Publishers, 1974); and *Truthfulness and Tragedy* (Notre Dame, IN: University of Notre Dame Press, 1977).

consequences or alter given circumstances? And what is the influence of an insidious moral pride: the subtle self-righteousness, condescension, and arrogance toward others that can develop when a person becomes aware of his better qualities and begins to seek or create opportunities to exercise them at the expense of others?

Both finitude and guilt contribute to the hero's downfall, merging in the blindness that accompanies a tragic error. The traditional motif of blindness in tragedy points to the need for reflection on a neglected issue in ethics: the significance of various kinds of inattentiveness or perceptual bias in the moral agent. Because of the unique perspective which characterizes each individual's outlook on the world, inadvertence, ignorance, negligence, and a tendency to misinterpret certain kinds of events are all aspects of even the most admirable persons. A person's purposive attentiveness to certain values or individuals means he cannot help but neglect other ones. This mental bias, so minor a flaw in itself (if it is one at all), can have momentous consequences, as any number of examples from tragic literature show. A moral agent's character gives his life direction, concentration, and focus; it also makes him or her habitually inattentive to or ignorant about certain aspects of life which can prove crucial in some situation.

Extremely significant theoretical work linking the concepts of virtue, narrative, and tragedy has been done recently by Alasdair MacIntyre and Stanley Hauerwas.[37] These two thinkers argue that because different virtues can conflict within one person's life or within a society, tragedy is sometimes an inescapable part of moral experience. Both writers deny Aristotle's and Aquinas's belief in the necessary unity and harmony of the virtues within the life of the individual good person or in the good society. Opposition and conflict are central in human life, and moral agents are sometimes unable to meet all the moral obligations that confront them. Hauerwas and MacIntyre acknowledge the possibility of tragic conflicts within the moral life and yet also assert the need for a conception of human life as a whole, which helps a person deal with tragic decisions without subjective arbitrariness. For both thinkers, paradigmatic narratives reveal a community's conception of the good of human life as a whole. I have offered elsewhere an assessment of the work of these thinkers.[38] In the context of the present study it can only be stressed that their work provides the most promising theoretical account of the significance for ethical reflection of our central categories—narrative, tragedy, and virtue—and of

[37] Alasdair MacIntyre, *After Virtue: A Study in Moral Theory* (Notre Dame, IN: University of Notre Dame Press, 1981) and Stanley Hauerwas, *A Community of Character: Toward a Constructive Christian Social Ethic* (Notre Dame, IN: University of Notre Dame Press, 1981).

[38] John D. Barbour, "The Virtues in a Pluralistic Context," *The Journal of Religion* 63 (1983), pp. 175–182.

their interconnections. However, this study has not confirmed MacIntyre's claim that Jane Austen is the last representative of the tradition of thought about the virtues. Certain modern narratives, such as the four tragic novels examined here, are centrally concerned with exploring connections between the practice of the virtues and moral tragedy. Philosophers and theologians would do well to follow MacIntyre's lead in turning to tragic narratives as a source of significant insights into the characteristic moral problems and values of particular societies and traditions.

Tragedy can present a sharp conflict between two virtues, or a conflict between some virtue or duty and a powerful human passion, as in *Macbeth* or *Dr. Faustus* or the several nineteenth-century novels dealing with an adultress. By posing such a conflict, tragedy raises the perennial problem of the relationship between virtue and happiness. Any comprehensive moral theory must define the connection between the moral life and the broader human quest for well-being, without reducing virtue to the menial status of being simply the most efficient way to happiness. Ethical thinkers have found it very difficult to avoid subordinating, one to the other, either the concept of happiness or that of virtue. By far the most common tendency has been to subordinate the search for happiness to the imperative of moral duty. It is understandable—indeed the point of their work—that ethical thinkers emphasize this aspect of life. Furthermore, it is realistic about human nature to assume that most of us do not need much encouragement to see to our own interests but rather need reminding to look beyond them to the needs of other persons. However, there is a danger that ethical thought will sever the moral life from broader conceptions of "the good life."

The issue of the relationship between virtue and happiness is continually raised anew by the tragic spectacle. Tragedy is terrifying because it shows how a person's virtue can lead not to happiness, but to the greatest suffering. It raises all our lingering doubts about the connection between happiness and virtue, and arouses the fears and uncertainties that we moralistically deny in order to reassure ourselves. Tragedy makes us ask why a person should try to live a morally good life when it seems that the good man suffers most. The tragic spectacle does not lay our minds to rest; it makes us question the adequacy of our theoretical (philosophical and theological) explanations for the good man's suffering. By raising such doubts, tragedy not only functions as an incentive to further reflection, but may help us perceive more compassionately the misery of others. The humanizing potential of tragedy lies in its ability to shatter settled notions about blame and responsibility by presenting in poignant detail the suffering of others. It may help us to see in a new way suffering to which we grow accustomed or hardened, inured by moralistic views.

Yet if tragedy challenges various explanations of the connection between virtue and happiness, it also shows how particular characters have reconciled these two concerns, not theoretically, but in their own experiences. Even the tragic hero who has been morally corrupted reveals that his deepest happiness is bound up with an ideal of moral virtue. The fates of Nostromo and Willie Stark show that though a protagonist may commit some crime or evil, his conscience will not let him rest; he cannot forget that his lasting satisfaction and peace of mind depend on his being the kind of person he aspires to be. A Macbeth feels the agony of worldly success achieved through moral damnation. For most tragic heroes, true happiness cannot be attained apart from the realization of moral ideals and the fulfillment of responsibilities to others.

We recognize the stature of another kind of tragic protagonist by his or her capacity to undergo suffering for the sake of a moral ideal or value. Neither Ike McCaslin in Faulkner's *Go Down Moses* nor Sophocles' Antigone discounts the value of material well-being and security, and so their suffering involves a real sacrifice. But such a tragic hero believes that these constituents of happiness must sometimes be subordinated to protect or further some crucial moral value. While shaking us from our unthinking assumption that we can be morally good without sacrifice, tragedy offers a representation of the moral life which is strangely consoling; we see the nobility and courage that may, despite adversity or failure, identify the pursuit of genuine happiness with the requirements of virtue.

Tragedy discloses, too, the roots of virtue in a way of life involving metaphysical and religious perspectives on the world and convictions about the ends and the ultimate meaning of life. Tragedy shows how moral beliefs are embedded in and finally justified by deep-rooted attitudes and religious presuppositions about the fundamental purposes of human existence. It provides a valuable resource for understanding what "considerations capable of determining the intellect" influence a person to accept as normative a particular ideal of virtue.[39] And tragic literature shows how moral notions are bound up with broader human aims and capacities so that not only the intellect, but the emotions and the will, are actively and affectively engaged in trying to live according to a particular vision of the good life.

A much disputed question is whether "the tragic vision" is compatible with monotheistic religious faith. Karl Jaspers has claimed that "Christian

---

[39] In "Principles of Morality," *Philosophy* 31 (1956), 150, Stephen Toulmin adopts Mill's distinction between formal proof and "considerations capable of determining the intellect" in explaining literature's unique ability to show that the ultimate justification for moral principles lies in their contribution to a whole way of life: "Once we reach the turning-point in moral argument, the real matters of principle or the really fundamental ends, the time for formal proof is past. From now on what we need is considerations capable of determining the intellect either to give or to withhold its assent. This indeed is something the Tolstoys of the world can provide for us; and do in a way that we philosophers cannot hope either to improve on or, I suspect, to formalize."

salvation opposes tragic knowledge. The chance of being saved destroys the tragic sense of being trapped without escape. Therefore no genuinely Christian tragedy can exist."[40] On the other hand, Paul Tillich, Miguel Unamuno, Langdon Gilkey, and especially Reinhold Niebuhr have argued that Christian faith requires the recognition of tragedy as an aspect of human experience. Yet they all argue that Christian faith enables the believer to move "beyond tragedy."[41] When theologians affirm that Christian faith involves an appreciaion of the tragic dimension of human life, they usually take this to mean a recognition of human evil and sinfulness. They do not claim to share the tragic apprehension of a wicked deity. It may be, however, that the tragic presentation of divine responsibility for the mystery of evil is not ultimately antithetical to a theology that stresses the hiddenness of God and the ambiguous and unfinished character of Providence in history. Paul Ricoeur has argued that one crucial value of tragedy is its power to remind believers of the mystery of "the wrath of God."[42] Perhaps the task of accounting for the tragic aspects of life still lies ahead for Christian theology.

Tragedy explores inconsistencies between moral notions and other fundamental beliefs, and glaring discrepancies between both moral and epistemological presuppositions about the world and the actual shapes of human experience. Tragedy raises a basic religious question: how can the worth of human existence be affirmed in light of our experience of evil and suffering, and in light of our knowledge of man's inhumanity to man? I share Freud's doubts about the value of interpreting a certain sort of thinker (for example, an author like Conrad) as somehow religious despite their own self-understanding:

> Critics persist in describing as "deeply religious" anyone who admits to a sense of man's insignificance or impotence in the face of the universe, although what constitutes the essence of the religious attitude is not this feeling but only the next step after it, the reaction to it which seeks a remedy for it. The man who goes no further, but humbly acquiesces in the small part which human

[40] Karl Jaspers, *Tragedy Is Not Enough*, trans. Harald Reiche, Harry Moore, and Karl Deutsch (Boston: Archon Press, 1952), pp. 38–39.

[41] Reinhold Niebuhr, *Beyond Tragedy* (New York: Scribner's Sons, 1937). See also Nathan A. Scott, Jr., "The Tragic Vision and the Christian Faith," in *The Broken Center* (New Haven: Yale University Press, 1966), pp. 119–44.

[42] Paul Ricoeur, *The Symbolism of Evil*, trans. Emerson Buchanan (Boston: Beacon Press, 1967), p. 322: Tragedy contributes to our understanding of the Adamic myth two things: "On the one hand, pity for human beings, who are nevertheless accused by the Prophet; on the other hand, fear and trembling before the divine abyss, before the God whose holiness is nevertheless proclaimed by the Prophet. Perhaps it is necessary that the possibility of the tragic God should never be abolished altogether, so that Biblical theology may be protected from the platitudes of ethical monotheism, with its Legislator and its Judge, confronting a moral subject who is endowed with complete and unfettered freedom, still intact after each act."

beings play in the great world—such a man is, on the contrary, irreligious in the truest sense of the word.[43]

On the other hand, even so bleak a work as Conrad's *Nostromo* offers a "reaction . . . which seeks a remedy" insofar as, even when the protagonist has failed or been defeated, his virtues are reaffirmed as the qualities that best enable persons to recognize and respond to life's evil and suffering. In this limited sense, the reader's experience of tragedy involves a process of recognition and thought that can be interpreted as religious in its ultimate significance for human life. For tragedy usually does offer a reaffirmation of a particular kind of virtue, and of a particular conception of human excellence, after having taken into account all the ways that virtue can fail or lead to evil. This movement of reassurance is analogous to what many philosophers and theologians see as the primary function of religion in human life: the provision of trust or confidence in the worth of human existence in spite of its threats and terrors and failures. In any case, whether or not the reader's experience of tragedy can be compared to this functional view of religion, religious thinkers can ill afford to ignore tragedy's vision of the dilemmas of moral experience. Religious positions which deny or slight the tragic aspects of experience limit or distort our understanding of the moral life.

Tragedy offers a critique of virtue: it invites readers to understand how a person's most admirable qualities can help destroy both him and others. "In being the bad conscience of their time," "by applying the knife vivisectionally to the chest of the very *virtues of their time*," the authors of tragedy perform the service Nietzsche demanded of the ideal philosopher.[44] To the degree that we, too, value the kind of character the author has created, our recognition of a virtue's potential susceptibility to tragedy requires the courage to be skeptical of our own convictions. Tragedy can help us take a critical perspective on our moral absolutes, which all too often justify our inflicting suffering on other persons. Yet if tragedy helps us to imagine the potential liabilities and dangers in particular ideals of virtue, it also forces us to recognize that a person's deepest moral beliefs are indispensable not because they are always successful in action but because even in failure they remain commanding as ideals or requirements for the self. Tragedy requires a recognition of the fallibility of particular moral ideals and aspirations; it involves, as well, the most powerful, because profoundly self-critical, reaffirmation of the ultimate value and significance for human life of particular forms of moral virtue.

[43] Sigmund Freud, *The Future of an Illusion*, trans. W. D. Robson-Scott (1927; New York: Doubleday Anchor, 1964), p. 52.

[44] Friedrich Nietzsche, *Beyond Good and Evil*, in *Basic Writings of Nietzsche*, trans. and ed. Walter Kaufmann (New York: Modern Library, 1966), p. 327.

Index